English Teaching
and Evangelical Mission

CRITICAL LANGUAGE AND LITERACY STUDIES

Series Editors: **Professor Alastair Pennycook** (*University of Technology, Sydney, Australia*) and **Professor Brian Morgan** (*Glendon College/York University, Toronto, Canada*) and **Professor Ryuko Kubota** (*University of British Columbia, Vancouver, Canada*)

Critical Language and Literacy Studies is an international series that encourages monographs directly addressing issues of power (its flows, inequities, distributions, trajectories) in a variety of language- and literacy-related realms. The aim with this series is twofold: (1) to cultivate scholarship that openly engages with social, political, and historical dimensions in language and literacy studies, and (2) to widen disciplinary horizons by encouraging new work on topics that have received little focus (see below for partial list of subject areas) and that use innovative theoretical frameworks.

Full details of all the books in this series and of all our other publications can be found on http://www.multilingual-matters.com, or by writing to Multilingual Matters, St Nicholas House, 31-34 High Street, Bristol BS1 2AW, UK.

Other books in the series

Collaborative Research in Multilingual Classrooms
Corey Denos, Kelleen Toohey, Kathy Neilson and Bonnie Waterstone
English as a Local Language: Post-colonial Identities and Multilingual Practices
Christina Higgins
The Idea of English in Japan: Ideology and the Evolution of a Global Language
Philip Seargeant
Gendered Identities and Immigrant Language Learning
Julia Menard-Warwick
China and English: Globalisation and the Dilemmas of Identity
Joseph Lo Bianco, Jane Orton and Gao Yihong (eds)
Language and HIV/AIDS
Christina Higgins and Bonny Norton (eds)
Hybrid Identities and Adolescent Girls: Being 'Half' in Japan
Laurel D. Kamada
Decolonizing Literacy: Mexican Lives in the Era of Global Capitalism
Gregorio Hernandez-Zamora
Contending with Globalization in World Englishes
Mukul Saxena and Tope Omoniyi (eds)
ELT, Gender and International Development: Myths of Progress in a Neocolonial World
Roslyn Appleby
Examining Education, Media, and Dialogue under Occupation: The Case of Palestine and Israel
Ilham Nasser, Lawrence N. Berlin and Shelley Wong (eds)
The Struggle for Legitimacy: Indigenized Englishes in Settler Schools
Andrea Sterzuk
Style, Identity and Literacy: English in Singapore
Christopher Stroud and Lionel Wee
Language and Mobility: Unexpected Places
Alastair Pennycook
Talk, Text and Technology: Literacy and Social Practice in a Remote Indigenous Community
Inge Kral
Language Learning, Gender and Desire: Japanese Women on the Move
Kimie Takahashi
English and Development: Policy, Pedagogy and Globalization
Elizabeth J. Erling and Philip Seargeant (eds)
Ethnography, Superdiversity and Linguistic Landscapes: Chronicles of Complexity
Jan Blommaert
Power and Meaning Making in an EAP Classroom - Engaging with the Everyday
Christian W. Chun
Local Languaging, Literacy and Multilingualism in a West African Society
Kasper Juffermans

CRITICAL LANGUAGE AND LITERACY STUDIES: 21

English Teaching and Evangelical Mission

The Case of Lighthouse School

Bill Johnston

MULTILINGUAL MATTERS
Bristol • Blue Ridge Summit

Library of Congress Cataloging in Publication Data
A catalog record for this book is available from the Library of Congress.
Johnston, Bill, 1960- author.
English Teaching and Evangelical Mission: The Case of Lighthouse School/Bill Johnston.
Bristol: Multilingual Matters, [2017] |
Critical Language and Literacy Studies: 21|
Includes bibliographical references and index.
LCCN 2016040549| ISBN 9781783097074 (hbk : alk. paper) | ISBN 9781783097067 (pbk : alk. paper) | ISBN 9781783097104 (kindle)
LCSH: English language–Study and teaching–Polish speakers. | Education–Religious aspects–Poland–21st century. | Bilingualism–Poland.
LCC PE1129.S6 J67 2017 | DDC 428.0071/0438–dc23 LC record available at https://lccn.loc.gov/2016040549

British Library Cataloguing in Publication Data
A catalogue entry for this book is available from the British Library.

ISBN-13: 978-1-78309-707-4 (hbk)
ISBN-13: 978-1-78309-706-7 (pbk)

Multilingual Matters
UK: St Nicholas House, 31-34 High Street, Bristol BS1 2AW, UK.
USA: NBN, Blue Ridge Summit, PA, USA.

Website: www.multilingual-matters.com
Twitter: Multi_Ling_Mat
Facebook: https://www.facebook.com/multilingualmatters
Blog: www.channelviewpublications.wordpress.com

Copyright © 2017 Bill Johnston.

Front cover image: Fra Angelico: *The Annunciation* (detail)

All rights reserved. No part of this work may be reproduced in any form or by any means without permission in writing from the publisher.

The policy of Multilingual Matters/Channel View Publications is to use papers that are natural, renewable and recyclable products, made from wood grown in sustainable forests. In the manufacturing process of our books, and to further support our policy, preference is given to printers that have FSC and PEFC Chain of Custody certification. The FSC and/or PEFC logos will appear on those books where full certification has been granted to the printer concerned.

Typeset by Deanta Global Publishing Services Limited.

Contents

	Series Editors' Preface	vii
	Acknowledgments	xiii
1	Introduction	1
2	A Nation of Many Faiths?: Religion in Poland in the 21st Century	9
3	The Road to Lighthouse School	19
4	The School with a Soul	40
5	Curriculum and Materials	51
6	In the Classroom	69
7	False-Bottomed Friendships?: Relation at Lighthouse School	99
8	Empty Meeting Grounds?: The Cross-Cultural Encounter at Lighthouse School	126
9	Conclusions	153
Appendix A	Transcription Conventions and A Note on Translation	165
References		166
Name Index		171
Subject Index		173

Series Editors' Preface

There is much for many audiences in this wonderful addition to the Critical Language and Literacy series. Though primarily an ethnographic account of an Evangelical Christian language school in Poland, *English Teaching and Evangelical Mission* is a multi-layered text with connotations that extend beyond the proffering and enticements of faith. For one, there is the author himself and the unique talents and experiences he brings to this project. Bill Johnston, a professor of comparative literature at Indiana University, is a renowned and multiple award-winning translator of Polish literature. His translation of Wiesław Myśliwski's *Stone upon Stone* (2010), as one prominent example, received the PEN 2012 Translation Prize, culminating in the Officer's Cross of the Order of Merit, awarded by the President of the Republic of Poland. Johnston expertly knows the language and national context of which he writes, and he applies a meticulous wordsmith's attention to the lexical tempo and detail with which he describes the people and events at Lighthouse School as well as broader transitions and re-alignments in the sociopolitical and religious landscape of Polish society.

The depth of contextualization is indeed impressive. For those interested in religion and culture, Johnston outlines the historical prominence of Catholicism in Poland, its relative submission under communism and its resurgence after the break-up of the Soviet Union and Eastern Bloc. As background to Lighthouse School, Johnston also introduces readers to aspects of religious history less commonly known: i.e. the longstanding presence and diversity of Polish Protestantism, and more relevant to the story at hand, the tensions and attractions that Evangelical Christianity currently poses for one of Europe's most Catholic nations. Johnston draws attention to new forms of religious syncretism, for example, an emergent charismatic Catholicism. At a more local and personal level, Johnston's interview data reveal religious Poles who find themselves in both 'camps' at once, negotiating and reconciling seemingly contradictory identity positions, as in the case of Pippa, a devout member of a Catholic congregation, on the one hand, and a committed evangelical missionary, on the other. Such contradictions are overcome, in part, by what Johnston describes as an ideological concordance between American evangelical conservatism and Polish Catholic conservative discourse in which creationism, homophobia, and anti-abortion sentiments are firmly established.

Johnston is also keenly concerned with *how* we come into words that are at first 'foreign' to the senses and require considerable effort in order to become part of our linguistic and semiotic repertoires. As he states early on, 'I write as someone committed to quality language teaching who is at the same time deeply interested in the identities and beliefs of language teachers, and how these impact classroom interaction and the quality of experience afforded the learners'. These are commitments and interests to which Johnston has already made significant contributions as a language teacher educator, scholar and researcher in applied linguists, and early in his career, as an English as a Foreign/International Language teacher in Poland. Many of the issues and perspectives Johnston explores at Lighthouse School thus build on and extend earlier studies, notably, his innovative work on values in English Language Teaching (ELT) (Johnston, 2003), the development of theory and practice related to language teacher identity (Varghese *et al.*, 2005), and perhaps most pertinent to this book, critical inquiry into evangelical teachers in the ELT profession (Johnston & Varghese, 2008; Varghese & Johnston, 2007).

These scholarly interests neatly converge in Johnston's discussion and underpin his views regarding ongoing debates and disputes over the place and purpose of evangelical Christianity – and religion, in general – in language teaching programs (see Edge, 2003; Pennycook & Coutand-Marin, 2004; Wong & Canagarajah, 2009; Wong & Mahboob, in preparation). Johnston carefully avoids doctrinal or idealistic proscriptions that are unlikely to further dialogue amongst critical, secular and evangelical language professionals. And certainly, this stance has been shaped by Johnston's own research experiences of being a participant observer, sometimes consulted for his ELT expertise, at Lighthouse School. Such ethnographic proximity fosters empathy and respect for his evangelical participants, leading him to comment critically on the hypocrisy and 'virulence of non-evangelical attitudes toward evangelical Christianity' in the ELT profession.

At the same time, this research intimacy generates newfound awareness of the ethical and professional boundaries oftentimes breached under the guise of language instruction and close teacher-student relationships. For example, we learn about Sydney – one of the Lighthouse teachers – and her impromptu 'mini-sermons' during class; we also learn about 'false-bottomed friendships', reflecting some students' concerns that the warm, interpersonal relationships fostered by Lighthouse teachers serve an ulterior goal of conversion and integration into the local evangelical community. Unconscious or taken-for-granted ideologies are similarly illuminated. One of the more egregious examples that emerge from Johnston's data is the inequality of language relations at the school, in which Polish students struggle to learn English while their Canadian and American teachers make little to no effort to learn Polish. Johnston's study thus serves as a template for a principled, critical opposition in ELT: in short, if non-evangelical researchers wish to voice their ethical and professional concerns regarding evangelical language teaching, then they need to gather empirical data with which to substantiate and specify the problems they perceive and wish to challenge or change. Johnston's detailed ethnography, of course, fulfills this requirement in exemplary ways.

Ethnography has featured prominently in a number of books in this series (Blommaert, 2013; Chun, 2015; Kral, 2012). In keeping with the strengths of this research tradition, Johnston foregrounds local uniqueness and complexity through sustained participant observation, the emic perspectives of participants and multiple sources of data (e.g. interviews, curriculum documents, lesson observations, site descriptions and histories) with which to triangulate his analyses. Again, given the controversy around his topic, Johnston's ethnographic approach adds authority to his multi-faceted discussion. We learn of the complexity and depth of evangelical teacher identities, particularly of Sydney, who otherwise might be reduced to stereotype or one-dimensionality based on her faith. We also come to appreciate Sydney's strengths as a language teacher and her ability to negotiate inter-faith tensions – what Johnston describes as *ecumenical discourse* – in a cultural and religious environment in which women are discouraged from taking on leadership roles. Johnston's detailed analysis of the unique, Bible-based curriculum and observations of its implementation and reception are also illuminating. We are invited to witness the pedagogical integrity of many language-learning activities, but we are also made aware of the proselytizing currents that often run through them, as in several reading lessons observed on Daniel Defoe's *Robinson Crusoe*, which is reinterpreted as a spiritual redemption text, notably void of any reference to racism and colonialism in its textual underpinnings. This is one of several examples in which the Bible-based curricular strategy of 'digging deeper' around course content is selectively and narrowly applied at Lighthouse. It is also a critical perspective that arises through careful ethnographic attention and site familiarity.

As noted, Bill Johnston is an accomplished linguist and scholar across several disciplines and languages. These varied interests enrich this timely addition to CLLS and expand the book's readership and relevance beyond its primary focus of Evangelical Christian language schools in ELT. As Johnston points out in his conclusions, *English Teaching and Evangelical Mission* reaches publication at a time in which words of profound difference or alterity are rarely 'heard' in public spaces – or only on ideologically narrow terms that contain the threat they might pose for entrenched beliefs. Even just a cursory glance at current political events suggests that we occupy spaces of increased polarization, intolerance and aggression often fueled by shrill, hyper-partisan discourse. Johnston's final advice is based on the insights he has gained from his engagement with Evangelical Christians: 'It is my deepest belief that understanding and dialogue are the only valid way to engage with those different from ourselves. The alternative is disrespect, dismissal, scorn, fear – and, eventually, conflict and violence. This book has been my small attempt to listen and to understand'. Readers of this important book are likely to find Johnston's self-assessment far too modest for what he has achieved.

Brian Morgan, Alastair Pennycook, Ryuko Kubota

References

Blommaert, J. (2013) *Ethnography, Superdiversity and Linguistic Landscapes: Chronicles of Complexity*. Bristol: Multilingual Matters.

Chun, C. (2015) *Power and Meaning Making in an EAP classroom: Engaging with the Everyday*. Bristol: Multilingual Matters.

Edge, J. (2003) Imperial troopers and servants of the lord: A vision of TESOL for the 21st century. *TESOL Quarterly* 37 (4), 701–708.

Johnston, B. (2003) *Values in English Language Teaching*. Mahwah, NJ: Lawrence Erlbaum Associates.

Johnston, B. and Varghese, M. (2008) Neo-imperialism, evangelism, and ELT: Modernist missions and a postmodern profession. In J. Edge (ed.) *(Re)Locating TESOL in an Age of Empire* (pp. 195–207). Basingstoke: Palgrave Macmillan.

Kral, I. (2012) *Talk, Text and Technology: Literacy and Social Practice in a Remote Indigenous Community*. Bristol: Multilingual Matters.

Myśliwski, W. (2010) *Stone upon Stone* (trans. B. Johnston). Brooklyn, NY: Archipelago Books.

Pennycook, A. and Coutand-Marin, S. (2004) Teaching English as a missionary language (TEML). *Discourse: Studies in the Cultural Politics of Education* 24 (3), 338–353.

Varghese, M. and Johnston, B. (2007) Evangelical Christians and English language teaching. *TESOL Quarterly* 41, 9–31.

Varghese, M., Morgan, B., Johnston, B. and Johnson, K. (2005) Theorizing language teacher identity: Three perspectives and beyond. *Journal of Language, Identity, and Education, 4*, 21–44.
Wong, M.S. and Canagarajah, S. (eds) (2009) *Christian and Critical English Language Educators in Dialogue: Pedagogical and Ethical Dilemmas.* New York: Routledge.
Wong, M.S. and Mahboob, A. (eds) (in preparation) *Spirituality and Language Teaching: Religious Explorations of Teacher Identity, Pedagogy, Context and Content.* Bristol: Multilingual Matters.

Acknowledgments

Many, many people have helped to make this book possible. Above all, I owe an impossible debt of gratitude to Sydney, Taryn and the teachers, learners and administrators at Lighthouse School, for their hospitality, understanding and kindness. Dziękuję z głębokości serca. 'I was a stranger, and ye took me in'. Thanks too to all the teachers I interviewed in N. and all around Poland.

I thank the Fulbright Commission of Poland for the funding that enabled me to spend a year at Lighthouse; Professor Elżbieta Tabakowska of the Jagiellonian University for hosting me during my time in Poland; and Indiana University for supporting this study.

One of the main things that sustained me as I collected data was the interest shown by many of my friends in what I was doing. I want to thank all those whose curiosity and questions forced me to organize my thoughts and begin to put them into words. In this regard, I offer special thanks to Krzysztof and Kinga Koehler.

Many of my colleagues at Indiana University helped me with advice, information and encouragement. I thank all of them, especially Candy Gunther Brown, Maria Bucur, Padraic Kenney, Sarah Phillips and Steve Stein.

The roots of this study lie deep in discussions I had in the field of TESOL. I want to thank all those who have helped me to reach this point. My special thanks go to Julian Edge, Cary Buzzelli and above all Manka Varghese.

Thanks too to Zach Scalzo for his meticulous work on the manuscript.

Lastly, I want to convey my special thanks to Victor, for showing me that dialogue is possible.

1 Introduction

There is something altogether fascinating about the idea of evangelical Christian missionaries operating a language school and teaching English to adults and children in present-day Poland. The most obvious question is: How can you 'convert' to Christianity a nation that accepted the Christian faith over a thousand years ago, and is known today for its allegiance to the Catholic Church? Following on the heels of this central puzzle, others soon occur to us: Are the missionaries 'successful'? (We'll leave aside for a moment the matter of how 'success' in missions is and can be judged, and by whom.) What do Polish Catholics think of efforts to win them over to the evangelical churches? After this, when we have had time to reflect a little more thoughtfully on the subject, more nuanced questions emerge: Why is Poland a particular target of evangelical missionary efforts in the first place (as it has been for some time)? Are all Poles in fact Catholics, in name, practice or belief? Do the missionaries indeed aim to 'convert' the Poles, or may the goal of their mission work be rather more subtle? And last but by no means least, what is English teaching doing in all of this? How is evangelical Christianity related to the global spread of the English language?

The present book is an attempt to address some of these questions, through a close look at the work of a single evangelical language school in Poland. Like the academic I am, I won't promise straightforward answers to the questions raised above, for the simple reason that often, they will turn out not to be the right questions after all. It will transpire that things are far more complicated than they seem; I hope to show some of this complexity, on the way reflecting on why it is that we persistently find ourselves imagining situations of this kind as being more black-and-white than they are in reality.

Anyone picking up this book is likely to be asking another major question, one that I can answer right away (albeit unwillingly); let me do so while you're still browsing the first page or so. The question is this: Who is the author? More specifically, where does he stand in terms of religious beliefs vis-à-vis the people he is studying? Well, as I hinted in the first sentence of this paragraph, I'm strongly opposed to identitarian writing of the 'as a white middle-class heterosexual male' variety. Yet, in the present case, I realize it may be hard for the reader to know how to interpret the text without a sense of who is writing, so here goes: I am an atheist. My interest in evangelical Christianity is as a complete outsider. I first became fully aware of the major evangelical presence in the field of English teaching as an outcome of my work on the moral dimensions of English language teaching (Johnston, 2003), and in particular my work on language teacher identity. My colleague Manka Varghese and I both found the matter compelling, and we conducted a study of evangelical Christian teachers in training in the US (Varghese & Johnston, 2007). This study, though deeply interesting to its authors, was limited in scope, and it was clear that the matter deserved a much more extensive inquiry. That was one of the germs of the present project.

I find evangelical Christians fascinating people to be around, partly because they are so profoundly different from me. Evangelicals see everything around them as being tied to God. Both good and bad things that happen in the world are directly related to the will of God, and specifically to their own relationship with God. For evangelical Christians, that relationship is the core of their existence; everything else flows from it, or should. As a key aspect of this central belief, evangelical Christians constantly look to the figure of Jesus Christ as a living example of how to lead one's life; they regard the Bible as the Word of God, taking this quite literally in many cases; and they believe that every evangelical has a spiritual duty to bear witness to his or her faith. This duty often (though not always) involves attempts to contribute to the Great Commission, Christ's last recorded instruction to his disciples, in which he commanded them: 'Go ye therefore, and teach all nations, baptizing them in the name of the Father, and of the Son, and of the Holy Ghost' (Matthew 28:19). (A different and widely used translation says, 'make disciples of all the nations'.)

As an atheist, I believe none of these things. Yet, even as I write those words – 'as an atheist' – I am conscious that such a formulation implies that I'm bound by some doctrine which obliges me to believe or not believe certain things. This, however, is not the case – I believe what I believe not because someone else has decided that that's what atheists have to believe, but rather because in my innermost being I find absolutely no shred of conviction that God exists, that the Bible is His word or that Jesus was His son. Since my own conviction comes from within, not from an outside authority, I must accept that evangelical Christians too believe what *they* believe not because their pastor or their parents told them so, but rather because deep within themselves they are convinced of the rightness of the way they see the world. This is the fundamental attitude of respect that I sought to bring to my study.

There is also another important reason why evangelical Christians are interesting to someone like me: As an atheist, I represent a very small minority both in my adopted home country of the US, and more widely in the world at large. Most people in the world believe in some form of divine being. Evangelical Christians, in particular, constitute a huge and ever-increasing percentage of the population, not just in North America but across Central and South America, Africa, Asia and also Europe. In a word, an interest in evangelical Christianity means an interest in a set of beliefs that are common to a significant portion of humanity.

A further personal motivation in pursuing the research that led to this book lay in the attitudes toward evangelical Christians that I encountered in those with whom I work. To put it plainly, such attitudes usually range between condescension and scorn, rarely straying beyond these boundaries. Let me give a small but telling example. At the beginning of each new academic year, the department where I used to work held an orientation and get-to-know-you session for new graduate students in our masters in teaching English to speakers of other languages (MATESOL) program. As part of this event, new students were asked to introduce themselves and say something about why they had entered the program. At one orientation session, a young man from Korea told us his name, then explained that three years previously he had come to know Jesus Christ as his personal lord and savior and that Jesus had pointed him in the direction of pursuing a master's degree in his chosen field, that of English teaching. I glanced around at my colleagues and saw several of them rolling their eyes; afterward, they made deprecating comments about the student in question.

Such reactions are a staple in non-evangelical circles throughout North America; one need only look at how evangelicals are portrayed in the media. A recent Google search using the term 'Crazy Christians' yielded 6 million results. Of course, many evangelicals in the public eye do indeed set themselves up for satirical treatment (examples are so common I will forgo repeating any here). But, more than with any other self-identified group, I believe we fall into the trap of tarring all its members with the same brush of intolerance, extremism and ideological fanaticism. Few, if any, of the evangelicals I know can be classified this way; yet, as non-evangelicals, we continue to dismiss all evangelicals regardless. Indeed, no other religious group is treated with such cavalier contempt by supposedly open-minded liberals. Going back to the orientation session mentioned in the previous paragraph, my strong suspicion is that the reaction would have been very different if the student had expressed his spiritual convictions as a Buddhist, a Jew or a Muslim; even non-evangelical Christians, such as Catholics, would have gotten off lightly. Anti-evangelical reactions are so strong, so predictable and so formulaic that one cannot help asking the question: Why? What is it about evangelical Christianity that non-evangelicals in North America and elsewhere find so objectionable? My work on the project described here led me repeatedly back to this question, and I will address it in some detail later.

As with many large-scale projects, the present one was also set in motion by very specific things I read and heard. In particular, I found myself returning over and over again to comments made by Julian Edge and by Alastair Pennycook and Sophie Coutand-Marin in articles about evangelical Christians in TESOL. Edge (2003) expressed particular concern about the use of deception – the practice, endorsed by some missionaries and missionary organizations, of using English teaching as a convenient cover for mission work. Edge asked his readers – TESOL professionals – to imagine being on the receiving end of this practice:

> Perhaps one way to understand the threat involved is to reverse the relationships. We need to imagine ourselves as constrained to encourage members of our community, perhaps send out our children (for as anyone involved in worldwide TEFL knows, both in the public and private sectors, the major growth area is in the teaching of English to ever-younger learners) to learn a language essential for their educational development and material well-being. We are required to do this in the knowledge that an unknown number of the teachers of that language are there with the express purpose of subverting our most deeply held beliefs and taking those people, those children, from us. They hope to do this at first surreptitiously, and then with the same discourse of 'choice' that those in power always like to affect when they take what they can, leaving the disadvantaged to put up with what they must (Mitchell, 1994). (Edge, 2003: 705)

Pennycook and Coutand-Marin (2004), in turn, express significant misgivings about several aspects of what they label somewhat facetiously 'TEML' – teaching English as a missionary language. Citing comments on a website run by a missionary organization entitled Christian Outreach International, they say that for this organization:

> ...there appears to be no concern about viewing the increased demand for English as 'a gold mine rich with mission opportunity'. Nor does the question of gaining students' trust in order to preach the gospel appear to raise ethical questions about this pedagogy. According to missionaries' testimonies, English classes are the most efficient

way to attract people. Indeed, for some organisations, using ELT has become an identifiable 'approach' to missionary work. (Pennycook & Coutand-Marin, 2004: 340)

Pennycook and Coutand-Marin (2004: 348) also state that 'Christian missionary work typically preys on the weak, using English to gain access to vulnerable non-Christians'. Finally, they criticize the noncritical nature of TEML, claiming:

> [T]he moral project of TEML all too often lacks an adequate ethics. While religious thinking is supposed to encourage engagement with hard ethical questions, all too often it does little more than promote a prior moral absolutism. (Pennycook & Coutand-Marin, 2004: 351)

Both these quotations formed part of the rather acrimonious exchange that emerged in the early 2000s about the intersection of TESOL and evangelical mission work (see Chapter 3 for a more detailed account of this literature). In thinking about the quotations, two feelings struck me. One was embarrassment – as a scientist, I was discomfited that as a field we were making such generalizations with no empirical data to back them up. The second feeling was curiosity. Were these things actually true? Were evangelical Christian missionaries using English teaching as a platform for mission work; were they doing so covertly; and were they indeed 'preying on the weak'? I decided rather quickly that the best way to redress my embarrassment was to go out and collect some data in the best way I knew how – by conducting an in-depth, data-based study. The present book is the result of these twin feelings of embarrassment and curiosity, and constitutes not just my response to the writers quoted above (and to their critics), but also, I hope, a contribution to the ongoing debate.

Another question that is bound to occur to the reader at the outset is: Why Poland? I should preface my answer to this question by saying that I believed strongly from the beginning that it was important to focus on a single setting for my study – that is, an ethnographic approach was called for. The encounter with faiths and cultures that mission work involves is so complex that I feel that any more superficial attempt to study it – via polls, or interviews alone, across numerous settings – would signally fail to capture the reality of any actual context. Only a painstaking look at the individuals and individual relationships involved could convey an accurate picture of at least part of the reality.

For me, Poland was an obvious choice. I lived in Poland for eight years in the 1980s and 1990s, and I often spend a month or more there every year. I speak fluent Polish (I am a translator of Polish literature), and have extensive knowledge of Polish culture and history. This knowledge would give me a head start in understanding the encounters in a language school from both sides.

But convenience alone is not a sufficient motivation for the choice of site, and I was initially leery of this option. I have always found Poland immensely interesting, but I was not sure whether it was an appropriate location for the study I had in mind. It was only after I discussed the idea with colleagues in religious studies that I became convinced that Poland is indeed an exceptionally interesting location for a study of evangelical mission work. In general, the evangelical focus on Europe is itself a notable phenomenon (see Chapter 2 for more details). What used to be 'Eastern Europe', in turn – that is, the former communist bloc – is interesting for its own reasons. And Poland in particular – the country that gave us Pope John Paul II and is widely regarded as one of the 'most Catholic' countries in the world – would seem to be, to put it mildly, a tough nut to crack for evangelical missionaries. For all these reasons, then, the case of Poland is a particularly compelling one.

I need to say very clearly from the outset that I am an applied linguist, not a theologian or a sociologist of religion. I have drawn on the literature of the latter two disciplines as well as that of other relevant fields (Slavic studies and Polish studies, anthropology, history, religious studies), but the center of my attention has been the language classroom – the place I know best, and the locus where the encounter I am writing about primarily took place. Where I write about religious belief, it is above all as an interested and relatively well-informed non-specialist, and, I hope, as a well-disposed or sympathetic non-believer. I'm not qualified to go into details about the niceties of religious dogma or practices, nor do I wish to do so. I write as someone committed to quality language teaching who is at the same time deeply interested in the identities and beliefs of language teachers, and how these impact classroom interaction and the quality of experience afforded to the learners. By the same token, it is my great hope that the present book will be accessible to those from outside my own discipline. I believe strongly that when examining religious and spiritual beliefs, and also educational practice, it is both possible and desirable to avoid unnecessary specialist terminology and to write in a way that any intelligent and interested reader can follow.

Simply put, my goal in the present study was to find out what a mission-based English language school *looks like*. I wanted to do an in-depth, relatively extensive study of a single school to capture the particularity of experience in one location. I was especially interested in understanding and conveying the perspectives of the participants, including teachers, students and others involved in the school. On the way, I found that much of what I was doing was learning what such a school does *not* look like – that is to say, dismantling my own preconceptions (many of which I was not initially aware of) and those of others I have spoken to about the project or whose work I have read. A perhaps inevitable side result of the research was a confrontation with my own religious and spiritual beliefs. But more of that later.

I was determined not to take an overly theoretical approach to the phenomena I was studying. At the same time, I was coming into the project with certain fairly obvious interests and theoretical preferences, and it was inevitable that these would color even the initial data collection. These entering perspectives included the question of identity; the processes of globalization and the view of the school's work as representing the front line of the transglobal encounter; and discourse analysis, in particular discursive psychology, which suggests that a careful analysis of the ways that people talk can be a major source of understanding of their motivations, world views and relationships. Other theoretical perspectives – notably those coming from gender studies – emerged during the course of the study. But I have chosen not to structure the present report around a single theoretical framework, preferring instead to call upon different theories at different moments to help understand aspects of what I found. In this project in particular, I felt that it is the substantive facts of the case that are most interesting, and I did not want to lose sight of these by immersing myself too much in theory. This seemed particularly important because the present study, to the best of my knowledge the first of its kind, is very much exploratory in nature, and I would like to leave room for a range of theoretical approaches. I've chosen then to sketch out a few such possibilities without committing wholly to any one theoretical lens.

The book is structured as follows: After the present introductory chapter, Chapter 2 gives a brief overview of the social, political, cultural and religious landscape of present-day Poland. Chapter 3 describes the background to the study reported in the rest of the book, including a review of the relevant professional literature both within applied linguistics and in other domains; a discussion of the research methodology employed in data gathering; and an overview of the theoretical sources used to frame the findings.

Chapter 4 introduces Lighthouse School: how it came to exist, its mission and its teachers and staff – above all its two founders and directors, Sydney and Taryn. Chapter 5 takes a detailed look at the extensive curriculum developed by Taryn and Sydney for use at Lighthouse School, with special attention being paid to the materials used in the classes observed for the study.

Chapter 6 considers the fundamental encounter that the school represented by looking in detail at data from three different Lighthouse classrooms, as well as school-related encounters in other settings. Chapter 7 extends this analysis by looking at the central topic of relation as it was perceived and enacted by various participants in the work of the school. In particular, I look at further evidence from transcripts of classroom interaction to locate examples of what I call 'ecumenical discourse', a discursive strategy that enabled the teachers to address spiritual issues across the denominational gulf between Polish Roman Catholicism and North American evangelical Christianity. Chapter 8 considers this gulf in more detail, framing it in the broader context of the cross-cultural encounter constituted by the work of Lighthouse School.

Finally, Chapter 9 pulls things together and offers thoughts on the big picture – what the present study can and cannot tell us about the use of English teaching for missionary purposes; where the study leaves us; what sorts of theory might usefully be brought to bear on some of the puzzles thrown up by this research; and what future research should aim to investigate.

2 A Nation of Many Faiths?: Religion in Poland in the 21st Century

The Religions of Poland

In the public imagination of the late 20th century, the name 'Poland' became so indelibly associated with Roman Catholicism that it was very easy to lose sight of two important facts. The first is the extraordinary variety of faiths represented in the Polish-speaking lands before World War II. By far the most significant religious faith after Catholicism was, of course, Judaism: Jews constituted about 10% of the overall population of Poland in the interwar period. But prewar and 19th-century Poland was also home to a wide array of other religious groups, including the Eastern Orthodox and Uniate Churches, Protestants of various hues (mostly Lutherans and Calvinists), Muslim Tartars and numerous others. Religious diversity was mirrored by ethnic diversity on a large scale – 'Polish' territory was home to Jews, Germans, Austrians, Ukrainians, Belarusians, Lithuanians, Roma, Tartars, Czechs, Hungarians, Lemkos, Hutsuls, Cassubians and many other ethnic groups.

The second fact that is easily forgotten in the linking of Poland with Catholicism is that in the late 20th century too, the country was not exclusively Catholic. Of course, religious diversity in the country was shattered as a direct or indirect result of World War II. The great majority of the country's Jews were murdered by Nazi Germany, while many of the rest left after the end of the war. In the redrawing of the Polish borders that Stalin imposed in 1945, most Germans were expelled from the West, while millions of Ukrainians, Belarusians, Lithuanians and others were forcibly resettled to the Soviet Union. Subsequent ethnic cleansing operations by the Polish government led to the breaking up of many small ethnic communities – the 1947 Operation Vistula, for instance, forcibly uprooted Ukrainians, Boykos, Lemkos and others from their traditional homelands in southeast Poland, moving and often scattering them to the newly acquired Western voivodeships (provinces). When I first became interested in Poland in the 1970s, I clearly remember reading and hearing that Poland was '99% Catholic'. Yet, it later transpired that this statistic was misleading. Largely as a result of the communist unwillingness to acknowledge religious identity in general, as well as linguistic, cultural and ethnic minorities in particular, official statistics misrepresented the situation. In fact, during the communist period, Poland contained significant populations of Jews, Germans and German-speaking communities (e.g. Silesians), Lemkos, Hutsuls, Cassubians, Belarusians, Slovaks, Roma and other groups. As the previous paragraph suggests, this ethnolinguistic diversity was mirrored by the presence of numerous religious traditions and practices beyond Roman Catholicism.

I mention the religious, ethnic and cultural richness of Poland's recent past because it ought to complicate our image of Poland as a Catholic country, and it has particular significance in trying to understand present-day Poland's encounter with evangelical Christianity. The fact is that Protestantism has been a major presence in Poland for centuries, and that churches that we in the West would think of as evangelical, such as the Baptist Church, have existed in Poland for decades. This makes the evangelical 'invasion' described below much more ambiguous and much more interesting.

According to polls by CBOS (Centrum Badania Opinii Społecznej, or the Public Opinion Research Center), Poland's official organization for research on social attitudes and practices, in 2009, 94.7% of Poles self-identified as Catholics; 0.4% were Eastern Orthodox Christians and 0.4% Protestants, while 2.1% stated that they were atheist, agnostic or otherwise without a denomination (the remaining percentage was made up of non-specified religious affiliations) (CBOS, 2012). Interestingly, only three years later the percentage of Protestants had doubled to 0.8%, as had that of atheists and agnostics (4.2%). The number of Catholics was largely unchanged at 93.1%.

The first Protestant churches appeared in Poland in the 16th century, soon after the Reformation, and many have remained since that time. The largest Protestant church in Poland is the Lutheran Kościół Ewangelicko-Augsburski, which according to its own website has about 80,000 members (Luterański Kościół Ewangelicko-Augsburski, 2012). In the 19th century, evangelical churches also began to appear on Polish-speaking territory. According to an unsourced article on Wikipedia, the first Baptist congregation was formed in 1872 ('Baptist Union of Poland', 2012). The Polish Baptist Union was created in 1922, and continues to operate today under the name of Kościół Chrześcian Baptystów w RP or the Church of Baptist Christians in the Republic of Poland. Its website states that at the end of the 1980s there were about 3000 members in 60 congregations, and that in November 2007 there were 86 congregations with almost 5000 members (Seweryn, 2008). There have also been Polish Pentecostals since the early decades of the 20th century. The Kościół Zielonoświątkowy w Polsce (2012) or Pentecostal Church in Poland says on one of its websites that in 1987 it had 84 congregations and 6,000 members, while by December 2010, the last date for which figures are given, there were 13,179 members in 219 congregations. It is also important to mention that according to their own statistics, the Jehovah's Witnesses (Świadkowie Jehowy) currently have over 126,000 members in 1,814 congregations in Poland (Watch Tower Bible and Tract Society of Pennsylvania, 2012). Since 1977, there has also been a Mormon community in Poland, headed by an American president, though membership figures were not available from the church's Polish website (Kościół Jezusa Chrystusa Świętych w Dniach Ostatnich, 2012).

For the Protestant churches to have survived at all during the wartime and communist periods is an achievement in itself. Any kind of religious practice was frowned upon under communism. Polish Catholics at least had strength in numbers, the political backing of the Vatican and an awareness shared by all Poles of the historical significance of the Catholic Church. The Protestant churches enjoyed none of these advantages. Indeed, they were not recognized as separate churches at all by the communist regime, which lumped all Protestant denominations together in a single category. That Lutheran, Baptist, Pentecostal and other communities retained their sense of identity until the fall of communism in 1989 is a sign of remarkable strength.

What 'Evangelical' Means

At this point, it is important to clarify exactly what is meant by 'evangelical Christianity'. Among non-evangelicals, this term is widely misunderstood; given its central place in the present book, I should explain how I am using it here.

From the perspective of Church structure and hierarchy, what 'evangelical' means can be hard to pinpoint. Practices in particular denominations vary widely, and individual churches also display great variation. There is no centralized authority, and so individual personal charisma assumes huge importance; anyone with sufficient innate authority can found a church, even a denomination. This leads to a bewildering array of churches, many of which carry the same or similar names – 'Church of God', 'Church of Christ' and so on. Quite different beliefs are held by fundamentalists than, say, Pentecostals. Some churches engage in political activity; others, like the Mennonites, do not vote and refuse to do military service.

In place of a central overarching authority, evangelicals are united by a set of beliefs common to all, though they are not formalized or written down in any official creed. I follow Noll (2002), Bebbington (1989) and other scholars in identifying four key tenets. First is crucicentrism: the centrality of Jesus Christ, and the importance of developing a 'personal relationship' with Christ and emulating him in every possible aspect of life. Second is biblicism, the central importance of the Bible as the revealed Word of God. Third is conversionism, the pivotal experience of being born again or 'saved'. Fourth is the crucial significance of witnessing to one's faith, which is often though not necessarily equated with the need to evangelize – that is, attempt to bring others into the church.

In all my experience conducting research on evangelicals, these four central beliefs have proved to be common to all evangelical denominations. No evangelical I have ever spoken with has ever disagreed with this definition – and I tried it out on every evangelical I interviewed for the present study. It is common to all evangelical denominations I have encountered, including Baptists, Mennonites, Brethren, Pentecostals and others. Furthermore, it has been my consistent experience that evangelicals generally do not place great importance upon distinctions *among* the various denominations, and in fact generally move from one kind of church to another without difficulty. When they change churches, it is rarely because of doctrinal differences, but rather because they are searching for the right kind of community, a pastor they feel comfortable with or for other reasons of a more personal nature. Hence, differences of doctrine and practice among the different denominations are not generally a subject of interest in the present study, except in a few cases that I will mention.

Missionary Work in Poland since 1989

Though there was some missionary activity in Poland under communism, it was the fall of the communist regime in 1989 that opened the floodgates. The perhaps coincidental appearance in the same year of the Manila Manifesto, a pan-evangelical call reinvigorating Christ's Great Commission to 'teach all nations' and baptize them, undoubtedly underlined the significance of the fall of communism in Central and Eastern Europe for missionary opportunities. Just as Western governments, and governmental or quasi-governmental agencies like the US Peace Corps, the British Council and the British organization VSO (Voluntary Service Overseas), began or significantly expanded operations in Poland, so too did the evangelical churches organize intense missionary campaigns to numerous countries in the region. (The same was true of religious denominations such as the Jehovah's Witnesses and the Mormons.)

In the case of the evangelical Protestant denominations, many missions were attached to existing churches or congregations – the large Southern Baptist mission in N., for example, was affiliated with the long-established Polish Baptist congregation in the city. As explained further in Chapter 8, relations between Polish and American adherents of what was supposedly the same denomination were in fact somewhat troubled; communication and collaboration were not always straightforward. Many evangelicals on both the Polish and North American sides told me of disagreements and misunderstandings, something that is echoed in Wanner's (2007) study of evangelism in Ukraine, a country that at the fall of communism had a much more extensive indigenous evangelical presence than did Poland.

In many ways, the early 1990s were the heyday of evangelical missionary work in Poland. Many of the Polish evangelicals I spoke to for this study had converted from Catholicism at that time, often under the influence of American or other Western missionaries. A typical story was that of Ola, a woman of about 40 who was taking classes at Lighthouse School at the time of the study. Encouraged by her sister, Ola had gone to an evangelical church and had been positively surprised by the simplicity of the language being used in comparison with the Catholic Church she was used to; subsequently, she and her sister were invited by Jane, an evangelical missionary, to a Bible study in Jane's home. As Ola told the story:

Ola: When I started going to Jane it really opened my eyes, because all those spiritual puzzles I was struggling with began to fall into place; she spoke in such a clear way about, you know, why Jesus came into the world, and the whole question of salvation, life after death, it all started to 'make sense' [Ola used this phrase in English], and all those things that I'd heard before in the Catholic Church that were just meaningless phrases, you know I'd heard them but I didn't understand them, but now they began to make sense. Then the prayer about devoting your life to God that I'd heard at the [evangelical] church I attended, which had been so straightforward, I started to think about it all, and I realized that I was more aware of what it was all about and that, speaking for myself of course, my life was too much to cope with on my own, and that it was better to hand over the reins of my life to someone who knows what they're doing, in other words the Lord God. And I remember that one evening I said that prayer. I sometimes joke that I was reborn twice; the first time was when Jesus gave me eternal life and the promise of going to heaven, whereas the second time was more deliberate, I really knew what I was doing, and it was more a matter of submission.

Ola was baptized into the local Baptist church in 1993.

Though subsequently less successful in terms of acquiring numbers of new church members, evangelical missionary work continued unabated in Poland from that time. And of course, what I am calling 'indigenous' Polish evangelical congregations – those affiliated with Polish church organizations, with Polish pastors and services in Polish serving almost exclusively Polish worshippers – continued to grow in number, and to pursue their own evangelizing work. At the time of the study, in the town of N. (a city of approximately 750,000 inhabitants) there were about 14 Polish-language evangelical churches, including three churches affiliated with the official Polish Baptist Church, two independent Baptist churches, two Pentecostal congregations and several others, including the church to which Lighthouse School was attached and one church with a more international congregation where bilingual services were held in English and Polish, involving simultaneous translation.

It should be noted here that though numerous evangelical churches flourish in Poland, many Catholic Poles retain a suspicion of what they regard as nonconventional forms of religion. Such religions are sometimes labeled as 'sekty', which in popular parlance is used to mean something like 'cults'. The label has at various times been applied to Mormons, Jehovah's Witnesses, the Hare Krishna and other groups. Like 'cult', the Polish word 'sekta' (the singular) carries connotations of brainwashing and other undesirable excesses. The word 'sekta' is sometimes bandied about in reference to evangelical churches, and in fact there was concern among some friends and relatives of Lighthouse participants that the school was run by a 'sekta'.

What 'Catholic' Means

It is equally necessary to begin to question what is meant by the term 'Catholic' in the context of 21st-century Poland. What exactly is Polish Catholicism, and how has it changed in the years since the fall of communism?

Of course, in one sense the Roman Catholic Church is easier to talk about and define than the loose affiliation of denominations described above. On the face of it, the Roman Catholic Church is entirely different in nature. It comprises a rigid hierarchy with a single leader, the Pope, who is God's vicar on earth. The content and form of a Catholic church service is determined to a high degree by the authority of Rome – one example of this is the recent 2011 change of translation for the English-language version of the Mass, which was imposed by Rome and has caused much grumbling among English-speaking Catholics (Richert, 2014). Any change in practice or belief is laid out in a Papal edict or bull. The Catholic Church adopts standard views on such issues as abortion, evolution and other fraught topics. At first glance there seems little room for maneuver.

Yet, in fact, there are significant differences in practice, both from one country or culture to another, and from one parish to another in the same national setting. Perhaps because of the very nature of the Catholic Church's strict hierarchy, a great deal of moral authority is invested in the parish priest; as a result, individual priests play an important role in shaping attitudes and (perhaps to a somewhat lesser extent) behaviors among their parishioners.

The Catholic Church in Poland in the post-1989 period was very heavily influenced by Pope John Paul II, who was elected to office in October 1978 and served till his death in March 2005. Of course, many volumes have been written about John Paul II and his legacy, and I doubt I can say anything new here. All I can do is give some indication of his influence on Polish Catholicism and more generally on religious practices in the country. John Paul II was extremely influential because he was a Pole and thus an insider who understood the country and its complex and troubled history. But his influence also came from an extraordinary personal charisma that Catholics and non-Catholics alike found compelling, and that in some cases seemed to mask, or even run counter to, the conservatism of some of his teachings.

Even before 1978, the Catholic Church had come to be regarded as something of a bulwark against the communist regime. In the post-World War II decades, while the influence of the Church in most communist countries waned, in Poland it grew stronger, with concomitant increases in church attendance, numbers of priests and churches (Zuzowski, 1992: 119). The reasons for this exception lie beyond the scope of the present book, but are undeniable. As Zuzowski describes, after two and a half decades of maintaining a low profile and restricting itself to purely religious matters, in the early 1970s the Church extended its activities to broader cultural and political spheres. The election of Pope John Paul II (formerly Cardinal Karol Wojtyła) in 1978 and the emergence of Solidarity in 1980 only intensified this process; as Zuzowski (1992: 119) states, 'By the late 1980s the Roman Catholic Church in Poland probably had more authority than ever in its entire existence'. During the 1980s, sometimes despite the misgivings and cautionary words of Church leaders (Porter-Szűcs, 2011: 259ff.), the Solidarity movement became indelibly associated with Catholicism, especially after the murder of Father Jerzy Popiełuszko by government agents in October 1984.

The fall of communism in 1989 was a moment of triumph for the Polish Roman Catholic Church; it was also a point of crisis, since the decoupling of religious belief and political struggle, along with the coming growth of material well-being (and materialism) that led in the same direction as the already largely secularized West, posed a huge threat to the Church's position. Sensing this, the Church acted quickly; a series of agreements between the Polish government and the Vatican, notably the 1993 concordat, served to solidify the Church's presence, for example ensuring that (Catholic) religion classes were offered in all Polish schools, and militating for the introduction of laws virtually banning abortion – Polish abortion laws remain among the strictest in all Europe whether within the European Union or beyond (a fact that can be seen in striking visual form on a Wikipedia map in which Poland stands as a single yellow patch in the middle of a sea of blue: 'Abortion Laws', 2013).

Though the Church remains highly influential in Polish public life, including in the political sphere, it is also the case that since 1989 there have been marked declines in church attendance, and in numbers entering the priesthood and religious orders. For example, as reported by CBOS in 2012, those stating that they attended church at least once a week dropped from 58% in 2005 (the year Pope John Paul II died) to 52% in 2012 (CBOS, 2012). The Catholic Church's own statistics put that number at 39.1% nationwide in 2013 (Instytut Statystyki Kościoła Katolickiego, 2013b); in 2009, it had been 41.4% (Instytut Statystyki Kościoła Katolickiego, 2013a). A 2009 article in *Gazeta Wyborcza*, one of Poland's leading newspapers, stated that in 2008 the number of students entering seminaries to train for the priesthood had dropped by over 10% from the previous year, and almost 40% since 2005 (695 students in 2008 vs. 1145 in 2005) (Wiśniewska, 2009); there was an even more dramatic decline in the numbers of people wishing to enter monasteries and especially convents – for the latter there had been a drop of over 20% in two years.

At the same time, the great majority of Poles still call themselves Catholics. In contrast to church attendance and the other indicators described above, the number of respondents self-identifying as Catholic has barely changed: according to one source, 94.6% declared themselves to be Catholic in 2005, and 93.1% in 2012 (CBOS, 2012). (Incidentally, the same poll reports an 800% rise in the number adherents of Protestantism in the same period – from 0.1% to 0.8% of the population.) Roughly equivalent numbers of Poles baptize their children, have church weddings and seek a Catholic burial. How can this discrepancy be understood? It will help to adapt a term used by many evangelical missionaries. They use the phrase 'cultural Christians' to refer to evangelicals who go through the motions of religious adherence – church attendance, the rites of baptism and marriage and so on – without a deep spiritual consciousness of what they are doing. It seems that in the case of Poland, we can suggest that many Poles are 'cultural Catholics'. For them, the social and cultural – i.e. identitarian – aspects of Catholicism are more important than its spiritual dimensions. Such an understanding further implies that, despite formal membership of and allegiance to the Roman Catholic Church, spiritual practices and needs may be more in flux than might initially seem to be the case.

A final important part of the picture is Radio Maryja. Radio Maryja ('Maryja' is an older spelling of Maria, the Polish name for the Virgin Mary) is a conservative Catholic radio station based in Toruń in Central Poland and run by Father Tadeusz Rydzyk, a Redemptorist priest. It was founded in 1991 and continues to thrive today; its operations include not just the radio station but a TV channel called 'Trwam' ('I abide') and a daily newspaper, *Nasz Dziennik*. Radio Maryja offers religious broadcasting, but is also deeply engaged in politics; it is closely aligned with the far right wing Prawo i Sprawiedliwość (Law and Justice) party. Father Rydzyk and his station have been repeatedly accused of anti-Semitism; they are staunchly nationalist, xenophobic (they remain, for instance, strongly opposed to Poland's membership in the European Union, which it joined in 2004) and socially conservative (Rydzyk and his associates are militantly opposed to abortion, for example). The Catholic Church seems unsure what to do about Rydzyk – Church authorities have been by turns critical and forbearing. Part of their hesitation lies in the fact that, though by no means all Catholic Poles listen to Radio Maryja, it wields a powerful influence in the cultural, spiritual and political life of the country. This is due partly to the sheer stridency of Rydzyk's media voice, but also to his capacity to mobilize – as Grabowska (2008: 13) points out, for example, in the 2005 elections voter turnout was 41%, whereas 65% of Radio Maryja listeners voted. Whatever one thinks of Radio Maryja, it is an undeniable presence on the religious, social and political scene in 21st-century Poland.

Thus, Poland's religious landscape is much more complex than a cursory glance might reveal. The Catholic Church, though still highly influential in political and social terms, has lost much of its spiritual drawing power beyond the ritual mileposts of baptism, marriage and death. While some Poles have been drawn to the nationalist extremism of Radio Maryja, others have moved progressively away from the Church. At the same time, there are other enduring religious traditions, including various forms of Protestantism; the latter takes the form of both indigenous Polish-language communities and an extensive missionary presence.

This, then, was the situation in Poland in 2008 when I began my study.

3 The Road to Lighthouse School

TESOL and Evangelical Christianity

The confluence of evangelical Christian mission work and English language teaching has proved to be one of the most contentious topics facing the field of TESOL (teaching English to speakers of other languages) in recent years. Indeed, in all my 30 years in TESOL, I cannot think of another issue that has riled people up the way this one does. For reasons that I hope I shall be able to go into in more detail in the course of the present book, this matter feels a lot more emotional and personal than any other controversy in the field – process vs. product in writing, debates over methodology or even the role of politics in language teaching. I've never before seen TESOL authors putting their considerable intellectual resources to work at expressing ideas of such emotional power. In the present chapter, I will review the debate thus far over evangelical Christianity in English teaching, and then move on to describe the current study: how it came to be, how it was designed and conducted and how it relates to what has already been written.

In the broadest sense, Christian mission work has by its very nature – that of encounters across cultural and linguistic space – been interwoven with language and language instruction since it first began (Spolsky, 2003; Willinsky, 1998). In what we might term the heyday of 'old-style missions' – the period between initial European contact with the peoples of the rest of the world, especially North and South America and sub-Saharan Africa, after 1492, and the breakup of colonial rule in the 20th century – missionaries served as language specialists in numerous ways. Some learned indigenous languages and translated the Bible and other religious materials into them; others, or the same ones, taught English, Spanish and other colonial languages to the 'natives'.

The present, ever closer relationship between evangelical Christianity and English language teaching, however, has more recent roots. Evangelical Christianity as a phenomenon within the Protestant churches can be dated to revival movements in British and American Protestant churches in the early 18th century (Balmer, 2010), though the present-day character of the evangelical churches has also been shaped in crucial ways by developments primarily in the US in the first half of the 20th century. Cox (1993), for example, dates the beginning of the Pentecostal movement, one of the most successful of all evangelical denominations, to the Azusa Street Revival of 1906 that took place in Los Angeles, California. Another key moment was the emergence around the time of World War II, partly in the aftermath of the Scopes trial of 1925, of a loosely associated but influential group of charismatic evangelical preachers such as Billy Graham and Dwight L. Moody. The North American roots of revivals and preaching have meant that in the late 20th and early 21st centuries, evangelical Christianity has been, for better or worse, indelibly associated with the US, though as many authors have pointed out (e.g. Wanner, 2007), the strong growth of evangelicalism in Europe, Africa and South America has in fact largely been due to the emergence of local churches without strong North American ties, and so these days the movement can rightly be considered global in a more interesting sense.

Another turning point came in the late 1970s. It was at this time that the evangelical movement found a political voice and emerged as a major player on the American political scene as a supporter of what is often dubbed 'cultural conservatism' – the defense of 'family values', which includes the struggle to illegalize abortion and, in more recent years, the fight against the legalization of gay marriage. Alan Peshkin (1986), in a book I will review below, happened to be conducting an ethnographic study of an American fundamentalist Christian high school in 1979–1980, during the US presidential campaign. He describes how the church affiliated with the school that he was studying became deeply embroiled in electioneering. Interestingly, the fundamentalist churches, like many other evangelical churches, chose to back the Republican but non-evangelical Ronald Reagan, the candidate they saw as being closer to them in the kind of 'values' they were interested in supporting, rather than Democratic contender Jimmy Carter, who unlike Reagan was 'one of them' – a fellow evangelical Christian. Since that time, the 'Christian Right' has constituted a significant political lobby in the US, a state of affairs that continues today (*The Economist*, 2016). Dudley (2011) describes the 'big four' issues that the lobby has engaged with: Along with the fight against abortion rights and gay marriage, there is the struggle against the environmental movement and the battle of intelligent design (creationism) over Darwinian natural selection (evolution).

A final crucial moment shaping the present-day situation of evangelical Christian mission work came in 1989. The fall of the Berlin Wall and the end of communism in Central and Eastern Europe and (two years later) the Soviet Union left a vast swath of the Earth available for proselytizing efforts. (Previously, there had of course been largely covert mission work behind the Iron Curtain, but this was inevitably on a relatively small scale, given the difficulties and dangers involved.) Coincidentally (or perhaps not), in Manila in July 1989, a pan-evangelical congress reaffirmed the Great Commission; the resulting 'Manila Manifesto' (Lausanne Movement, 2016) set out to attempt to 'evangelize the world' by the year 2000, aiming at 'the reaching of unreached peoples', that is to say, bringing the word of God to 'all nations' (Matthew 28:29). These two developments, along with numerous related events such as the relative democratization of many other countries in Asia, Africa and South America, led to a surge in missionary numbers in the final decade of the 20th century.

The emergence of TESOL as a distinct professional field can be dated to around the 1960s. The TESOL organization was founded in 1966, and its flagship professional and research journal, *TESOL Quarterly*, began publication in 1967. In Britain, the International Association for Teachers of English as a Foreign Language (IATEFL) organization dates from 1967, though the major British professional periodical in English teaching, the *English Language Teaching Journal*, had first appeared in 1946. Of course, the English language had been taught before this time for as long as it existed; but it was the 1960s that saw the emergence of a sense of profession and identity among English teachers.

For several decades, professional publications in the field of English teaching retained a narrow focus on the practical issues of instruction and research conceived in a somewhat narrow way. Though many English as a second language (ESL) and especially English as a foreign language (EFL) evangelical Christian teachers combined teaching and mission work in various ways, this fact somehow never attracted the attention of researchers (even though many of those researchers were also evangelicals). To the best of my knowledge, the first exchange of fire between evangelicals and non-evangelicals, in written form at least, came in 1996–1997 with a series of short pieces in *TESOL Matters*, a bimonthly newspaper-style magazine published at that time by the TESOL organization. In the opening salvo, a front-page article entitled 'Keeping the Faith', Julian Edge (1996b: 1) referred to a TESOL convention plenary by H. Douglas Brown which mentioned 'teachers whose greater aim in getting involved in TESOL is to bring more people closer to Jesus'. In response to this, Edge (1996b: 1) said: 'very clear to me is the conviction that taking on educational responsibilities under false pretenses is utterly repellent'. Crucially, in a quotation I shall return to, Edge (1996b: 1) stated:

> If there are people overtly engaged in TESOL with the covert purpose of exporting their moral and/or religious certainties to the rest of the world, they are engaged in a project that deserves the accusations of linguistic and cultural imperialism that are leveled against it.

In a letter written in response, Earl Stevick (1996: 6) recounted how he had entered the field of teaching with exactly the aim that Edge referred to, but that he was 'quite open about it, so there were no false pretenses'. Stevick (1996) focused on the word 'export' in the above quotation, and said:

> *Export* certainly can mean 'force or pressure other people to accept', which is what I get from your [Edge's] context. But of course it can also mean 'make attractive and available in a free market'. I agree there's no place for the former, but I find nothing sinister in the latter. (Stevick, 1996: 6; emphasis in the original)

I've dwelled on what are in fact two very short pieces of writing for the simple reason that the arguments set up in this exchange anticipate much of the future debate.

After the exchange, nothing else appeared in print for some time. Then, round about the beginning of the 21st century, all of a sudden people started paying attention. I'm still not quite sure what caused it all. Partly, it may have been the field's delayed reaction to the increased public presence of evangelicals in the US and elsewhere, as described above. Certainly, 9/11 and the subsequent invasion of Iraq played an important part. One of the first publications in what this time became an extended ongoing discussion in print (I hesitate for the moment to use the word 'dialogue') was Edge's (2003) short article 'Imperial Troopers and Servants of the Lord: A Vision of TESOL for the 21st Century', which juxtaposed US neo-imperialism with missionary efforts in the Muslim world in particular. Yet, even before then, in 2000, my colleague Manka Varghese had drawn my attention to the significant presence of evangelical Christians among the MA students in the program she was working in at the time; this led to a mention of the topic in a book I was working on at the time (Johnston, 2003), and eventually to a study (Varghese & Johnston, 2007) that I believe was the first empirical – that is to say, data based – piece of research in our professional field on this subject.

But to return to Edge's article and the responses it provoked – what was it about? What was at stake?

As I suggested above, much of Edge's 2003 article was hinted at in the earlier exchange with Stevick. In the second article, Edge gave examples of calls by evangelical Christians to use English teaching as a platform for mission work. Edge (2003) criticized the use of covert methods (see the quotation in Chapter 1), and made an appeal for what he termed 'transparency', stating:

> If, for some people, religious conversion is their goal and TESOL is their means, then I believe that these people have a moral duty to make that instrumental goal and means relationship absolutely explicit at all stages of their work. (Edge, 2003: 704)

It's also significant that, as the title of the article indicates, Edge explicitly identifies global evangelism as a neo-imperial project to be compared to, or perhaps better aligned with, the US invasion and occupation of Iraq in 2003.

TESOL Quarterly published two responses to Edge's article, by Purgason (2004) and Griffith (2004), both evangelicals themselves. Purgason (2004) objected to Edge's use of emotive language, pointed out the commitment to professionalism among many evangelical ESL teachers and suggested that learners and their families should be credited with the ability to evaluate what is being offered by their English teachers. Griffith (2004: 714–715), in turn, argued that 'all teachers teach out of their worldview', and that TESOL as a field has an agenda beyond teaching language. Griffith (2004: 716) also dissociated English from the specific interests of the US, suggesting that 'one safeguard against domination by English-speaking societies is the diffusion of the English language'.

At around the same time, other critics of the use of English teaching in mission work were raising objections similar to Edge's. In one of the articles most militantly opposed to the use of English teaching for mission work, Pennycook and Coutand-Marin (2004) reviewed website and other information concerning, among other things, teacher training programs for those planning to engage in mission work using English teaching. They then drew links between global Christianity and the agenda of the Christian Right in the US, and further, challenged the notion of English teaching as Christian service by questioning the benignity of the whole enterprise of teaching English around the world. Pennycook and Coutand-Marin (2004: 350) concluded by arguing for what they called a 'critical approach' as being preferable to what they labeled 'TEML' or 'Teaching English as a Missionary Language'. Among their objections to the latter, they repeat Edge's (1996b) concern about the concealment of the teacher's purposes;

they call for 'a position of respect and engagement with students' cultures and ideas' (Pennycook & Coutand-Marin, 2004: 350) which they see lacking in evangelical approaches; and they claim that 'the moral project of TEML all too often lacks an adequate ethics. While religious thinking is supposed to encourage engagement with hard ethical questions, all too often it does little more than promote a prior moral absolutism' (Pennycook & Coutand-Marin, 2004: 351).

Edge, and Pennycook and Coutand-Marin, were correct in saying that these issues had hitherto been ignored in the field – that there had been, in Pennycook and Coutand-Marin's (2004: 338) words, 'massive global silence' about them. It is also true that evangelicals themselves had kept a low profile in the profession. Part of the reason, undoubtedly, was that evangelicals in TESOL were still thinking in terms of what Balmer (2010: 49) calls the mid-century 'era of separation', during which evangelicals 'withdrew... from any culture outside of their own subculture' (Balmer, 2010: 49) and 'burrowed into their own subculture' (Balmer, 2010: 49–50) – certainly this separationist attitude seemed to prevail at the TESOL conventions in the early 2000s when I was starting to take an interest in the Christian Caucus, a special interest group within the TESOL organization. It's also true, though, that, often because of the deep-seated hostility of non-Christians toward evangelical Christianity, many evangelicals felt that there was no room in the professional discourse for them to defend themselves or, less confrontationally speaking, to present their views.

At the same time, evangelical Christians were engaging in a professional discourse of their own. Their work, though, was appearing outside of the publishing arena of the discipline at large, in houses (like Eerdmans) and journals (e.g. *Christianity and Language Teaching*) that are largely unfamiliar to non-evangelicals. Many leading TESOL specialists essentially led parallel writing lives, addressing evangelical and non-evangelical audiences in very different arenas and ways. A telling example is that of Don Snow, a well-known figure in TESOL. Snow's (1996) book *More Than a Native Speaker*, a teacher training and professional guide for 'volunteers teaching English abroad', was published by the TESOL organization, and is widely known and still extensively used and referred to in the field. Yet, a few years after this book appeared, Snow (2001) also brought out *English Teaching as Christian Mission: An Applied Theology* with Herald Press, a Mennonite publishing house. This book, widely referred to by evangelicals in TESOL, is virtually unknown to non-evangelical TESOL professionals. Likewise, an engaging book entitled *The Gift of the Stranger* (Smith & Carvill, 2000), focusing not on ESL but on foreign language teaching, was published by

Eerdmans, a publisher of 'religious literature', and is similarly unknown to non-evangelical language teaching professionals (see also Smith, 2009; Smith & Smith, 2011).

It was something of a milestone, then, when Baurain (2007) took the bull by the horns and succeeded in publishing, in a highly regarded journal (*Language, Identity, and Education*), an evangelical response to critics like Pennycook and Coutand-Marin (and myself, as it happens). Baurain's article constitutes the first major piece of writing in the professional literature that, from an overtly evangelical standpoint, counters the objections raised by Pennycook and Coutand-Marin, Edge and others. While acknowledging the undesirability of covertness, Baurain (2007: 205) focuses mainly on the matter of 'respect for persons', specifically offering an answer to this question: 'Can Christian witness – the desire for people to convert to the Christian faith – and the value of respect for persons be reconciled?'. Baurain points out that all teaching aims at changing those being taught; he goes further, and compares the efforts of Christian missionaries to the actions of 'believers' in critical pedagogy (Baurain [2007: 213] refers to the latter approach as Pennycook's 'gospel') as they strive to win over students and student teachers – that is, to do 'their energetic best to persuade others to believe and act in the same ways as themselves' (Baurain, 2007: 213). Last, while acknowledging that Christians do in fact believe in some absolute truths, he argues that though this can sometimes lead to arrogance, for Christians it should be, and often is, accompanied rather by humility. He ends by observing that in any case 'conversion' must be a freely chosen act and cannot be forced on someone against his or her will.

I have spent some time over relatively few articles because together they contain most of the major points made on either side of the debate, such as it is, about the use of English teaching for missionary purposes. Many of these arguments are expanded upon in Wong and Canagarajah (2009), which remains the single most extensive discussion of the matter. This book contains essays both by evangelical Christians and non-evangelicals (a group somewhat misleadingly labeled 'critical educators'), many of which center around personal anecdotes and perspectives (indeed, lest there be any doubt that the identity of each writer was to be seen as a crucial part of the picture, the editors saw fit to solicit and publish a 'spiritual identification statement' from each contributor).

Wong and Canagarajah (2009) constituted an important step forward in the willingness of both sides to engage with one another and forge efforts at dialogue across what remains a vast intellectual and spiritual chasm. For my purposes, though, a major shortcoming of the book was not its spiritual positioning so much as the fact that with only a couple of exceptions – the chapters by Bradley (2009), Loptes (2009) and Wong (2009) – the 30 contributions do not draw on empirical data. It was precisely the dearth of data-based research that had led Manka Varghese and me in 2003 to gather data for a study that was eventually published in 2007. For this study, we interviewed undergraduate teachers in training at two evangelical universities, one in the Pacific Northwest and one in the Mid-South. Though purely interview-based research has its limitations, this study at least included the voices of actual evangelical Christian teachers in research conducted by non-evangelicals, and more broadly, was written with a view to countering generalizations and essentializations on both sides.

Since this time, though, it remains the case that very little empirical inquiry has appeared in print. Indeed, it seems that the non-evangelical community has somewhat lost interest in the matter. The two major contributions to empirical research in the last few years have both been from evangelical researchers. Brad Baurain's (2013) dissertation examined the importance of religious beliefs in mostly evangelical Christian ESL teachers working in Southeast Asia. In the same year, Wong *et al.* (2013) offered an edited volume of empirical studies on various aspects of the intersection of English language teaching and evangelical Christian faith; all the contributions are from evangelical Christians, and in the foreword, Canagarajah (2013: xxiii) claims that in general the volume 'ushers in a tradition of research on faith-based teaching'. Yet, both these contributions rely almost exclusively on interview or survey data, and both focus on teachers and teacher identity only. Broader contextual information and analysis are missing.

Other Points of Reference

Though no study like the present one has been reported in the professional literature, much has been written on related topics in a number of disciplines and fields (anthropology, religious studies, Slavic studies, education, sociology and so on). There is of course a vast literature on Christianity, on Protestantism and on evangelicalism; much has also been written about Christian missionary work. I will refer to this literature selectively at various points throughout the present book. Certain studies in particular, though, are close in spirit if not exactly in subject matter to my project, and I'd like to mention them here.

First, many years ago, the educational ethnographer Alan Peshkin (1986) published what remains one of the best and most detailed empirical investigations into the intersection of evangelical Christianity and education – *God's Choice*, an 18-month ethnographic study of a fundamentalist Christian high school in Illinois. Reference to this study will be made at various points in the present book. For now, I shall only say that, for me, Peshkin served as an inspiration, as a non-Christian with a profound and abiding interest in evangelical Christian schooling, and as a researcher who was able to set aside his own views, feelings and reflections for long enough to gain a deep knowledge and understanding of the setting and the people he was studying.

Another key book in terms of my own project was historian and anthropologist Catherine Wanner's (2007) *Communities of the Converted*, an extensive empirical examination of evangelicalism in post-Soviet Ukraine. The historical tradition of evangelicalism (primarily involving the Baptist and Pentecostal Churches) was much stronger in Ukraine than in Poland, and Wanner reveals tensions between indigenous evangelicals and foreign, primarily (though not only) North American missionaries. She also shows evangelical practices among Ukrainian emigres to the United States. Above all, as indicated by her subtitle – 'Ukrainians and Global Evangelism' – she locates church activity and mission work in post-1989 Ukraine within the movements and activities of 'global Christianity' – the worldwide enactment of the Great Commission, which involves participants from all around the globe. Indeed, the largest evangelical church, not just in Ukraine, but according to Wanner in the whole of Europe (see also Vu, 2008), the 30,000-member Embassy of the Blessed Kingdom of God, located in Kyiv, is run by a Nigerian pastor, Sunday Adelaja; Adelaja's church sends missionaries to numerous other countries, including the US.

The phenomenon of American teaching overseas, in turn, is examined somewhat quizzically but in engaging detail by Jonathan Zimmerman (2006) in *Innocents Abroad: American Teachers in the American Century* – that century, of course, being the 20th. The story of American teachers traveling to teach in other countries is to a significant extent one of missionary efforts on behalf of various churches (though Zimmerman also looks at the extensive involvement of the Peace Corps, which among other things sent large numbers of often unqualified young people to teach English in Central and Eastern Europe after 1989). Balancing what he calls 'the story of American innocence and the story of American iniquity' (Zimmerman, 2006: 212), Zimmerman reveals the ambiguities of attitude in many Americans teaching overseas, especially in the latter half of the century, and reminds us that the encounters between Americans and their hosts around the world were varied and complex. At the same time, Zimmerman (2006: 216, emphasis in the original) notes that the essentializing of cultural identities into 'American' and 'local' 'blinded them [the American teachers] to diversity *within* the cultures they encountered and – especially – to values they might have shared with their hosts'. Zimmerman's work will be mentioned elsewhere in the present book; his focus on innocence, in particular, will resonate with attitudes and ideas expressed by the various missionaries in the city of N.

Lastly, two in-depth qualitative studies also impacted the content and form, respectively, of the present project. Catherine Prendergast's (2008) *Buying into English* looks at the role of English teaching and learning, and of the English language more generally, in post-communist Slovakia, Poland's neighbor to the southeast, and a country that is in economic and social terms rather comparable. Prendergast provides many concrete insights into the ways in which English has become an almost universally unquestioned 'good' in post-1989 Central Europe; her work was a constant reminder of the geopolitical, social and cultural context of the work of Lighthouse School. James S. Bielo's (2009) *Words Upon the Word*, in turn, an ethnographic study of Bible study groups in evangelical communities in central Michigan, was a fine example of the sort of small-scale, detailed research I was aiming to do. Through the in-depth study of seemingly unremarkable encounters, Bielo succeeds in revealing profoundly interesting aspects of interaction in a very concrete setting. This will be my goal in looking at classroom interaction at Lighthouse.

The Present Study

Soon after completing the study with Manka Varghese mentioned above, I began to contemplate a large-scale study that would provide more in-depth empirical data, and a deeper level of engagement with the subject matter than had been possible in the short format offered by book chapters and journal articles. At the same time, my central aim was to move beyond the confrontational forms of discourse that we were becoming trapped within, and to allow myself extended contact with the evangelical Christian teaching world of which my non-evangelical colleagues were so leery.

After deciding on Poland as a location for my study (see Chapter 1), I started by doing extensive research on the internet to see what information I could glean, both about evangelical missionary work in Poland in general, and about language schools attached to missions in particular. It turned out that there were large numbers of evangelical missionaries in the country, primarily from the US, but also from other countries such as Britain, Canada and Nigeria. My web-based research identified approximately 120 long-term evangelical missionaries based in Poland in various capacities, along with a much greater number of short-term missionaries present at any given time. I found about six evangelical-run language schools (a few more came to light during the time I was actually in Poland), located both in larger cities and small towns around the country.

At this point I should say what I mean by 'language school'. Throughout Poland, as in many other countries, there are numerous private schools that offer language classes to adults and children. They are not affiliated with state-run educational systems. Learners typically attend perhaps two or three classes a week. The schools vary widely in terms of their materials, focus, and the experience and qualifications of their teachers, as well as in size; some are part of a recognized chain (such as International House); some have a governmental affiliation (the British Council, the Institut Français); others are locally owned and often though not always standalone. At the time I conducted my research in 2008–2009, in the city of N. alone there were several dozen such schools. Among other things, this means that competition for learners is considerable.

It is also the case that Poles have always been avid language learners; language schools existed even under communism, and their numbers exploded in 1989. English is by far the most popular choice. Children are sent to such schools by parents concerned that classes in the public education system are inadequate; many adults choose to study English to improve their career options, or simply for pleasure. Poland's accession to the European Union in 2004 only intensified the hunger for language instruction. In the aftermath of the accession, hundreds of thousands of Poles moved to the United Kingdom to work, and the desire to remain in contact with family members who had made this move, or indeed to join them, added an important incentive for those back home in Poland to learn English.

As I investigated the language schools run by evangelical missionaries, from the very start the most intriguing was a place called Lighthouse School (like almost all personal and proper names in the present book, this is a pseudonym). When I first found out about Lighthouse, in about 2006, it was located in the small town of D. about 50 miles outside Warsaw, and it offered what was described as a 'Bible-based curriculum'. I immediately paid attention, since this seemed to ensure that the encounter I was becoming interested in – between North American missionary teachers and Polish Catholic learners – would be, as it were, forced into the open.

Over the following months, I kept an eye on Lighthouse via the internet. As I submitted applications for funding to allow me to be in Poland for the academic year 2008–2009, I never identified Lighthouse specifically since I had not obtained permission to conduct my study, nor even met the two women who ran the school, yet it was always Lighthouse that I imagined as the site of my study.

The study was designed as a standard ethnography by participant observation (Glesne & Peshkin, 1992; Marshall & Rossman, 1989). I proposed spending a whole school year at an evangelical-run language school in Poland, observing, recording, interviewing and collecting materials. The exact nature of my 'participation' leaned strongly toward what Glesne and Peshkin (1992: 40) call the 'observer end' of the participant–observation continuum; it matched their description of the 'observer as participant', in which '[t]he researcher remains primarily as an observer but has some interaction with study participants' (Glesne & Peshkin, 1992: 40). As a non-believer, I could not take a role in the functioning of the school: teachers have to be not just committed Christians but official missionaries. At the same time, as will be seen later, at certain moments I did find myself playing a more active part in lessons and school activities than I had anticipated. Nevertheless, in principle I remained an outsider, observing lessons and other aspects of the life of the school, and attempting to be 'minimally intrusive' (Marshall & Rossman, 1989: 81).

By the time I heard that I had received funding, in the spring of 2008 – in the form of a Fulbright Research Award – Lighthouse School had moved to N., a sizeable city in the southern part of Poland. This made it an even more attractive proposition, since the larger urban setting meant that more interesting things would be happening around the school. Nevertheless, I decided I should approach the selection of a site in a systematic way. I traveled to Poland in May 2008 to make site visits to four schools I had identified – of the original six I had found, one closed at the end of the 2007–2008 school year because of financial concerns, while another seemed to have shut down some time before.[1]

Lighthouse was the first school I visited. I had to meet with Sydney and Taryn, the directors of the school, the day after my arrival, as they were leaving for the summer the following day. I was extremely apprehensive about the meeting, since the opportunity to work at the school hinged entirely on this first encounter. To make matters worse, I was badly jet-lagged. Nevertheless, Sydney and Taryn turned out to be extremely agreeable people, and we had a very pleasant conversation. We seemed to take a liking to one another, and both Sydney and Taryn expressed their willingness to have me present at their school the following year. (The school is described in detail in Chapter 4.)

Despite this promising step, knowing how hard and drawn-out the matter of gaining entry can be, and also for the sake of thoroughness, I continued to visit the other schools on my list. I was received very graciously in two of them. The first was run by Anabaptist (Mennonite) missionaries from the US and was located in a small town outside Warsaw that served as a dormitory suburb for those working in the city. The teachers were all American missionaries. The problem here was, firstly, that the institution was not formally a 'school', but rather the teachers were 'giving lessons'. This meant that administratively there could be problems. Second, the lessons offered had no religious or spiritual content – regular EFL teaching materials were used.

The second school I visited was affiliated with a well-established Polish Baptist church. It was the oldest school of its kind in Poland, having been founded in 1989, and was located in another large city in the south. The teaching faculty was a mixture of Poles and missionaries from a variety of English-speaking countries including the US, Britain and Australia. Here too, the lessons themselves constituted straightforward EFL teaching with commonly used textbooks.

On this visit, it proved impossible to visit the fourth school on my list, which was located in the same city as the preceding one. I emailed and called the director and secretary of the school several times, but was not able to obtain an appointment. I found out later that the school was in difficult straits, and was threatened with closure as a result of internal politics connected with the church it was affiliated with a different Baptist assembly. I never did manage to see any lessons, though I eventually got to meet with the director, who proved to be one of my most interesting informants (see Chapter 8).

After these visits, I was quite sure that Lighthouse was the school I wanted to observe. Aware that its Bible-based curriculum was atypical, I felt this aspect of the school's work would provide the most direct way of addressing many of the questions and concerns raised in the literature reviewed above, especially since I planned to focus on adult classes (though Lighthouse offered classes for young children and teens as well as adults). Was coercion or deception being used? Did classes target the poor and vulnerable, as some suspected? Was the school preaching the 'gospel of prosperity' and promoting conservative values like militarism and homophobia, as Pennycook and Coutand-Marin (2004: 343–345) suggested? How many Poles were converting? Lighthouse seemed an ideal venue to explore these and related questions.

After returning to the US, I wrote to Sydney and Taryn and asked them formally if they would agree to my conducting my study at Lighthouse. As I had promised them during our meeting, I sent them a draft of the Human Subjects application I was filling out for the study, and explained that the ethical aspect of my research was of great importance to me. I explained too that all personal names, names of institutions and place names would be changed to maintain confidentiality. Sydney and Taryn, in turn, promised to pass my request on to the board that oversaw their mission.

Eventually, I received the school's permission to conduct my study, and some time after that, approval from my university's Human Subjects Committee or IRB (Institutional Review Board). I traveled back to Poland at the very beginning of September 2008. I began observing in the school during the registration period for the first semester in early September 2008, and stayed until the end-of-year graduation party in mid-May 2009.

In terms of research methods, the study employed data collection procedures widely used in ethnographic inquiry (Fetterman, 1989; Glesne & Peshkin, 1992; Marshall & Rossman, 1989). I observed classes, gathered materials used in teaching and in the work of the school and conducted interviews with teachers, students, administrators and other stakeholders. I also attended church services most Sundays at different churches – in all, I visited about half of the more than a dozen evangelical churches in the city of N. One church, which was led by a US-based Southern Baptist mission and whose services were in English, I attended regularly throughout the school year, and interviewed several of the missionaries working there. Lastly, during the second semester, I spent several days traveling around Poland and conducting observations of, and interviews with, teachers at other evangelical language schools.

As mentioned above, I was present as a participant observer, with the emphasis on 'observer' – that is to say, I sat in on classes but did not take part in the work of teaching. Yet the extremely small size of the classes (see Chapter 4) meant that my presence was much more noticeable than it would have been with larger class sizes. Because of this, I felt it was particularly important to accustom the students to my presence from the very beginning. The school offered classes to learners of all ages, but I was especially interested in the classes for adults, because I was most curious about how mature adult Catholics responded to the evangelical endeavors of the school, whatever these might be. Furthermore, I felt that the higher the level of students, the more likely it was that there would be interesting interactions in class. At the same time, I wanted to be able to see the Bible-based curriculum I had read and heard about. For this combination of reasons, at the beginning of the school year I selected a class labeled 'intermediate' for regular observation. This label may have been somewhat optimistic, but the learners were in fact capable of discussing linguistically demanding topics in English, as shall be seen. The class used materials based around the novel *Robinson Crusoe* in an adaptation prepared by the school itself. Much more will be said about this curriculum below, especially in Chapter 5.

The teacher in the fall semester was Allie, a missionary from Texas in her mid-twenties. The class met twice a week on Tuesday and Thursday evenings from 7.30–9.00 pm.

I attended the class from the very beginning, and with only one interruption for a week-long business trip back to the US, I observed every class throughout the semester. During an introductory period of about six weeks, I observed without recording or taking notes, so the students could get used to my presence. I sat to the side of the class, keeping my head down, though this wasn't always enough to remain inconspicuous, and from time to time Allie would call on me with a language question or occasionally to form a pair for pair work. I quickly came to accept this infringement of my non-participatory status, though at the same time I made every effort to minimize such interactions in length and frequency.

After the initial six weeks, I began recording classes, and did so until the end of the semester. I recorded using two Olympus WS110 Digital Voice Recorders placed at different points in the classroom. I also took notes. At this point too I began interviewing. I started with the teachers; through the course of the semester I interviewed each teacher, multiple times in the case of Allie and of Jean, the school's acting director while Sydney and Taryn, the regular directors, were on furlough in North America. I also began the process of interviewing students.

It was also at this time that I began attending the Friday 'team meetings' of all the teachers, along with Agnieszka, the Polish officer manager, which were held in Jean's apartment on a Friday morning, a day without classes. These meetings I also recorded.

Toward the middle of December, Sydney and Taryn returned from furlough and resumed their positions, while Jean and Allie left. As the new semester began, Sydney took over the class that Allie had been teaching, and I continued to observe and record it. With only a couple of breaks for short trips and one brief illness, I attended and recorded every class throughout the semester – 25 classes out of about 30. I also continued to conduct interviews and attend as many team meetings as I could. In addition, Taryn was offering a book-club style class centered around William P. Young's *The Shack*, a bestselling novel on spiritual themes widely read in the evangelical community. I observed this class once a week, on Tuesday mornings (the same group's Thursday morning classes were devoted to grammar teaching, which was of less interest to me), and recorded the classes. In this way, I was able to conduct extended observations of three different teachers in the school: Allie, Sydney and Taryn.

All through the year, I paid visits to other classes in the school, observing almost every class at least once, including the children's classes, and I attended numerous extracurricular events at the school. Throughout the period of data collection, I also kept a research journal, which I wrote immediately after each observation, interview or other school-related experience. The journal allowed me to record facts and impressions, and also gave me an opportunity to begin to reflect on, analyze and synthesize what I had seen and heard.

All in all, I collected the following: 44 classroom recordings from the 3 classes observed extensively; 45 interviews with about 28 different individuals; 134 pages of notes from classroom observations; about 200 pages of the research journal; several hundreds of pages of documents, including the entire curriculum of the school's adult classes; and extensive email correspondence.

With this mass of data, I have had to be selective. Aware from the very beginning that I would have neither the time nor the resources to transcribe all the classroom data, I made detailed notes during my observations to identify the parts that were of interest to me, primarily when spiritual and religious matters were being discussed, or when other topics of interest came up. This allowed me to find these moments on the recordings and transcribe them as needed. The interviews were another story – though I made notes in my journal about especially interesting topics and statements, there was so much I wanted to listen to again that I went through each of the interview recordings and transcribed relevant passages. The documents were used selectively – I was primarily interested in the Crusoe materials, and these are analyzed in some detail in Chapter 5.

As mentioned above, I decided that the study should be carried out as a straightforward ethnography. At various points, I considered alternative, extra ways of collecting data – focus groups, questionnaires and so on – but in the end, the data I gathered through the 'traditional' means of observations, interviews and document gathering were so rich, and my informants, teachers and students alike, so forthcoming, that I felt I had more than enough material to do what I wanted to do.

I call the present study an *ethnography of contact*. Most ethnographic studies are interested in 'the' culture of a given setting – village, school, classroom, whatever it might be. In the case of Lighthouse, what interested me most of all was the encounter of two significantly different cultural worlds that met in the space of the school, and more particularly in the classroom. In Chapter 8, as well as throughout the book, I say more about these cultural worlds, of course problematizing the very idea of 'culture' as a monolithic thing. But *prima facie* it seemed reasonable, and extremely interesting, to wonder what happens when the values, practices and assumptions of North American evangelicals encounter those of Polish Catholics in a sustained and intimate setting.

The idea of contact came from the work of Mary Louise Pratt (1992), and specifically her use of the term 'contact zone', which she defines as:

> the space of colonial encounters, the space in which peoples geographically and historically separated come into contact with each other and establish ongoing relations. (Pratt, 1992: 6)

As this quotation suggests, Pratt is concerned primarily with encounters in colonial space, and her book focuses on European accounts of cultural encounters elsewhere in the world. Indeed, it is important to acknowledge that the above quotation continues: '...ongoing relations, usually involving conditions of coercion, radical inequality, and intractable conflict' (Pratt, 1992: 6). Such conditions cannot be said to obtain in any obvious way in the relation between North Americans and Poles in the 21st century, and in general it might seem odd to regard the evangelical–Catholic encounter in Poland as a colonial one. Nevertheless, as I will repeatedly attempt to show in this book, there is a significant colonial dimension to relations between North American evangelicals and 'indigenous' Polish Catholics in early 21st-century Poland, and the use of a suggestive colonial framing device is quite deliberate. Pratt (1992: 7) further emphasizes the way in which what she calls 'a "contact" perspective' sees 'relations among colonizers and colonized... not in terms of separateness or apartheid, but in terms of copresence, interaction, interlocking understandings and practices'. Once again, I have omitted the final clause of the quotation: '...often within radically asymmetrical relations of power' – in order to underline the applicability of Pratt's framework to a much broader set of concerns and locations than she originally perhaps intended. Indeed, Singh and Doherty (2004: 11) explicitly employ the idea of contact zones – which they describe as 'spatial temporal locations that have already been constituted relationally and that enter new relations through historical processes of displacement' – to analyze English language teaching in the 'global university'.

The present study was also guided by the broader idea that our very notion of 'pure cultures' is fundamentally mistaken, and that the true business of life in fact always goes on in places where these so-called cultures are constantly blurring as they come into contact with one another. Singh and Doherty (2004), for instance, quote Clifford as writing: 'Cultural centers, discrete regions and territories, do not exist prior to contacts, but are sustained through them, appropriating and disciplining the restless movements of people and things' (Clifford, 1997: 3, quoted in Singh & Doherty, 2004: 12). Many anthropologists have made the same claim. At the same time, I am mindful of the way in which many cultural encounters, especially in the often vapid space of the postmodern, can become what MacCannell (1992) chillingly but tellingly calls 'empty meeting grounds' – places where ideas and peoples come into proximity but do not ultimately impinge on one another. One aim of this study is to explore the extent to which the sustained 'contact' provided by English classes at Lighthouse School can and should be seen as a genuine interpenetration, in the way Pratt and Clifford suggest, or whether in fact the sides in the encounter are relatively unchanged by it, as MacCannell contends.

Another key ethnographic question is the extent to which Lighthouse School can be said to be 'typical' of its kind. As the research methodology experts rightly urge us to ask: If the present book is a case study, what is it a case *of*? To what extent is Lighthouse like or unlike other language schools run by evangelical missionaries in Europe and around the world?

Of course, this is both a legitimate and an unfair question to ask. It is legitimate because any study has not just a 'what' but a 'so what' – a claim to be of interest beyond its own boundaries. It is unfair, in turn, for several reasons. First, ethnographies do not claim to be generalizable. Rather, as Lincoln and Guba (1985) point out, the aim is the opposite: to *particularize*, that is, to say something that is true of the case under consideration *in particular*, initially without regard for whether this truth extends to other comparable cases and settings or not. Second, a fundamental underlying assumption in qualitative inquiry is that each setting or context is in significant ways unique and unrepeatable, just as human beings, and relations between them, are always also unique. Third, in many qualitative studies a case is chosen precisely because it *is* in fact different from other comparable cases; the researcher hopes that the unusual aspects of the case will reveal particular insights into the setting and, possibly, others in its category. Such was definitely the case with Lighthouse School, whose Bible-based curriculum set it apart from all other English language schools run by evangelicals in Poland (see Chapter 9).

As always in such cases, to a significant degree the onus is on the reader, not the writer, to determine the extent to which findings in one context are or are not relevant to attempts to understand other contexts. This is decidedly the case here. I will do my best to provide thick description, and to convey the realities of Lighthouse School as they were seen and expressed by those who took part in the life of the school, including myself. I believe firmly that the missionary teachers I spoke with and observed over my months at Lighthouse have much in common with other missionary teachers working elsewhere in Poland, across Europe and around the world. I will suggest at various points what I think those commonalities might be. But it is up to you, the reader, to determine whether what I say rings true for other individuals, relationships and settings with which you may be familiar.

As befits a study that is the first of its kind, I have refrained from taking a heavily theoretical stance. Above all, I was interested in the phenomenon itself – Lighthouse School, what went on there, the people and relationships involved. This is perhaps itself theoretical, and one might say my approach is phenomenological, in the sense of giving a reflective account of my own unfolding experience of the school. In any case, a large part of my endeavor here has been to gather some facts about Lighthouse School, and to convey experientially what it was like to teach and to learn there. At the same time, no study is devoid of theoretical underpinnings, and many of these will be explicitly mentioned or implicitly hinted at in the following pages. My orientation toward discourse, which is not merely methodological but arises from a strong conviction that much of our understanding of reality is mediated to a significant level through language, has informed both my methodological choices (e.g. the close study of classroom interaction and of the written materials made by Taryn and Sydney) and my understanding of my own task as a researcher. Much previous work looking at the use of English teaching for evangelical purposes, including some of my own (Johnston & Varghese, 2008), has explored the neo-imperialist and neocolonial dimensions of US-based mission work, and these perspectives are very much present in my ways of thinking about Lighthouse School; the same is true of critical approaches, in particular critical pedagogy, a line of thinking that remains very influential in my ideas about teaching and learning. When working with evangelicals, gender issues are rarely far from the surface, and gender-based theoretical approaches will emerge here from time to time. In Chapter 9, I explore further the theoretical possibilities for coming to terms with the phenomena observed at Lighthouse School. But through the rest of the book, I have deliberately chosen to employ a light touch when utilizing theoretical resources.

Positioning Myself

Lastly, if ever a researcher needed to position himself or herself with respect to an ethnographic study, it is with this one. Usually, when people hear about my project the first question they ask is: So are you an evangelical? Of course, this choice itself is telling – I'm never asked if I am a Catholic, for instance. Such a guess reflects a general assumption that only evangelicals should be, are or could be interested in their own work. One of the major goals of this book is to counter such an assumption, and to argue that non-evangelicals equally would do well to take an empirical interest in evangelicals and in evangelical mission work.

As I stated in the opening pages of this book, I am an atheist. I don't believe in the existence of any divine being. It follows that I do not regard the Christian Bible (or any other text) as the Word of God, or as morally authoritative. I'm quite comfortable in my atheism – for many years I wrestled with matters of faith as an agnostic, and when I finally concluded I could not believe in a divine being, I felt a sense of relief; many things fell into place, and I felt that my doubting phase was over.

I could write much more about my reasons for being an atheist, but that is not what this book is about. Suffice it to say that for me, they are many and strong.

The study I describe here was motivated above all by a desire to encounter and seek to understand an Other whom I found, and continue to find, profoundly different from myself. It was my own human curiosity that led me deep into the world of evangelical Christianity. In many ways, I am what you might call an unreconstructed humanist – I carry a powerful belief in the value of each unique human life, and the concomitant conviction that, in Terence's words, *humani nil a me alienum puto*: I count nothing human alien to me. For me, evangelical Christians constitute one important limit case for this credo. The most foreign place I have ever been was the small Christian university in the Mid-South where I conducted interviews for Varghese and Johnston (2007). Belief in a god is one thing, but to yield so utterly to that believed-in god so as to organize one's life around him and the ancient text that is claimed to be his word – a way of life one encounters with many evangelicals, and all the more so with evangelical missionaries – this to me is passing strange. And, both as a researcher and as a human being, I believe firmly that the only right course of action is to seek dialogue and understanding, to whatever degree either is possible. Such an impulse seems particularly crucial when one considers that about a third of all Americans identify as evangelical, as well as tens of millions of people around the world; and also when one sees the continual erosion of dialogue – which is to say, good-faith listening – in public discourse, whether written or spoken.

During the period of data collection for this study, various evangelical Christians witnessed to me innumerable times. They did so in more or less subtle or invasive ways, but the underlying desire – their wish that I should come to know Jesus Christ as my personal lord and savior – was essentially the same. The same motivation led to many prayers being said for me, both in my presence and when I was absent. There were times when, inwardly, I took offense – usually because a prayer or 'approach' overstepped what I consider the bounds of privacy (I am an extremely private person). I will share an example of this in Chapter 7. But, ultimately, I do not hold it against my interlocutors, some of whom became friends, that they tried to convert me. They believed it was in my best interests; it pained them (and no doubt pains them still) that I remain resistant to 'coming into the Word'.

Besides, who am I, finally, to say that I am absolutely, 100% convinced that I am right and they are wrong? A little bit of doubt never did anyone any harm, and I refuse to be categorical. Many of my relatives are practicing Catholics; I have close friends who are Jewish or Muslim or Buddhist. I would see it as the height of arrogance to dismiss all these belief systems out of hand. Rather, since I am firm in my own beliefs, I would prefer to let other people be firm in theirs. The spirit of the present study is that of dialogue, of listening, rather than of dogma. I have tried to convey this attitude in my writing, and I hope that my readers, whatever their prior experiences and views, will read with the same spirit in mind.

Note

(1) This latter school, the Godson School of English, was run by John Godson, a Nigerian-born pastor who had taken Polish citizenship. He ceased his pastoral activities in 2008, and became involved in Polish politics. He is currently a member of the Sejm, the Polish Parliament.

4 The School with a Soul

Introducing Lighthouse School

Lighthouse School – the 'School with a Soul', as it was advertised – was located in a suburb of the city of N. The school sat close to the boundary between two administrative districts of the city, both of which bordered the city limits. It was about a 40-minute ride by bus and tram into the historic center of the city. Twenty years before, the neighborhood had been semi-rural, with farms and smallholdings alongside regular residential houses. Since the fall of communism in 1989, and especially as a result of the big housing boom in the years immediately preceding the study, several new housing developments had appeared within a couple of kilometers of the school, with more under construction, mostly consisting of apartment buildings. As a result, in at least two distinct locations in the vicinity of Lighthouse, what might be thought of in the American sense as 'neighborhoods' had emerged – areas that have their own stores, facilities and services, name and sense of local identity.

As was the case with much new housing of this kind in Poland, apartment prices were not cheap, and the whole area felt very middle class – residents generally drove nice new cars and appeared well-heeled. This fact is not insignificant in terms of the intended and actual clientele of Lighthouse School. More will be said about class later in the context of the school's work.

The school was located in a pleasant, light, airy, L-shaped building that was newly constructed when the school moved in in 2006. Sydney and Taryn, the school's directors (I'm using this term somewhat loosely here, though I'll be more accurate later in this chapter), had taken care with the interior design, and as a result the whole place had a warm and friendly feel. It looked new and smart: a sharp contrast with many educational settings in Poland (I'm thinking of everything from run-down university lecture halls to run-down public school classrooms and hallways). The rooms where the school itself was located had originally been intended as residential apartments; as a result, there were fully appointed bathrooms and other quirky but agreeable features.

The school had four classrooms of different sizes. Each room was decorated according to a particular theme, and was also sometimes allotted unofficially to one teacher. No room was particularly big. The biggest one, 'Sydney's Room', was known as the Caribbean Room; it had a photomural of a beach scene on the back wall, other beach-related pictures and was decorated with objects such as dried starfish and seashells. There was also an inspirational poem on the wall. The room contained three garden tables with parasols and matching blue chairs. The space seemed full when as few as 10 students were present (which rarely if ever happened). The smallest, the Green Room, had a single large table with bench seating, and could accommodate perhaps six or eight people. A third room, the Blue Room, was generally used only for children's classes; it was decorated with charts and various inspirational posters, some overtly religious (e.g. with Bible inscriptions or references to God), others not. The furniture consisted of children's plastic chairs and three or four easily movable small tables; the room was reconfigured for different classes. The final room, 'Taryn's Room', was labeled 'the Grand Canyon Room'. It contained pictures of the Grand Canyon, and also unrelated inspirational posters. There were two small coffee tables, and wicker chairs arranged around the edge of the room. The room would have seemed full with perhaps six or eight students, though I never saw that many in there.

The pride of Lighthouse School was Coffee Central, a fully appointed cafe. The seating for Coffee Central was located in the biggest room in the school, which had large windows and a small balcony opening onto the side of the building. There were about six cafe-style tables with upright seats, and also a sofa and a couple of matching armchairs. The school rearranged the cafe on a fairly regular basis – every few weeks the configuration of the chairs and tables was changed, giving the place a fresh feel. It was also spotlessly clean. There was a half-door with a shelf that opened to the kitchen area; cookies, chips, candy and other snacks for sale were laid out on and below the shelf, while the top half of the door functioned as a serving hatch – people buying coffee or other beverages would stand at the hatch and be served by those in the kitchen. The cafe had an espresso machine and served a variety of espresso drinks, regular and herbal teas, hot chocolate, cold bottled sodas and other drinks.

Unlike other cafes in Poland, this one served no alcohol (I'll say more about Poland, evangelicals and alcohol later), just as in general there was never any alcohol in the school as a whole. Also, unlike most cafes in the country, there was no smoking[1] either in the cafe or anywhere in the school. During the more than nine months I spent there, I never saw anyone connected with the school smoking, even outside the school or during the outdoor graduation party in May; this fact also differentiated the school from almost any other place in Poland.

Students and their families were encouraged to hang out in the cafe, and many did so; Mavis, who staffed the cafe kitchen, and the teachers would accompany them, often playing card games and the like with the children or chatting with the adults. Class activities sometimes spilled over into the cafe. The space was also used for various special evening events, some of which are outlined in Chapter 7. Last but not least, the room was used for Sunday services of the church with which Lighthouse School was affiliated.

There was also a small square hall space that served as a spillover area for the cafe and as a general meeting place. It was located between the cafe and the Grand Canyon Room, and contained a couple of extra cafe tables and some chairs. There was a coat rack, as the hall was on the way from the outside door to the cafe, so it was often here that new arrivals would be greeted and would take off their coats. Two bathrooms led off this hall. In addition, opposite the Grand Canyon Room there was a good-sized Teachers' Room with a large worktable in the middle and bookshelves with books and materials.

Aside from the classrooms and the cafe – the public areas or what Goffman (1959) calls the 'front region' – there were also two storage and work rooms off the Blue Room and the Caribbean Room. Lastly, off another hallway to the left of the stairs was the secretary's office. In that hallway, there was a bookshelf containing English-language books available for students to borrow (though I never saw anyone using it). The books were almost exclusively what is known as 'Christian fiction' – that is, fiction aimed explicitly at an evangelical Christian readership.

The school was accessed via a gateway that was always open during the day. Visitors came round the base of the 'L' and entered a door in the crook of the letter. From a small entrance hall with nothing but a table, stairs led up to the hallway of the school. To the right was the cafe and beyond; to the left, classrooms and the office; and straight ahead the children's room. Though the entrance door was left unlocked during class hours, members of the Lighthouse team kept an eye on things, and made sure to greet any new arrivals.

The school was on the upper floor, occupying about the base of the L and half its long side. Below the school were two businesses, one selling electronics and one dealing in auto parts. I saw little traffic in these offices, though their entrances were on the other side of the building to that of the school, and I rarely found myself on that side of the building. In any case, the whole place was rather quiet aside from the school itself.

The back end of the building's upper floor – the top of the L – contained the apartments where Sydney, Taryn and the other teachers lived. The school rented three apartments. The largest one was shared by Sydney and Taryn. The smallest was assigned individually to the teacher with the longest commitment – in this case, Briana. The other, somewhat bigger apartment was shared by the teachers with shorter commitments: Louise, Mavis and Allie at the time of the beginning of the study. Agnieszka, the secretary-cum-office manager of the school up until the February of the year I was there, was the only staff member who did not live in the school – she rented an apartment in a nearby housing development.

Transportation between the school and the city center was not particularly easy. The school was on a number of bus routes, but no route went directly into the center – most terminated in adjacent neighborhoods. To get 'into town', you needed to change bus or tram at least once. Sydney and Taryn owned a car, though it was off the road a lot of the time I was there. They used it mostly for large shopping trips, when they bought supplies for the school or the cafe. There were small local grocery stores for everyday needs, and a huge Tesco hypermarket a couple of miles into town where the teachers did a lot of their shopping. There was a decent-sized parking lot around the building of the school, and most learners came to the school by car. I was living on the outskirts of a different side of the city, and did not have a car; it typically took me about an hour and a half on public transportation to reach the school, a trip I made three or four times a week during the time of the study.

The immediate surroundings of the school were not particularly inspiring. It was located close to a major T-junction. There were bus stops almost right outside the school, with a few small businesses nearby – a newspaper kiosk that was open in the morning, a grocery store, the companies downstairs and a couple of other establishments. A mixture of old and new was clearly visible – next to the school was an established farm with turkeys and other livestock, but there were also newly built villas. The new prevailed, however, and like the housing estates a little further away, this was a middle-class area, something I subsequently found reflected in the clientele of the school (see below). Like many middle-class, educated Poles, the inhabitants of this neighborhood had chosen to live further from rather than nearer to the center of town, and judging by the cars and clothing of the people I would see in the vicinity of the school – and the absence of such phenomena as public drinking on benches and in parks, something widespread in many parts of the city – this was by and large a 'nice' neighborhood.

Lighthouse School: Learners and Teachers

Lighthouse offered classes for children, teens and adults. Classes were *very* small – I never saw more than eight in a single class, and in fact most classes I observed had between two and five students, whether for adults, teenagers or kids. Classes took place Monday to Thursday, with each given class meeting twice a week, in most cases Monday–Wednesday or Tuesday–Thursday. There was a small number of classes in the mornings for adults who either did not work or worked afternoons or evenings. But the busiest time for the school began at around 3pm and went on until 9pm. Child and teen classes were arranged both by age and by language level, adult classes by level. A single children's or teens' class lasted an hour; for adults each class was 90 minutes, with a break.

The adult learners who attended the school were, as far as I could tell, exclusively what I would describe as urban middle-class professionals. They included architects, university professors, engineers, businesspeople, teachers and artists. In the classes I focused on most closely, all the learners were women; though some of them were not currently working, all were highly educated, with at least a *magisterium* or five-year initial degree, usually considered the equivalent of a BA plus MA in the American system, and had worked in jobs related to their qualifications before becoming homemakers; some were actively looking to return to work.

As mentioned above, in the first semester Sydney and Taryn were in Canada on furlough, an obligation every few years for missionaries. In their absence, and at their request, the school was run by Jean, a missionary and English teacher from Texas, whom they knew from a short-term mission trip Jean had made to Poland in the recent past. (Much more will be said about all of the teachers in the school as this book develops; for now I'm just providing brief introductions.) Jean was in her fifties and had been working in the field for about 10 years; she ran her own evangelical English teaching organization. Jean brought with her Allie, a missionary teacher in her mid-twenties who had just completed four years teaching in an evangelical middle school in Mexico with which Jean's company was affiliated. At the beginning of the year, it seemed that Allie was a kind of protégée for Jean. The remaining expatriates at the school were all young Canadian women in their early twenties. Briana was completing the second year of a three-year commitment at the school, while Louise had signed up for a year to fulfill the internship requirement of her Bible college degree. Lastly, Mavis had been recruited for a semester to run the cafe as well as help out in the school. Alongside the North American teaching staff, there was Agnieszka, a young Polish woman in her mid-twenties who was the secretary-cum-admin person at the school.

In the second semester, Sydney and Taryn returned, while Jean and Allie left. Mavis's commitment was over and she returned to Canada. Briana and Louise stayed on. In February, Agnieszka returned to the central city of R. to resume her university degree; her place was taken by Kinga, a Polish woman in her late thirties who had been a learner at the school.

As can be seen, the teaching and administrative staff at the school during the year I observed was exclusively female. The only man on the horizon, so to speak, was Rysiek, the 40-year-old pastor of the church with which the school was affiliated. Formally speaking, Rysiek was the director of the school. In the previous year, he had attended team meetings on Fridays, but early in the year that I was present, there was a reshuffle at the church owing to a bereavement, and Rysiek was promoted from assistant pastor to main pastor. He did not attend team meetings, but he met regularly with Sydney and Taryn and took an active part in the running of the school.

The Origins of Lighthouse

Sydney and Taryn, both from Canada and both lifelong evangelical Christians, had first met in the mid-1990s when Sydney moved to the Western Canadian city where Taryn lived, and joined the church at which Taryn was a group leader. At the time, Sydney had a well-established career as a district sales manager dealing in women's clothing, while Taryn was head of training for a major Canadian telecommunications company – in a word, both had successful careers in business. A study group at the church led to the idea of a short-term mission trip; a church member who was a Polish immigrant had mission contacts in Ukraine, Belarus and Poland, and in the end, a trip was arranged to Poland to lead a summer Bible camp and visit the country. Sydney and Taryn traveled with three other women. They spent 18 days in Poland in the late summer of 1997. This was the first time either woman had been in the country, and in Sydney's case, her first mission trip (Taryn had been on mission trips in Mexico before).

In preparing for the trip, each woman had been assigned a job or role in what was billed (somewhat bizarrely) as a 'singles camp'. Taryn would lead Bible study, while Sydney was asked to teach English for a few hours a day. She had never done this before, nor did she have any other experience as a teacher, tutor or trainer. Nevertheless, she agreed to give it a try, and went off to Staples to buy 'flashcards and flipcharts', in her words.

After the camp was over, the camp director, Mariusz, who led an evangelical church in the small town of D. in North Central Poland, asked Sydney and Taryn separately (but not the other women on the mission trip) if they'd consider coming to his church on a more permanent basis, Sydney to teach English, Taryn to help with a church planting (the establishment of a new church). Both women were flattered but didn't reflect much more on the suggestion. They promised to pray about it, and returned to Canada. About a month later, Mariusz called up and, through an interpreter, asked if Sydney and Taryn had prayed about his request. Even more taken aback, they confessed that they hadn't really given it a lot of thought. Once again, he urged them to pray about it and to at least consider the possibility.

For some time yet, Sydney was skeptical of such a radical step. Nevertheless, the idea started to take hold, and for the first time she and Taryn found that they needed to give it some serious consideration. They made a list of various obstacles that needed to be overcome before they would be able to move ahead. This included everything from concerns about aging relatives, through stock options, to the matter of who would support them as missionaries. To begin with, the barriers they had listed seemed insurmountable, and more obstacles appeared – for example, it turned out that their own church could not send them as they were already at their maximum level of support for overseas missions. After a while, though, things changed, and at this point, as Taryn put it, 'stuff started dropping off the list almost instantaneously. We said, it has to be a God thing, because there were too many things to be a coincidence'. One after another, resolutions were found for their personal issues, while support was found from a church in Eastern Canada where Sydney's brother was an elder. This church could also ordain the women as missionaries. The final hurdle was overcome when Sydney's boss, a practicing Jew, helped her resolve her financial problems with stock options and, more importantly still, gave her his blessing – as he put it, if God was calling her, he would not stand in her way. At this point, Sydney knew she was going. It was February 1998.

Sydney and Taryn used up their vacation time (and a lot of their own personal funds) in making preparations. They got some cross-cultural training in Louisville, Kentucky, took a training course in Bible-based materials from Literacy and Evangelism International, an 'inter-denominational, inter-mission fellowship' (Literacy and Evangelism International, 2015) based in Tulsa, Oklahoma, and traveled east to be ordained as missionaries at Sydney's brother's church. They also took a TESOL course offered by Atlantic Overseas Institute in Nova Scotia.

Eventually, a year to the day after last leaving Poland, Sydney and Taryn returned and took up residence in the town of D., population about 30,000. They were given an unfurnished apartment in the church building. They did not speak Polish and had never run a language school. They did not teach during the first semester, but spent the time getting to know the country, the culture and the town, as well as the people of the evangelical church that had invited them (though Mariusz, the original inspiration for the project, had moved to take up a position in Warsaw). Above all, they laid the groundwork for their school, with the help of a new friend who for several years had been running an evangelical language school in Warsaw, and with assistance from many other people. Eventually the preparations were complete. Advertisements were placed in the local newspaper and elsewhere. The school opened its doors at the start of the second semester, in the winter of 1998–1999. During the initial registration and placement period, over a hundred applicants were tested, and in the end 90 students signed up for classes. Lighthouse School was a reality.

From the beginning, Lighthouse School formed the heart of a mission, and that mission was aimed at the middle classes of Poland. This idea originated from Mariusz, the former pastor of the church at D., who had first invited the Canadian women to his town and his church. As he presented the matter, the church in D. had done a good job of 'reaching out' to the homeless, but had not been able to do the same for professional people. This focus was retained as Lighthouse grew, developed and subsequently moved, and was very much still the primary concern of the school in its incarnation in N.

Another idea originating from Mariusz was that of using Bible-based materials. Since this is such a crucial aspect of the work of Lighthouse, I will discuss it in much more depth in Chapter 5, but for the moment it is important to note that the idea itself came from the Polish side that invited Sydney and Taryn in the first place.

In the early days in the small town of D., Sydney and Taryn were the only teachers in the school, and classes were offered Monday through Friday. Over the first few years, registration held steady at between 95 and 120 students per semester. Lighthouse School quickly became popular in D. Its clients included the deputy mayor of the town as well as judges, lawyers, businesspeople and other professionals, as had been the intention. When the school opened, it was the 'only show in town' – the only language school operating there. By the time Sydney and Taryn left D. there were five other language schools offering English to adults, but Lighthouse remained popular because classes were taught exclusively by native speakers, and also because the content and form of the classes were different from other establishments.

After a couple of years, a third teacher joined the school, a young woman of 20 from Western Bible College in Canada who came to teach at Lighthouse as an internship requirement for her program; she stayed for four years. From this point on, there were always at least three teachers at Lighthouse at any given time.

Sydney and Taryn began teaching with no more than a one-month TESOL training course to prepare them for their job. As Sydney explained, much of the first couple of years involved learning to teach at the same time as they were actually teaching. They drew on internet resources as well as published secular course books (notably the *Cambridge English Course*) and teachers' reference grammars in order to first understand, then be able to explain, the various points of English grammar. In this beginning period, Sydney and Taryn referred to themselves as 'language coaches', not language teachers, in deference to teachers who were qualified and experienced.

To begin with, Sydney and Taryn used materials that they had obtained from Literacy and Evangelism International (2015), which produced first-language literacy and English as a second language (ESL)/English as a foreign language (EFL) materials with the prime goal of enabling illiterate students to 'read the Word of God'. But they found these materials too fast-paced and lacking a sufficient number of activities to accompany the texts. After trying a number of alternatives, including photocopiable supplementary materials and children's books, in the fourth semester of teaching, the fall of 2000, they began creating their own materials. They selected Bible stories (such as the life of Joseph) and also classic literature, including novels like Daniel Defoe's *Robinson Crusoe* and Mark Twain's *The Prince and the Pauper*, either for their overt religious content (in the case of the former) or their spiritual dimension (in both cases). These materials – which will be discussed at length in Chapter 5 – were immediately piloted with learners and subsequently revised.

Sydney and Taryn had originally made a commitment to stay in Poland for three years. However, as this time neared they felt that they were only just beginning to get into their stride in terms of the mission and the work of the school – it was only in the third year that they started working seriously on their new materials, for example. The church planting model that had been assumed when they originally left Canada was one by which North American missionaries would 'train up' locals to take over, then they would leave – a sustainability model, to put it in development terms. However, the longer they stayed in Poland, the more Sydney and Taryn realized that this model was not appropriate for their context – their students had actually rebelled when faced with the idea of being taught by Polish teachers, explaining that a large part of the school's draw was the fact that it employed only native English-speaking teachers (the prejudice claiming the preferability of native speaker teachers remains widespread in Poland). Lastly, the church authorities in Warsaw told Sydney and Taryn that from the moment a person hears the gospel ('really hears it'), it takes five to seven further meaningful encounters with the Word before that person is ready to accept Jesus as his or her personal Lord and Savior; this usually translates into about seven years. For all these reasons, Sydney and Taryn signed on for another stint in D.

To begin with, only adult classes had been offered at Lighthouse. This continued for several years. Eventually, the school started classes for children and teens, which became popular.

After several years of good relations with the church in D., things started to change in 2005. The pastor left, and one of the church elders took over the running of the church. His beliefs were somewhat different than those of the pastor who had left, including in the domain of gender roles. There are ongoing debates in the evangelical churches over the role of women in the ministry. Churches and individuals alike hold a wide range of views, ranging from absolute equality (very much a minority position) to the total exclusion of women from ministry roles. Most evangelicals I have spoken with believe in at least certain restrictions on the participation of women – many suggested, for example, that women could lead 'small groups' (supplementary activities such as youth groups within the community of a particular church), but should not serve as principal pastor.

The new leader of the evangelical church in D. held more conservative views than his predecessor. He believed that it was not right for women to teach the Bible. As a result, Sydney and Taryn were given an ultimatum by the church authorities: either stop teaching with Bible-based materials, or leave town. Lighthouse's students rallied behind their school and petitioned the church; Sydney and Taryn themselves suggested that they move to a different location elsewhere in the town. But the church wanted to avoid the appearance of a split, and this was not an acceptable solution to them. Sydney and Taryn felt that they had not come to Poland to be embroiled in trouble of this kind, and they decided to move.

They consulted with the Warsaw-based head of the Christian Fellowship Churches of Poland. He suggested four potential locations, all in major cities. A series of visits to the southern city of N. made it clear to Sydney and Taryn that this was a suitable location. A new church was being planted, and the school was to be seen as the 'front door' of the church in efforts to attract new members. Sydney and Taryn moved to N. in the summer of 2006. They found a suitable (and suitably priced) site for the school, as described above, in a predominantly middle-class suburb. They spent a semester learning the lay of the land, doing market research and getting to know the members of the new church. The new Lighthouse began offering classes for adults, teens and children in January 2007. When I started my study in September 2008, the school had three semesters under its belt.

I've devoted quite a lot of space to Sydney and Taryn's experiences in D., even though I was not able to observe that school directly myself and have only their account of the history. It was clear to me throughout the year that the earlier incarnation of Lighthouse was still very much a psychological and practical point of reference for both leaders, and learning about D. and what happened there helped me to understand a lot of what was and was not going on in the school in N.

Throughout the time of my study, enrollment in N. never reached the levels it had achieved in D. Numbers hovered around the 50–60 mark. Since the school aimed to be financially self-supporting, this meant that there was a subdued yet constant sense of brinksmanship and crisis – I had a number of conversations in the final semester of my data collection in which Sydney, Taryn and Briana considered what would happen if Lighthouse were to go under. As I left in May 2009 the school still had its head above water, but was by no means financially secure. At the time of writing – April 2016 – it is still in existence. Yet, like much of what happens in the mission field, its future was financially uncertain and dependent on forces that to a significant extent it could not control.

Note

(1) The situation regarding smoking in public places eventually changed. In February 2009, I saw a leaflet aimed at tourists that listed over a hundred totally or partially smoke-free cafes, restaurants and bars in the city of N. (some of these establishments had smoke-free sections or rooms). Then in 2010, smoking was banned in cafes and restaurants countrywide, with only a few exceptions. At the time of the study, though, the vast majority of eating and drinking establishments allowed smoking.

5 Curriculum and Materials

Bible-Based Curriculum at Lighthouse School

It was the term 'Bible-based curriculum', more than anything else, that first drew me to Lighthouse School. Once the first contact was made and I got to know Sydney and Taryn, I discovered many other reasons why this school was a fascinating place to do my research. The initial impulse, however, came from my curiosity about what a Bible-based curriculum might look like and how it would play out in an adult classroom in Poland. This chapter and the next set out what I found in this regard.

As mentioned earlier, the idea of employing Bible-based teaching in the school originated in the first instance not from Sydney and Taryn themselves but from Mariusz, the Polish evangelical preacher who first invited them to open a school in the small town of D. (see Chapter 4). It was Mariusz who first suggested that they use 'Bible-based material', as Taryn explained to me. In fact, Taryn went so far as to say, 'I don't think either of us would have been interested in the invitation if that hadn't been part of the invitation... it was, there's something more attractive to us personally because of our own relationship with God's word; so that was part of the allure'.

Taryn and Sydney, then, were immediately attracted to the idea of using materials based on the Bible. Initially, they believed that they would be able to use already available materials, and had no intention of creating their own. They began by surveying what was on the market. Much of what was there constituted Bible study in simplified English with no pedagogical language support. As outlined in the preceding chapter, they used materials produced by Literacy and Evangelical International (LEI). Though Taryn and Sydney looked at a number of different sets of available materials, including some intended for homeschooling, at that time (around 1998) the LEI-produced materials were the only ones commercially available that did *not* use the King James version of the Bible, something that as Sydney pointed out, 'isn't so practical when you're trying to be a conversation program'. Sydney went on:

> It was just really very difficult to try and figure out how you would teach this to someone. You know, there were words in there that we

> would have to learn ourselves, you know, how do you use this properly, I don't know how to use 'thees' and 'thous' appropriately, you know. I mean I've read it, I've read Shakespeare, I've read the King James Bible, but my goodness, I don't know how to use that. So, and then just, you know, words that have changed their meaning over the years, you know, it doesn't make sense.

However, the LEI materials also turned out to be inadequate for Lighthouse's purposes. In particular, there was a significant jump from the first year to the second year, the latter textbook requiring large amounts of reading and vocabulary with too little grammar, with the result that, as Sydney put it, 'we were dying out there'. Sydney and Taryn explored various solutions, including providing supplementary materials, using mainstream (non-evangelical) ESL/EFL materials, and using first language (L1) children's materials. As Sydney explained: 'We tried everything until finally we realized if we want something that is going to work well, and we want it to be Bible-based, which we do, we're going to have to create it'. This work initially proceeded in piecemeal fashion until, partly as a result of criticism from their students, they decided that a more organized and large-scale approach was necessary. At this point, things began to fall into place, though it was also a 'brutal' experience as the materials were being written while classes were going on, that is to say, for immediate use, and then adapted from year to year. (Sydney herself described the first version of the Joseph materials as 'scary'.)

Each part of the curriculum was designed for a two-semester sequence, and was mapped out by Taryn into a number of chapters that together covered the main language points that needed to be included. In figuring out an overall shape for the language part of the curriculum, Taryn and Sydney also made use of mainstream materials, finding the *Cambridge English Course* particularly useful as a model or 'guideline' in terms of scope and sequence.

> And we would just try and look at the different kinds of activities that they would do so that we could figure out what's going to give them the best variety so that they're not bored, something that is fun, something that's interesting, and still provide them with a comprehensive unit where they feel like at the end of this unit, aha, I've moved ahead. Maybe they haven't gotten it but they've at least moved ahead.

Taryn put it as follows: 'We want it to be natural and seamless so that the conversations happen naturally because of what they're reading and the English stems out of that and it's all part and parcel'.

In contacting and visiting other evangelical schools in Poland and elsewhere in Central Europe in preparation for setting up Lighthouse, Taryn and Sydney had found little support for using Bible-based curriculum. Teachers and administrators at already existing evangelically affiliated language schools in the region told them that they had tried using more overtly religious or spiritual materials, but that this had proved too difficult, there being too much resistance on the part of the learners.

Yet, Taryn and Sydney were convinced that it could be done, and persevered with developing their own materials. While they also met resistance, they found that when done in a non-confrontational way, it was in fact possible to address such topics in the adult language classroom. In Sydney's words, despite the discouragement conveyed by other evangelical language schools:

> We just kept encouraging one another, you know, don't give up; we came here with this purpose; I mean we were asked to use this kind of material; so let's fulfill what we were asked to do. And then once we got into it, we realized, I mean the doors for spiritual discussion just opened so easily.

As to why stories such as *The Prince and the Pauper* and *Robinson Crusoe* were selected for use, Sydney explained:

> [It was] because they were classics, and we felt like people would be interested in reading a classic in English. We felt perhaps they had read them in Polish, you know; we looked around to see what was available in Polish. Both of those stories are available; and so we thought, ah, well maybe this is something that they would remember from their childhood, or reading it at some point in their life, reading it to their kids maybe. And maybe that would be of interest to them.

Sydney also pointed out that Poles may well know these stories from literature 'whereas a lot of them don't know their Bible stories because they haven't really read their Bibles', an interesting observation that for many Catholics is true – study of the Bible is relatively rare among practicing Catholics, especially when compared to the extensive Bible study found in evangelical practice: Bielo (2009: 3) states that 'Bible study contends strongly for being the most consequential form of religious practice' in American evangelicalism, and it is widespread in evangelical churches and communities in other countries too. Lastly, an important financial consideration was that a text like *Robinson Crusoe* is in the public domain, which meant that there would be no problems with copyright.

Sydney explained in turn why *Robinson Crusoe* was chosen:

> It's a classic, and it's the story of the prodigal. You know, he leaves his father. I mean he refers to himself in the very first few chapters as the prodigal; and then you have his entire conversion experience. And basically he's the one that's telling the reader about the love of God and about Christ. It's not us saying, What do you think about this? It's him saying, This is what happened to me, this is my experience. And so there are a lot of moments in the story where he presents a challenge, and we just ask them to talk about that. And it, it has always been a very very well received text. They love it. Because they, they watch his life, they watch his stupid mistakes, they see themselves in him, you know, their own stubbornness and own unwillingness to yield to some things. And um, even today, you know, we had a good conversation about the fact that he says, You don't realize how much you love something until you've lost it. And so we talk about those kinds of things, you know. So, I think the text has gone over very well with people because they enjoy that, and yet for us it's not like we're standing up front saying, Well here's another Bible text that you need to read, and you know, we really want you to give in to the Bible. So we're trying to find a way to, to balance how to look at life. That life is not, it's not all Bible, because your whole life isn't about spending every day in the Bible all day. It's about figuring out what to do with that, and how you apply that to your life. And so we see him applying it to his life. [...] And so we're trying to choose texts that provoke conversation, that get people thinking, that have someone else present the Gospel or the truth, rather than it just coming from us, where they feel at some point like we're preaching at them. Because we don't want to, we don't want them to feel like we're preaching at them. And I think in those early days we felt like preachers, because we were, I mean we had these massive texts and it was just tough sledding through all of this Bible material day after day after day. And we really felt like it was too much. We absolutely want spiritual discussion to happen in the classroom at least once a week if possible, and we really want to be able to have people digging into the Word, but we don't want it to feel like it's being shoved down their throat.

Overview of the Lighthouse Curriculum

By the time I arrived to spend a year at the school, the Lighthouse curriculum was quite extensive. Materials had been developed for five levels of language learners, and were used with adult learners and in most cases, with certain adaptations, in children's classes too. Each set of materials was intended to cover a year of study at Lighthouse, translating into roughly 90 class hours. The sequence began with *The Prince and the Pauper*, built around an adaptation of the 1881 novel by Mark Twain. This was followed by *Survivor 1: Joseph*, based on the story of Joseph from the Book of Genesis. It then proceeded to *English Toolbox*, which augments modern-day situational dialogues and language work with discussions stimulated by biblical stories and parables. This was followed by *Survivor 2: Robinson Crusoe*, which will be described in detail in the present chapter. Finally came *Power Up 1*, a set of materials aimed at the adult professional audience that was Lighthouse's prime target (see Chapter 4). *Power Up 1* was organized thematically, with chapters focusing on such topics as risk-taking, integrity, perseverance, creativity and teamwork, as well as offering more advanced language work; it contained some biblical content, but much less than the other sets of materials. During my time at Lighthouse, all these sets of materials were in use either in the children's classes or those aimed at adults.

It is important to point out here that 'curriculum' in the understanding of Lighthouse School is definitely more driven by content and purpose than linguistic structures, and that from an educational point of view an argument can of course be made that content-based teaching is desirable. Such an approach, though, is predicated on there also being a language checklist or some such to ensure that major grammar structures, vocabulary, speech acts, situational language and so on are in fact also covered (Graves, 1996). The Lighthouse materials did include a heavy language focus, and I will look at this below as well as at their purpose-driven spiritual content.

Each set of materials had been carefully formatted, and had been copyrighted by Sydney and Taryn in their own names or that of Lighthouse Ministries. It was available for purchase by the students, and Taryn and Sydney made sure they had control over how and where it was distributed beyond the school. (I bought a copy for the purposes of my research.) This was necessary not only for reasons of intellectual property, but also because of the always precarious financial situation of the school, in light of which any additional source of potential income had to be exploited.

Survivor 2: Robinson Crusoe

The curriculum materials used in the course I attended throughout the school year were entitled *Survivor 2: Robinson Crusoe*, and were built around a simplified adaptation of English author Daniel Defoe's 1719 novel *Robinson Crusoe*, the full original title of which is: *The Life and Strange Surprizing Adventures of Robinson Crusoe, of York, Mariner: Who lived Eight and Twenty*

Years, all alone in an un-inhabited Island on the Coast of America, near the Mouth of the Great River of Oroonoque; Having been cast on Shore by Shipwreck, wherein all the Men perished but himself. With An Account how he was at last as strangely deliver'd by Pyrates. Like the title, the original text was considerably simplified linguistically (I'll show an example of the original and the adaptation below), which of course involved shortening it a great deal. The original novel is told in a single unbroken narrative; the Lighthouse adaptation was divided into 22 chapters and was designed to be covered in two semesters of study at the school. Most chapters were somewhere between 1000 and 1500 words long; the whole totaled about 35,000 words, which was a fairly ambitious amount of reading for the students. The reading of the book was completed somewhat hurriedly in the last few weeks of the second semester of classes that I observed. This was the second time that the Crusoe text had been used in its present incarnation at Lighthouse, and the second time Sydney herself had taught it.

The original book is written in what is today dated and difficult language, most of which is absent in the Lighthouse version. Though the adapted version was still quite difficult for learners at the level of the class (which the school defined as 'intermediate'), the story was made somewhat more accessible by being widely known from numerous film and television adaptations, and, as Sydney and Taryn rightly observed (see above), translations of the original are still read in Poland under the title *Robinson Cruzoe* or *Przypadki Robinsona Cruzoe* (*The Adventures of Robinson Crusoe*), in direct translations from the original English, and also in simplified adaptations for children.

Each chapter in the materials was organized according to a fairly regular template. After a title page, the chapter as a whole was about five pages long, with two pages of Crusoe text along with a filler illustration and three pages containing exercises and other activities. The latter part began with a series of sections revolving around vocabulary that was new in the chapter. In many cases, new words and phrases were defined, after which there followed exercises designed to use the words. Elsewhere, interactive activities (for example, asking learners to look the words up in a dictionary, draw pictures illustrating the meaning of a word or simply underline any new words in the story) were used to introduce new items as well as practice them.

The opening 'Vocabulary' sections offering dictionary-style definitions of new words and phrases were one of the aspects of language pedagogy at Lighthouse that betrayed the material writers' lack of professional training. In numerous cases, aside from the general pedagogical questionableness of presenting large amounts of vocabulary ahead of the text (see e.g. Nation, 1993), the definitions themselves suffered from a categorical confusion whereby the word or phrase and the definition failed to match in terms of grammatical category. For example, in Chapter 15 the initial section looked as follows:

VOCABULARY
Match the vocabulary word to its meaning

1. damaged
2. binoculars
3. skull
4. bones
5. presence

a) the bone of the head
b) something that is broken or destroyed
c) the noun which means someone or something is with you
d) something you hold up to your eyes to help you see long distance
e) the part of your body that makes the skeleton, what your muscles are attached to

Here, the verbally derived adjective 'damaged' is defined with a noun phrase 'something that is broken or destroyed'. The noun 'presence', in turn, is rendered as 'the noun which means something or someone is with you', which is both grammatically and semantically confusing. Such examples occurred in numerous chapters. In Chapter 2, for example, 'sensible (adj)' was defined as 'to have, or show or use good judgment', while 'profit (n)' is explained as 'to get something from a good business investment, or to gain from an experience'. In Chapter 3, 'naked (adj)' was given as 'to be without any clothing on'.

After the initial 'Vocabulary' section, there was a follow-up section entitled 'Vocabulary Practice' which offered further work with the vocabulary items in question. In Chapter 15, for example, to practice the words given above and other new lexis from the chapter, the following exercises were provided:

VOCABULARY PRACTICE
1. Fill in the blanks as the teacher reads this paragraph from the story.

In _____ a month I had made my second pen for the goats. I did all this because of the man's _____ I had seen. For two years I had been _____ because of that footprint. This fear had _____ my prayer life. Every minute I _____ to be killed and eaten

by wild men; and a mind _____ with thoughts of
_____, thankfulness, and love is much better for
_____ than a mind filled with _____.

2. Complete these sentences:
1. _____ with his binoculars.
2. The damaging fire _____.
3. He cracked his skull _____.
4. _____ and he broke every bone in his hand.
5. The invitation says your presence is requested _____.

3. Unscramble these words:

1. uamnh _____   6. dergowpun _____
2. potfornit _____   7. senob _____
3. oclbarinus _____ 8. tagos _____
4. magaded _____   9. otab _____
5. luksl _____   10. bache _____

Each set of vocabulary activities concluded with a section called 'Apply Your Knowledge', which invited discussion about topics suggested by the new vocabulary. A typical 'Apply Your Knowledge', from Chapter 10, in which vocabulary items included 'plenty', 'loneliness', 'depressed' and 'fulfilled', read as follows:

APPLY YOUR KNOWLEDGE
Talk to your partner about:

...what fulfills you.   ...what depresses you.
...what you have plenty of.   ...when you feel lonely.

In Chapter 12, whose new vocabulary included 'mould', 'compare', 'to give up' and 'severely', the following questions were found:

APPLY YOUR KNOWLEDGE

(1) What's the last thing that went mouldy in your refrigerator?
(2) Have you ever made foolish decisions during a project? What happened? What could have been different if you had planned better?

(3) Have you ever been tempted to give up on something or someone? Describe this situation.
(4) Using the word SEVERE, describe a weather situation you have experienced.

After the vocabulary came the reading itself, laid out in a smallish font, and typically between one and two pages long, single-spaced, with lines numbered in intervals of five.

The reading was followed by two regular sections. The first, 'Comprehension Questions', was aimed at checking understanding of the text, and included a variety of fairly standard text comprehension exercises such as true-false, informational questions, multiple choice and so on. A typical list of questions appeared immediately after the text in Chapter 11:

COMPREHENSION QUESTIONS

(1) How long has Crusoe been on the island by the end of chapter 11?
(2) How long did it take Crusoe to make a shovel?
(3) What was the name of Crusoe's parrot?
(4) How long did it take Crusoe to make his first two things from clay?
(5) What was the first thing Crusoe made in one of his clay pots?

In some cases, learners were asked to draw a picture, fill in a simple crossword or perform some other task of this kind. In Chapter 14, for instance, Question 1 in the 'Comprehension Questions' section asked:

(1) Draw a picture of Crusoe in the clothes that he describes in the second paragraph of Chapter 14. Have fun and use your imagination.

Beneath the question, half a page of blank space was left for the drawing.

The second regularly occurring section after the reading was entitled 'Digging Deeper'. The goal of this section was to open up issues, primarily of a moral and/or spiritual nature, that had been raised in the text, and offer learners an opportunity to personalize these issues and discuss them from their own point of view. Each Digging Deeper section contained about four to six questions. In many cases, as well as referring to the Crusoe text, the questions made overt reference to the Bible, sometimes including biblical quotations that were in many cases constructed from several different translations in order to make their language simple enough for the target students. Thus, for example in Chapter I the Digging Deeper section includes the following item:

(2) Robinson's father believed that being very poor or being very rich would make people unhappy. What do you think? Can you think of some examples to support Mr. Crusoe's opinion?

Does the Bible teach this? Read this proverb: *'Make me absolutely honest and don't let me be too poor or too rich. Give me just what I need. If I have too much to eat, I might forget about you; if I don't have enough I might steal and disgrace your name'.* Proverbs 30: 8-9[1]

Elsewhere, as well as other Bible quotations there was frequent reference to religious and spiritual practices such as prayer. For example, in Chapter 8 the Digging Deeper section read as follows:

DIGGING DEEPER

(1) Have you ever been so sick that you thought you might die? Talk to your partner about what happened and how you felt.
(2) Have you ever had a dream where you thought that an important message was being given to you?
(3) What do you think the message of Crusoe's dream was? Do you think he imagined what he saw, or do you think the dream was a sign from God?
(4) Do you believe that God speaks to people in dreams? Are there any popular books in your culture about interpreting dreams or understanding dreams?
(5) Can you think of any stories in the Bible where God spoke to people in dreams?

It was generally the discussion of the questions from the Digging Deeper sections that provided the classroom discourse I look at in the following chapter, since these were usually the times when spiritual and religious questions were talked about most extensively in class.

Finally, the chapter was often rounded out by a lighter activity, sometimes called 'Use It, Or Lose It!' and elsewhere 'Brain Twister', that presented a task such as a sentence in code that needed to be deciphered, or a language puzzle. These activities sometimes appeared at the end of the introductory Vocabulary part, before the reading, instead of after 'Digging Deeper'. Here is a typical example, from Chapter 10:

USE IT, OR LOSE IT!

Crusoe talks about animals in almost every chapter. In the sentences below you will find the animals he has talked about, but they are hidden in the sentences. The letters will always be in order, but sometimes you will need to skip a letter or word to find all the letters to spell the whole name of the animal.

(1) She chats with Mark every night on the internet. _____
(2) Do you love Phineas? _____
(3) My uncles pig likes to sleep on the mud piles. _____
(4) Tom, stop hurting Les. _____
(5) When he ran backwards, he dropped bits of bread on the ground. _____

(6) I will go at 6 p.m. _____
(7) I left my pen sitting up in my bedroom. _____
(8) It is important to do good things for people. _____
(9) Is it par for so many students to get such good grades? _____

(10) Did you find a nice pair of shoes? _____

Another example, from Chapter 11, presents lateral thinking puzzles:

BRAIN TWISTERS

Directions: To answer these questions, you have to let your brain think in different ways than you may be used to.

Question #1: A girl who was just learning to drive went down a one-way street in the wrong direction, but didn't break the law. How come?
_____

Question #2: How can you throw a ball as hard as you can and have it come back to you, even if it doesn't hit anything, there is nothing attached to it, and no one else catches or throws it? _____

Question #3: Two students are sitting on opposite sides of the same desk. There is nothing in between them but the desk. Why can't they see each other?
_____

From a pedagogical point of view, these materials showed the influence of the Cambridge English series upon which they were modeled, and incorporated many activities that drew on communicative and interactive approaches to language teaching, including matching activities, true-false and multiple-choice comprehension questions, cloze exercises and games and puzzles like crosswords. Within the chapters there was a heavy emphasis on vocabulary, which benefited from the items in question appearing in the reading texts. At the same time, the materials revealed their writers' lack of extensive professional training in that there was little attempt to create meaningful sequences from receptive to active knowledge or to utilize common concepts such as schema theory and the accompanying preference for thematically or conceptually linked items. Many of the activities such as unscrambling words, filling in missing letters and so on, were rather repetitive and of dubious usefulness. In fairness, it should be acknowledged that relatively little class time was devoted to these kinds of exercises.

While much more can be said about the Crusoe materials, rather than analyzing and evaluating the materials themselves in isolation it is much more interesting to see how they were used in classroom interaction – that is to say, within the broader ecology of the classroom (Guerrettaz & Johnston, 2013). For this reason, further discussion of the pedagogical use of the materials, and also of the Grammar appendix of *Survivor 2: Robinson Crusoe*, will be set aside until the following chapter, which looks at classroom interaction.

Adapting Robinson Crusoe

As concerns the adapted text of the novel that forms the backbone of these materials, it was abundantly clear that the developers of *Survivor 2* were foregrounding the religious dimension of the book. It is very much the case that *Robinson Crusoe* is in fact a religious text, among other things. Its author Daniel Defoe (c. 1660–1731) was brought up as a Protestant Dissenter, and his prolific writings included many texts of a religious nature, often offering moral advice. In the preface to *Robinson Crusoe*, he states, 'The story is told with modesty, with seriousness, and with a religious application of events to the uses to which wise men apply them' (Defoe, 1719/1968: 3). Sydney's reading of the book (see above) is not amiss. Yet, in the popular remembering of the story, the religious dimension is either secondary or completely overlooked. In his introduction to the novel, James Sutherland (1968: xi–xii) writes: 'To most readers *Robinson Crusoe* is simply an adventure story, and if they can hardly help being conscious of certain religious overtones, they are apt to write them off as a conventional and irrelevant commentary to be skipped over as quickly as possible'. This is certainly the way the book has been conveyed in movies and television adaptions; it's also true of other simplified readers prepared for children or language learners. One of these, for instance, the Penguin adaptation 'retold' by Nancy Taylor (2008), a text of just over 9700 words, does not include a single reference to God, the Bible or any spiritual or religious experience. Indeed, in the Teacher's Notes to *Survivor 2* this fact is commented on forcefully:

> Many publishing houses have chosen this classic as a text for second language learners and have condensed it to less than 100 pages. What we have noticed is this [sic], in most cases, the spiritual content has been brutally eliminated from the text and so we end up with a castaway story with no moral, no conclusion and no God.

(It is interesting that evangelicals seem not to be 'most readers', in Sutherland's phrase quoted above, and that Taryn clearly remembered the spiritual and religious content of *Robinson Crusoe* from having read the book as a child.)

The 'spiritual content' referred to in the Teacher's Notes is not just present, but prominent, in the original novel. Following are just two of the innumerable examples to be found in the book. The first occurs after the well-known scene in which Crusoe sees the footprint on the beach, and subsequently finds himself overcome by fear:

> I then reflected that God, who was not only righteous but omnipotent, as he had thought fit thus to punish and afflict me, so he was able to deliver me; that if he did not think fit to do it, 'twas my unquestion'd duty to resign my self absolutely and entirely to his will; and on the other hand, it was my duty also to hope in him, pray to him, and quietly to attend the dictates and directions of his daily providence.
>
> These thoughts took me up many hours, days; nay, I may say, weeks and months; and one particular effect of my cogitations on this occasion, I cannot omit, *viz*. one morning early, lying in my bed, and fill'd with thought about my danger from the appearance of savages, I found it discompos'd me very much, upon which those words of the Scripture came into my thoughts, *Call upon me in the day of trouble, and I will deliver, and thou shalt glorify me.*[2]
>
> Upon this, rising chearfully out of my bed, my heart was not only comforted, but I was guided and encourag'd to pray earnestly to God for deliverance. When I had done praying, I took up my Bible, and opening it to read, the first words that presented to me, were, *Wait on the Lord, and be of good Cheer, and he shall strengthen thy Heart; wait, I say, on the Lord.*[3] It is impossible to express the comfort this gave me. In answer, I thankfully laid down the book, and was no more sad, at least, not on that occasion. (Defoe, 1719/1968: 127–128)

In the second passage, Crusoe reflects on his happier state of mind after the appearance of Friday:

My grief set lighter upon me, my habitation grew comfortable to me beyond measure; and when I reflected that in this solitary life which I had been confin'd to, I had not only been moved my self to look up to heaven, and to seek to the hand that had brought me there; but was now to be made an instrument under providence to save the life, and for ought I knew, the soul of a poor savage, and bring him to the true knowledge of religion, and of the Christian doctrine, that he might know Christ Jesus, to know whom is life eternal. I say, when I reflected upon all these things, a secret joy run through every part of my soul, and I frequently rejoyc'd that ever I was brought to this place, which I had so often thought the most dreadful of all afflictions that could possibly have befallen me.

In this thankful frame I continu'd all the remainder of my time, and the conversation which employ'd the hours between Friday and I, was such, as made the three years which we liv'd there together perfectly and compleatly happy, if any such thing as compleat happiness can be form'd in a sublunary state. The savage was now a good Christian, a much better than I; though I have reason to hope, and bless God for it, that we were equally penitent, and comforted restor'd penitents; we had here the word of God to read, and no farther off from his Spirit to instruct, than if we had been in England.

I always apply'd my self in reading the Scripture, to let him know, as well as I could, the meaning of what I read; and he again, by his serious enquiries, and questionings, made me, as I said before, a much better scholar in the Scripture knowledge, than I should ever have been by my own private meer reading. Another thing I cannot refrain from observing here also from experience, in this retir'd Part of my Life, *viz.* how infinite and inexpressible a blessing it is, that the knowledge of God, and of the doctrine of salvation by Christ Jesus, is so plainly laid down in the word of God, so easy to be receiv'd and understood: that as the bare reading the Scripture made me capable of understanding enough of my duty, to carry me directly on to the great work of sincere repentance for my sins, and laying hold of a Saviour for life and salvation, to a stated reformation in practice, and obedience to all God's commands, and this without any teacher or instructer; I mean, humane [=human]; so the same plain instruction sufficiently serv'd to the enlightning this savage creature, and bringing him to be such a Christian, as I have known few equal to him in my life. (Defoe, 1719/1968: 177–178)

These extracts are typical of many passages that deal with Crusoe's spiritual state of mind throughout the novel.

At the same time, *Robinson Crusoe* is not only a religious-spiritual text, just as no novel has only a single dimension. (An excellent discussion of the multiple possible readings of *Robinson Crusoe* can be found in Booth [1988].) One striking aspect of the Lighthouse treatment of the book was the virtually complete absence of any critical purchase on its colonial assumptions. In many ways, *Robinson Crusoe* is *the* colonial text – the white man protecting his civilization from 'savages', then benevolently adopting one of them, the canonical 'Man Friday', to be his trusted servant. It is for this reason that the story has spawned so many postcolonial analyses and retellings (the latter notably include Michel Tournier's *Vendredi ou les Limbes du Pacifique* [1967, translated as *Friday, or the Other Island*] and J.M. Coetzee's *Foe* [1986]). This aspect of the text was hardly ever mentioned in class at Lighthouse, let alone being singled out for particular attention. I found this problematic, especially in light of the arguably neocolonial character of the missionary enterprise in general (see Chapter 9). It is a standard argument in critical approaches to say that the failure to problematize texts, discourses or situations is tantamount to accepting the status quo. There were certainly indications that this was the case with the use of *Robinson Crusoe* at Lighthouse. For instance, in the vocabulary exercises in Chapter 10, the word 'cannibals' is defined as 'native Indians that eat people', a highly problematic Othering move that went without comment. In Chapter 8, we will examine a moment in the classroom that indicated the general failure of both teachers and learners to perceive the highly tendentious portrayal of race and racial hegemony in the book. The only point at which anything along these lines was brought up occurred in the Digging Deeper section of Chapter 17, in which three of the six questions concern master–servant relations:

(1) Talk about Crusoe's desire for a servant. Do you think this is a healthy desire?
(2) Crusoe tells Friday to call him master. How does that make you feel?
(3) Do you think Crusoe will ever have a friendship with Friday or do you think it will always be a master/servant relationship? Why or why not?

Aside from this one moment, I found no evidence of a focus on the racial or colonial dimensions of the novel during the year I spent observing the book being taught.

For Lighthouse, *Robinson Crusoe* was overwhelmingly a redemption text that was to be used as such. The reasons Sydney gave for choosing this novel (see above) are clearly echoed in the Teacher's Notes to *Survivor 2*, where potential teachers of the materials read:

> The story is a wonderful text for the English class because it is Daniel Dafoe [sic] who tells the wonderful message of the Gospel, and we, the teachers have the pleasure of watching our students awaken to spiritual truths. There is enough real life drama and decisions gone wrong to keep even the atheist keen on Crusoe's journey.
>
> There is no need to preach to your students, Dafoe [sic], through the voice of Crusoe will take care of that for you. Don't forget, you are teaching PEOPLE not a programme. It is essential that they feel they are being taught and not pushed through a course. Enjoy this journey into a classic.

Elsewhere in the same document, in the general introduction to the sections entitled 'Digging Deeper' – which as I explained above were the springboard for most of the class discussions on spiritual and religious matters – the authors of the Teacher's Notes state:

> And of course, when it happens naturally, this [the introduction of personal topics] is where the spiritual discussions will come in class. Please always be prepared with your own thoughts and opinions and spiritually directive answers. BUT please also let your students speak so you can hear what is on their heart and in their minds. This is an English class where thoughts are free to flow and judgment is left at the door. This is NOT a place to preach, but a place to explore and share the wonderful message of God's truth.

This 'missionary' use of the novel finds further reflection in the language of the adaptation. While, as mentioned above, and in contrast to other abridged editions, the religious content is retained, it is also reworded in terms that align very concretely with contemporary evangelical discourse. Let us take a look at the equivalent adapted versions of the two passages cited above. The first comes in Chapter 14 of the Lighthouse version:

> I decided I needed to remember that God could save me, and that I needed to keep my hope in Him, pray to Him, and know He would take care of me everyday. I thought about these things for many hours and days, in fact I thought about them for weeks, and months I was lying in bed early one morning, thinking about being eaten by wild men, and these words from the Bible came to me, "Call on Me in the day of

trouble, and I will save you, and you will glorify Me." I happily got out of bed, and my heart was not only comforted, but I was also able to pray to God honestly about saving me. When I had done praying, I read my Bible and came to the verse, 'Wait on the Lord, and be happy and He will strengthen your heart'. It is impossible to tell about the peace and comfort this gave me. I wasn't sad again for a long time.

The second appears in Chapter 18 of *Survivor 2: Robinson Crusoe*:

So whether I helped Friday or not, I was thankful to him for asking questions. In my lonely life, I had had to look to heaven to find God, but was now being used to save the soul of my man Friday, that he might know Jesus Christ and have eternal life. When I thought about all these things, I was happy, and thankful that I was brought to this place, which I had so many times thought was the worst thing that could have happened to me.
    The talks between Friday and me made the three years we lived on the island together completely happy. He was now a good Christian, much better than I was. We had the Bible to read and we were closer to the Holy Spirit on the island than anywhere else.
    I read the Bible and let him know, as well as I could, the meaning of what I read; and he, by his questions, made me a much better Bible student than I would ever have been on my own. Reading the Bible, I had asked for forgiveness from my sins, had trusted in Jesus, had changed my mind, and obeyed God's commands, all without any human teacher. The same Bible teaching turned a wild man into a Christian.

While of course much could be said about the relationship between the original text and the Lighthouse adaptation, what I find most interesting here is the way in which Defoe's language has been 'translated' into contemporary evangelical discourse. Thus, in the second text for example, 'that he might know Christ Jesus, to know whom is Life eternal' becomes 'that he might know Jesus Christ and have eternal life'; 'we had here the Word of God to read, and no farther off from his Spirit to instruct, than if we had been in England' becomes 'we were closer to the Holy Spirit on the island than anywhere else'; 'a much better Scholar in the Scripture Knowledge' is rendered as 'a much better Bible student'. In these cases, and many more, those preparing the Lighthouse materials have created a text that from a discursive point of view is intermediary between Defoe's original novel and the language of 21st-century evangelical proselytizing. This discursive strategy is a textual analog to the 'ecumenical discourse' that I will examine in Chapter 8, by which the Lighthouse missionaries sought to inhabit a neutral discursive zone that functioned as a common discourse which Catholics and evangelicals could use equally.

It remains to say a few words about how the students found the materials. In a word, their attitudes were positive. None of the students I spoke to raised any objections either to the colonial or racial dimensions of the text, or the foregrounding of its spiritual and religious aspects. Ania, a Catholic, liked the Crusoe text, saying that it was not like the kind of text used in religious education, that it 'could come in useful in life' and that it 'makes you think more deeply, wonder what you'd do if you were in the same situation'; she said that it encourages the reader to 'live life consciously'. Marysia, like Ania a practicing Catholic, described the materials as 'really interesting... they make you think... I really appreciate that'. She pointed out the importance in language learning of involving the learner as a whole person. Magda, one of the two evangelical learners in the class, considered that the materials 'stimulated conversation on different topics'. Overall, the students appreciated the personal nature of the discussions, the heavy use of discussion as opposed to grammar teaching and drills, and the inherently interesting subject matter.

As mentioned above, looking at how materials are used in the classroom – their place in the classroom ecology (Guerrettaz & Johnston, 2013) – is of at least equal interest as examining them in isolation. Indeed, for me the heart of my experience at Lighthouse were the twice-weekly class meetings I attended during my two semesters at the school. In the next chapter we shall see the materials in action, and observe how the texts and exercises discussed above played out in classroom interaction.

Notes

(1) In the King James version: 'Remove far from me vanity and lies: give me neither poverty nor riches; feed me with food convenient for me: Lest I be full, and deny thee, and say, Who is the Lord? or lest I be poor, and steal, and take the name of my God in vain'. In the New Living Translation: 'First, help me never to tell a lie. Second, give me neither poverty nor riches! Give me just enough to satisfy my needs. For if I grow rich, I may deny you and say, "Who is the Lord?" And if I am too poor, I may steal and thus insult God's holy name'.
(2) Psalms 50:15; curiously, in the annotated edition that this and the following passage are taken from, the source of the Bible quotations is not given.
(3) Psalms 27:14.

6 In the Classroom

As in almost any school, at Lighthouse the primary locus of the encounter between teachers and students was in the classroom. In the case of Lighthouse, this meant that the classroom was also the place where the teachers could most count on having the kinds of conversations called for by the mission of the school. In other words, it was the principal site for beginning and sustaining discussions of a religious or spiritual nature. The curriculum outlined in the previous chapter was designed precisely for this purpose.

As explained in Chapter 3, I observed three classes in detail, attending the great majority of class meetings, recording them and taking notes. In this chapter, I will share some of my observations, in particular of the classes taught by Allie in the fall and by Sydney in the spring. For reasons that I'll explain later, Taryn's spring class designed around the novel *The Shack* (Young, 2007) proved somewhat less relevant from a research point of view. Nevertheless, there were some very interesting data and I include a section on this class toward the end of the chapter. But most of my comments and analysis will focus on the other two classes.

Given the number of classroom recordings I made – 11 in the first semester and 33 in the second for a total of 44 – it was neither practical nor desirable to prepare full transcripts. Moreover, I knew what it was that I was most interested in as I began the observation process, and since I personally observed every class I recorded, I was able to keep notes in real time (backed up by a journal written immediately afterward) and identify the passages of classroom discourse that were of special interest to me. These were not infrequent – because of the nature of the materials, and of the school, spiritual issues were raised in a large number of the classes I attended. It is these moments that will be the focus of attention in the present chapter.

All the adult classes at Lighthouse lasted 90 minutes. Allie's class, and Sydney's, which was its continuation, ran from 7.30 to 9.00 pm on Tuesdays and Thursdays. There was almost always a coffee break, usually of about 10–15 minutes, starting at around 8.15 or later. Classes comprised a variety of activities, including reading aloud from the story (*Robinson Crusoe*), language work on vocabulary and grammar, language games, and discussions, the last usually centered around the curricular materials. Each teacher started the class with some 'chat'; in Sydney's case especially, I realized at some point that this part of the class, far from simply being a warm-up as students arrived and settled down, was in fact integral to the relationship-building mission of the class and the school (I'll say more about this in Chapter 7). Each class concluded with a prayer, an element of the class described in more detail below.

One other salient feature of classes was the fact that, especially in the second semester, they were often enhanced by groups of native speaker visitors from Canada, the US and Great Britain. These groups, which were often quite large, were on mission trips and typically stayed in N. for a few days, including several visits to Lighthouse. During their visits, work on the regular curriculum was interrupted and activities were set up to allow the Lighthouse learners to interact in communicative situations with the visitors. The frequency of such contacts was undoubtedly an attractive feature of the school, especially since the contacts themselves often appeared enjoyable and fruitful for both sides.

Though Sydney's class was in the second semester and Allie's in the first, I have chosen to describe Sydney's class first, since it seemed a more 'canonical' enactment of the curriculum by a founder and veteran of the school and coauthor of the materials. Allie, on the other hand, though an evangelical Christian and a missionary, was in almost every other way an outsider; she was only in Poland for the single semester during which she taught her class, and from everything I could see, was in other ways also 'atypical', if this word can be applied to such a small and intimate setting. Thus, I will first describe Sydney's spring class as an illustration of what Sydney and Taryn were striving to do through their work at Lighthouse; then, I will present Allie's class as a 'variation on a theme' which may tell us more about other ways in which spiritual content can be handled in a language classroom.

Sydney: 'Opening that door a little bit'

As already stated, Sydney could be said to have 'inherited' her class from Allie, though in fact it was really the other way around – the fall class is one that Sydney would normally have taught, but Allie was brought in to teach it while Sydney and Taryn were in Canada on extended leave.

There were five students enrolled in the class during the semester that Sydney taught it, all of them women. Three – Ania, Marysia and Ela – were continuing from the previous semester, while two others – Zosia and Magda – joined the class for the spring. However, it was rarely the case that all attended at once – rather, there would usually be three or four students in class during any given lesson. Occasionally, they were joined by Marta, a student from a morning class taught by Sydney that was following the same curriculum; Marta came in the evening when she had not been able to attend her morning class.

The women ranged in age from twenty-something to fifty-something; all came from middle-class backgrounds and were college educated. Ela and Magda were evangelical Christians; the other women were practicing Catholics. More details about the learners will emerge in the course of the following chapters.

Much of Sydney's class was taken up with the usual content of language lessons: vocabulary, grammar, reading comprehension, language games and so on. I'll say a word about this aspect of Sydney's teaching at the end of the present section. While many of these activities were of course colored by the nature of the materials (see Chapter 5), of particular interest to me were the frequent moments when the spiritual dimension of the classroom rose to the surface. In this section, I'll concentrate primarily on three kinds of occasion when this happened: in classroom discussions that were usually generated by the curricular materials; in what I came to call Sydney's impromptu 'mini-sermons'; and last but not least, in the extempore prayer with which Sydney closed each class.

Intimate conversations

Perhaps the most striking feature of Sydney's classes – the one that struck me the most, in any case – were the numerous occasions when the class engaged in searching, often deeply personal discussions about moral and spiritual matters. I found this surprising for a number of reasons – not least of which were the extreme demands that the interactions placed on the linguistic resources of the learners, and consequently the degree of motivation they must have felt to repeatedly make such efforts.

These discussions usually arose from questions posed in the materials, mostly in the 'Digging Deeper' sections described in Chapter 5, and were moderated by Sydney in a way that maximized student involvement. It was in these parts of the lessons that Sydney's charisma and skill were most clearly evident. She succeeded on many occasions in provoking thoughtful, personal responses from the learners – and this despite the fact that Poles are often quite guarded about discussing in a relatively public forum such as a classroom what are perceived as private matters, such as how one prays or the qualities of one's spouse. In what follows, we will look at three examples of such discussions from Sydney's class.

'A mind for prayer'

On March 3, the class worked on Chapter 15 of the Lighthouse adaptation of *Robinson Crusoe*, the opening paragraph of which included the following:

> I did all this because of the man's footprint I had seen. For two years I had been scared because of that footprint. This fear had damaged my prayer life. Every minute I expected to be killed and eaten by wild men; and a mind filled with thoughts of peace, thankfulness, and love is much better for prayer than a mind filled with fear.[1]

The first question in the Digging Deeper section of the activities was this:

1. Crusoe gives a recipe for prayer. What is it? Do you agree? When do you find it most difficult to pray? When is it easier to pray?

The lively discussion that arose in response to this prompt ran in part as follows:

Sydney: Let's go into 'Digging Deeper'. [*5 secs*] Crusoe gives a recipe for prayer. What's a recipe?
Magda: Przepis?
Sydney: Yeah, when you're making supper, right, you use a recipe? 'Crusoe gives a recipe for prayer. What is it? Do you agree?' Line 3. Have a look. [*12 secs*] Zosia, would you read...
[*Zosia reads the passage cited above*]
Sydney: What do you think about this? He says, 'A mind filled with thoughts of peace, thankfulness, and love is much better for prayer than a mind filled with fear'. Do you agree? Disagree? [*4 secs*]
Marysia: Difficult to say, because, um, we, if we are [*pause*] if we are afraid, or we have, have fear, we can pray also, um, good I think, because we have a problem and we should try solve it.
Sydney: We're motivated, right?
Marysia: Yeah, we have, um, more motivation I think.
Magda: But around this problem only [*laughs*].
Marysia: Yes, it's true, but
Magda: It's problem think about, think, and love, and
Marysia: I think if you are a good pray-er
Magda: I'm not [*laughs*]
Marysia: It's better when you are thankful and you have love in your heart that, um, we should try to learn how to pray and I think we pray in this moment of our life if we are in trouble
Sydney: Mm. I think this is a very interesting [*??*]

Magda:	It's every situation [*laughs*]
Sydney:	It's training
Magda:	Yes
Sydney:	Right? If you are going to run a marathon you train.
SS:	Mhm.
Sydney:	I think what Marysia is saying is that you, you practice it, you have to train for it, you have to learn how to pray, and then when the difficult moment comes in the marathon you already know how to do it.
Marysia:	Yeah.
Sydney:	That's a very interesting point, because I think so often, when we get to this difficult point, we have two, two ways that we go. We either are praying like crazy, [*whispers*] Oh God, help me, help me, help me! [*continues in normal voice; students laugh*], or we are so afraid that we don't do anything.
S:	Mhm.
Sydney:	Right? So when do you find it personally the most difficult to pray? Or the easiest time to pray? Is there a time that's easier to pray for you than other times? [*9 secs*]
Magda:	For me easier is when I have problem [*laughs*]
Sydney:	It's easier to pray when you have a problem?
Magda:	Yes, because I want, um, I try find an answer and a way
Sydney:	Mhm
Magda:	Where I should go.
Sydney:	Mhm. So if God wants to hear from you more he has to give you more problems? [*laughs*]
Magda:	[*laughs*]
Sydney:	I'm kidding, Magda, I'm kidding
Magda:	[??]
Sydney:	But if, it is interesting, right? If God wants us to have this relationship with him. Hm, Yeah. What about you, Zosia, when is it easier or more difficult to pray?
Zosia:	I think with Magda, what I, when I have problem I um, can be, um, [*to Magda*] Jak jest skupiony? [=How do you say 'skupiony' (focused)?]
Ania:	Focused
Zosia:	Focused on my prayer. Um, then when I'm happy I, I want to talk with people and can't be focused on prayer only. But I think that when we have problem if [?] we pray for some advance and some solutions, and everything is after this is good, we really, um, I, um I often don't, don't remember to thanks God.

Sydney: Yeah. this is something that I found very interesting in this chapter. Something has changed about the way he's praying now. Because in the past we heard that he was crying out for help, he was asking God for help, to save him, for all of the things that he needed. And then on his anniversary he would say thank you for saving him. But now, in this chapter, three times he talks about thanking God. And I think, this is a very interesting point that you're making. How we ask, and ask, and ask, and how often do we stop and say thank you. We don't need to know. But it's interesting, isn't it? Yeah.
Marysia: But I think it's not really correct. Because we should pray always, not when we are in trouble.
Sydney: Mhm.
Marysia: That's, um, that's not really good for us. But we do it [*laughs*]

This discussion was fairly typical for the class in terms of length, complexity and general character. Many features can be noted here. As far as form is concerned, it's striking that all the students take part, and that turns are rather evenly distributed among all four learners. (Ania says little in the transcript, though my notes confirm that she was engaged in the class, as she always was, and was providing active backchanneling.) Sydney takes a couple of longer turns, but otherwise the conversation is spread among all those present. Also of note from the point of view of classroom discourse is the length and the syntactic and lexical complexity of the student contributions. These are considerable, especially given the fairly low level of the class. In addition, at many points the learners can be seen struggling with syntax or vocabulary, showing that they are at the limits of their linguistic competence – a desirable state in a language classroom.

From a pedagogical point of view, it's also worth noting the extended wait times that Sydney allows – something that is highly recommended in classroom management, yet often lacking in actual classrooms. For example, after asking: 'So when do you find it personally the most difficult to pray? Or the easiest time to pray? Is there a time that's easier to pray for you than other times?', she waits nine seconds before Magda responds. There are other long pauses in this excerpt from the transcript, indicating Sydney's willingness to give the learners time to formulate the content and form of their responses. Pedagogically speaking, the resulting conversation justifies these waits.

Yet, more than the form of the classroom interaction – which bespeaks an environment in which extended talk is the norm – it is the *content* of this talk that will strike many readers. In this classroom, Polish Catholics and Polish and Canadian evangelicals discuss one of the most spiritually intimate topics one can imagine – prayer, or one's private conversations with God – in the setting of a language class. They do so, moreover, enthusiastically and with a high level of interest, as the duration and depth of the discussion shows. They reveal unflattering and undesirable aspects of themselves (the fact that they do not pray when and how they should, but only when they are in need – that they are 'bad pray-ers'). And while engaging seriously in a manifestly serious topic, they do not shy away from teasing one another (as Sydney does to Magda) and from generally laughing at themselves and one another.

In a word, the discourse we see in this extract shows that in fact Sydney and Taryn were right – it *is* possible to stimulate deep adult conversation about spiritual matters using the Crusoe materials, without proselytizing (though I'll say a little bit more about this later on) and without alienating adult Polish Catholic learners. It is this kind of discussion – a couple more examples will be shown below – that for me was the most remarkable manifestation of the cultural encounter at Lighthouse.

What makes you jealous?

Discussion in the class of April 21 was stimulated by the following, the opening questions in the 'Digging Deeper' part of the activities accompanying Chapters 19 and 20:

(1) Why do you think Robinson became jealous of Friday? What kinds of things make you jealous?

The students were put in two small groups (one of two, one of three) and asked to address the questions. Sydney sat with Ania and Magda. Magda spoke first, and said that while later in life she might become jealous of someone with good health, for the moment she was not jealous of anyone. Ania said that the desire for material goods and the like was not really jealousy, and that it was something everyone experienced. But she said quietly and clearly that she felt something akin to jealousy when she saw a close father–daughter relationship, something she lacked in life and would want for herself:

Ania: When I see a good relationship between daughter and father. Because mine was very bad and sometimes, this, is, this is not jealous, [??] I'm not very very angry, but in my heart I feel—
Sydney: You want this

>
> **Ania:** I want this, yes, sometimes, sometimes when I see some very great relationship.
>
> **Sydney:** I understand that

At this, Magda changed her mind and agreed that this was something she also would like to have had but didn't, 'because I didn't have [a] father'.

I was struck by this small and perhaps otherwise undramatic moment, primarily because of the depths of emotional experience and longing that it brought to the surface, and also the calm and matter-of-fact tone in which Ania spoke. It showed the way that Sydney was able to create a space for learners to speak about things that were not just meaningful for them but emotionally important; and it also showed how the learners themselves felt comfortable enough to take advantage of this opportunity to reveal and discuss personal feelings and desires that, in my many years teaching, observing and reading about language classes, I have rarely seen brought up in the classroom. The level of self-revelation and vulnerability was remarkable.

How romantic is your husband?

The last example of an intimate conversation comes from a class that was held on February 12, two days before Valentine's Day. Sydney began the class with a game of hangman in which the phrases to be discovered were 'a box of chocolates' and 'a bouquet of roses'. She then asked the students whether their husbands were romantic. This turned into a lengthy informal conversation that had a similar quality to the frequent warm-up chats described in Chapter 7, but was more pedagogically focused. During the conversation, Ela – who was often teased by the group, especially by Sydney, because of the rather downbeat, pessimistic way she tended to present things – told a story of visiting a jewelry store with her husband where she had admired a particular watch. Subsequently, her husband had bought her an expensive watch, but it had not been the one she'd liked in the store. Ela told this story in a way that was critical of her husband. Later in the conversation, on an unrelated topic Ania made a joke about someone coming home and being surprised by a bouquet of flowers. At this point Ela resumed the floor.

>
> **Ela:** Two week, two weeks ago when I, I come back home, um, from English class,
>
> **Sydney:** Mhm, when I went home
>
> **Ela:** When I went home, um, I, my husband started very nervous and look at me and I don't know, what is it? but after one hour I go to my, um, bedroom –
>
> **Sydney:** Went.

Ela:	Went to my bedroom and I realized that it's flowers in, in my bed.
Sydney:	Flowers *in* your bed?
Ela:	Flowers in my, on my, on my bed
Sydney:	Flowers on your bed. Oh my goodness.
Ela:	Yes
Sydney:	What are we talking about?
Ania:	The most romantic! [*laughs*]
Sydney:	Oh, he's not very romantic! Oh, two years ago I got a watch I didn't like that was gold!
Ela:	[???]
Sydney:	Two weeks ago he's got flowers! You have to leave now because we have to [??].
	[*huge laughter*]
Sydney:	OK, so what kinds of flowers did you get?
Ania:	It's everything, but she wanted to have another thing.
Sydney:	It's the sign, in the story –
Ania:	Right!
Sydney:	That Crusoe has, right? The sign that Marysia was talking about on Tuesday night. What is it? Can you bring it, please, Ania! Find the one.
	[*general noise*]
Ela:	No!
Sydney:	It's so important!
Ania:	Yes. [*laughs*]
Sydney:	Listen, honey! When a man puts flowers on your bed, let me tell you [*lots of laughter from the other women*]. Especially after you've been married for twenty-five years. Whoo, baby! [*laughs*] Come on, girl!
	[*everyone calms down a bit*]
Ania:	*Jest* [=Here it is]. [*reading*] 'Some people can't enjoy what God has given them because they are looking at something that He has not given them'.[2] [*laughs*]
Ela:	Maybe yes.
	[*huge laughter*]
Ela:	A little bit.
Sydney:	A little bit? That is such a good story. You know, as Marysia was talking about [???that] the other night, how she just thinks that this is how so many people look at their life, you know.
Ania:	Yes.

Sydney: And I had to think about it for myself as I read this chapter. Because it's true, you know, we always want something that we don't have, and um, whether it's a more romantic husband or whatever it might be, you know [*laughs*]. Yeah. We need to be thankful for what we have.

In this extract, Ela tells an intimate story from her own life – perhaps made more poignant by the fact that her husband Jan was also taking classes at Lighthouse at the time, and so was known to Sydney and others in the class. Several aspects of the interaction are remarkable: first, the fact that Ela is willing to share this story (which after all, with its mention of the bedroom, borders on the risqué, especially for an audience of women she did not know especially well – and with me, a male outsider, present also). Second, the great teasing that goes on, coming not only from Sydney but also from Ania and others, denotes a closeness in the group – such comments could be neither made nor accepted among strangers maintaining a distance. Third, as so often in the class, Sydney was able to draw explicit links between the Crusoe materials being used and the personal interactions among teacher and learners. In this extract, Ela's story – which could not have been anticipated – resonated with a line from the chapter examined in the previous lesson, and Sydney had Ania track it down and read it aloud, thus folding the materials back into the intimate conversation she had set in motion.

Lastly, I was struck by Sydney's ability to empathize with her students not only across cultural lines, but also personal ones. Sydney is a single middle-aged woman who has never been married, and has devoted her life to her work as a missionary. Yet, she is able to take full part in a lighthearted conversation about romantic relationships, marriage and men. Her participation in this conversation betokens a worldliness in her attitudes and ways of talking: though personally choosing not to engage in certain worldly things, she does not shy away from acknowledging them and talking about them. This was an important dimension of the empathy that Sydney was able to bring to her work at Lighthouse.

Teaching into preaching?

There were moments in Sydney's class when she took the floor for extended periods of time and talked to the students in what I came to call mini-sermons. Her tone was distinctly informal, almost conversational, and the speech was very clearly directed at the particular people in the room; nevertheless, she was equally clearly using the opportunity to convey some spiritual message that she felt appropriate at the given time. Usually, this message was related fairly directly to the text or activities of the current chapter in the materials. A typical example came at the end of the discussion on prayer which was shown above. Here is the conclusion of that discussion; I include the turns immediately preceding Sydney's mini-sermon to show how the discussion transitions into it.

Sydney:	Yeah. Yep. there is, um, there's a verse in the New Testament, the Apostle Paul says, 'Pray without ceasing'—that means never stop—'Pray without ceasing, in everything give thanks'.³
Marysia:	Mm.
Sydney:	[*sotto voce*] Wow. [*normal voice*] This is difficult.
Marysia:	This is very difficult [*overlapping*]
Sydney:	When you have problems, to say thank you? [*laughter*]
Sydney:	You know, really, when we have these difficult, very difficult times in our lives, how, how do we, how do we say thank you?
S:	If I couldn't pray I couldn't fall asleep [*overlapping*]
Sydney:	Mhm.
S:	[*very quiet*] I couldn't
Sydney:	It's, it's very difficult, and you know that's why we need each other also. Because we, we know, and God knows, that we will have these times when we cannot pray. And then we need other people to pray for us
S:	Mhm.
Sydney:	And that's why we have this community. It's, it's absolutely essential that we support each other by praying for each other, because when we don't, how do we survive? This is why, when we look at, when we look at the New Testament, we look at the church, the first church, they were a group of people that were so close to each other
S:	Mhm
Sydney:	They cared for each other, they prayed for each other, they supported each other, and that's the way it's supposed to be. We're not supposed to be here alone trying to do our life by ourselves. We're supposed to be here for each other. To pray with each other, to pray for each other; because there are times we cannot pray for ourselves. It's too difficult. There are things that we can't, we don't even have the words to pray. And God knows that. [*5 secs*]. I found this chapter very very challenging personally, because he talks about this, this, what does it mean to pray. And what he says here at the beginning, where he says that the fear had

damaged his prayer life. I like this expression, his prayer life. Not just, you know, survival and living but this, this life, this heartbeat of prayer. I think it's a, it's a beautiful picture. And he says that a mind filled with thoughts of peace and thankfulness and love is better for prayer than fear. This is powerful for me; this is something I, I think we can think about this for a very long time and make this a personal practice to think about this. [*coughs*]. How are we doing for time? Woah! It is nine o'clock. So we will stop there.

As is common in actual sermons, Sydney starts her reflections with a Bible quotation. As is also common in North American evangelical practice, she personalizes what she says with frequent reference to her own experiences, preferences, spiritual needs and so on – a discursive move that is intended to render her voice more authentic and convincing (e.g. 'I found this chapter very challenging'; 'I like this expression'; and her exclamation 'wow'). It's also noteworthy that the transition to this passage is very smooth – it's linked firmly to the current chapter of the Crusoe text and the accompanying exercises (see above), and is thus rather naturally embedded in the classroom discourse. A clear indication that this is the case is the high level of student involvement in the talk, evident in the active student participation immediately preceding Sydney's long turn, as she is 'warming up' for her mini-sermon. More will be said about this aspect below.

It is also interesting to note Sydney's somewhat disingenuous reference to the phrase 'prayer life'. She says: 'I like this expression', implying it is from the book, whereas in fact this is one of the very many latter-day evangelical interpolations that she and Taryn inserted into the text as they rewrote it for the purposes of Lighthouse School. Where the Lighthouse version of the text reads, 'This fear had damaged my prayer life', Defoe's (1719/1968: 132) original is: '...and this I must observe with grief too, that the discomposure of my mind had too great impressions also upon the religious part of my thoughts'.

Finally, I can't help remarking on the fluency and beauty of Sydney's manner of speaking. Phrases like 'heartbeat of prayer' are powerful; in general, the students' silence shows that they were intent on listening to what Sydney was saying, a fact confirmed by my notes. (I comment elsewhere on the charisma that many students noted in Sydney.) At the same time, she keeps her syntax and vocabulary at a level that is accessible for these particular students – no easy feat, as any second language teacher will testify. This is a good example of the way in which she was able to captivate the students' attention for extended stretches of time, and to use the classroom for the purposes of raising and addressing spiritual issues in a meaningful yet accessible fashion.

The vocal student participation in the preceding extract is an indication that the learners did not feel lectured to, but rather considered Sydney's contributions merely longer-than-usual turns in an ongoing dialogue to which they had access at any minute. Further evidence that this was so came in the class of March 10. Toward the end of the class, Sydney began another mini-sermon in response to an extended contribution by Marysia about the need to learn to be happy for what one has (I look in more detail at Marysia's contribution in Chapter 7). Throughout Sydney's turn, Marysia continues energetic backchanneling, until in the end, without letting Sydney continue, she interposes her own voice, at which point a distraction brings both contributions to an end.

Sydney: Yeah. But like you said, this is something that you had to *learn*. It's not something that comes naturally. Because I think naturally, it's a little bit more like what Zosia said, you know? It's human nature that -

Marysia: Yeah.

Sydney: - we're kind of not happy with what we have. And so we have to learn this. And I think it's, it's like so many other things, it's training.

Marysia: It's training.

Sydney: We have to train our mind—no, you know, but look at what I have, what I have is fantastic.

Marysia: Yeah.

Sydney: And I, I need to be thankful for those things.

Marysia: Yeah.

Sydney: And you know, there's, there's this fantastic verse in the New Testament from the Apostle Paul. And, now the apostle Paul has been shipwrecked, like Crusoe.

Marysia: Mhm.

Sydney: He has been beaten because he was a, a follower of Jesus Christ. He has been put in prison. And he's actually writing a letter from prison to other people, to other Christians, and he says: 'I have learned to be content. I learned to be happy in whatever situation I find myself. And this has become something that I am trying to live out in my life. That whether I—' and then he gives a long list: 'whether I have a lot, whether I have nothing, whether I am hungry or whether I am full, whether I am shipwrecked or whether I am living in a home, whether I'm in prison or whether I'm a free man, I have learned to be content with these things'.[4] And I think, Wow! This, this is the way I want my life to be. And I have moments, oh my goodness, I have many moments where I'm like –

Marysia: Yeah, but –
Sydney: I'm not so happy with my situation [*laughs*].
Marysia: It's true –
Sydney: Yeah.
Marysia: but you, we must try to, um, make the best of the situation –
Sydney: That's true.
Marysia: and see to things why, um, why I have in this situation at this moment
Sydney: Yes.
Marysia: Because we can –
[*there's a distraction with objects in the classroom—one student can't find a working pen*]
Sydney: All right. So let's—whose turn is it to read?

The point of this extract is to demonstrate that, far from being an unwelcomed intrusion into the classroom discourse, Sydney's 'mini-sermons' are in fact taken by the students as an integral part of the ongoing teacher–student dialogue – that is, they are seen as one component of an extended conversation in which they (the students) have an equal right to speak. It is striking that Marysia, whose English resources are still somewhat limited, is able to take the floor from Sydney to express what she seems to regard as a supportive but supplementary point to that which Sydney is making. Yet, by the same token, her willingness to interrupt Sydney to present her own viewpoint demonstrates the absence of relations of power and coercion in this classroom. Furthermore, it strongly suggests that at those moments when Sydney is *not* interrupted during her mini-sermons, this is not because the learners are afraid to do so, or that they are bored, but because they are genuinely listening to her and that their willingness to pay attention has more to do with Sydney's inherent personal authority than with her position of power as a North American teacher. The learners are simply interested in what Sydney has to say, and regard it as worth listening to.

Closing prayer

Sydney ended each class with a brief extempore prayer. The prayer often referred directly to the preceding lesson and to events and issues in the students' lives, and mentioned class members and others by name. During the prayer, the students would bow their heads respectfully and remain silent; some would join in with Sydney's 'amen' at the end. The following example came at the end of the March 3 class on prayer, an extract from which was examined above. At a little over two minutes, this prayer is about twice as long as most end-of-class prayers in this class, but its other features are quite typical.

Sydney: So let me pray for you, because it's my privilege and my pleasure to pray for you. [*pause*] Father, it's true that it is sometimes very difficult to be able to pray. Sometimes life is so hard that we don't even have the right words. And sometimes we pray because we are just so stressed that we just cry for help, and we say, Help us, help us, help us. But father, tonight, I pray for each one of these people in this room, that each us would have this understanding that 'a mind filled with peace and thankfulness and love is better for prayer'. Father, I pray that you would help each of us to pray; not to have long, elaborate, elegant prayers, but to pray simply, to pray honestly, to pray from our hearts, that we would have this prayer life with you, Father, that would be beautiful, that would be something very special. And so, father, I pray for Zosia, and for Magda, and for Ania, and for Marysia, and for Bill, and for myself, that each of us would take time this week to say thank you. Thank you for the wonderful things that you have given us. For our family, for our friends, for our homes, for our food, for our clothes, for living in a great city, and that we would take time to spend with you, Father, by praying and thanking you for the goodness that you have given us. And Father, as Marysia has said, we need to learn how to pray, and practice it, and be ready for when we really do have the difficult, difficult days. Father, we pray that you would help each of us to learn this practice, to learn how to do this. And Father, I continue to pray for Ania, that you would heal her broken heart, and that you would give her strength for the next day. In Jesus' name I pray. Amen.

A number of observations can be made about this prayer. First, it is deeply embedded in the particular place and time when it was spoken. All those present are named (including myself); Sydney specifically mentions Ania, who had suffered a great personal loss a few weeks earlier (I write more about this in Chapter 7), asking God to 'heal her broken heart'. This emphasizes not just the centrality of the teacher–student relation, but also its intimacy – to speak in this way in the presence of both Ania and the other students indicates a significant level of closeness among the whole group.

Here as elsewhere, Sydney practices what Brian Morgan (2004) has called 'teacher identity as pedagogy', that is, the teacher making use of his or her own experiences, feelings, personal practices and indeed failings, as fodder for teaching. More will be said about these things in Chapter 7.

It is worth noting too that the materials are also referred to in this prayer: the phrase 'a mind filled with peace and thankfulness and love is better for prayer' is, as we have seen, taken directly from the chapter of *Survivor 2: Robinson Crusoe* that the class read that day, and the general topic of the prayer – which is the practice of praying itself – follows from the discussion looked at earlier, which was based in turn on the Digging Deeper section of the chapter. It was quite typical of Sydney to weave in references to the materials in informal discussions, prayers, mini-sermons and elsewhere – another example of this was seen in the discussion about romantic husbands quoted above, in which Sydney explicitly connected something said in conversation with an idea expressed in the materials, and had Ania go back to the text and read the relevant sentence aloud.

Finally, this chapter also looks forward to a phenomenon I examine in more detail in Chapter 8: that of 'ecumenical discourse', that is, the use by Sydney, Taryn and others connected with the school, of terms that can link to both Catholic and evangelical forms of discourse. The whole prayer above is spoken by an evangelical, but it is couched carefully in a way that makes it accessible to Catholics too – there is nothing in the prayer that a Catholic could object to, and much that she or he would recognize and endorse.

In the initial stages of the research, I often wondered what the Polish learners thought of these prayers. Or, more accurately, I assumed that they would be shocked and perhaps embarrassed, not only by the very practice of (non-Catholic) prayer in a language classroom, but also by the intimate character of many of the prayers and the informal nature of their form and content – for example, Sydney would say things like, 'thank you, God, that we have fun', not something I could ever imagine being said in a Polish Catholic context. Yet, as so often happened in the course of this study, I was mistaken, underestimating the learners and their reactions. None of the Catholic students found this practice objectionable. Ania admitted to having found the practice of prayer in class embarrassing to begin with, but she said she had 'gotten used to it' and that it 'didn't bother her'. Later, she came to see it as a way of showing friendship and empathy. Zosia found the practice of class prayers 'interesting' and 'cool' (*fajne*), and mentioned recent developments in Catholicism (which has strongly tended to favor more formulaic and elevated kinds of prayer) toward spontaneous praying.

Most enthusiastic of all was Marysia. When asked about the classroom prayers, she said:

> For me it's a valuable thing. I like it, because I know she's praying for me... It's a great gift that someone is doing something for your sake... What she gives us is completely disinterested, that's how I experience it. It's a disinterested gift that should be accepted. Plus, I try to join in the prayer myself in some way, you know?

Once again, my preconceptions concerning the gulf of theological belief and practice between Catholic and evangelical perspectives proved fundamentally mistaken. And once again, I was taken aback by the way these otherwise very different world views can harmonize at unexpected moments – something I look at in more detail in Chapter 8.

Regular pedagogy

As mentioned above, much of Sydney's class was taken up with the regular business of language teaching: vocabulary and grammar presentation and practice using a variety of activities. 'Regular' pedagogy both is and is not my subject in this chapter. On the one hand, I'm more interested in the overtly spiritual dimension of the classroom – the kinds of elements explored in the preceding pages. In terms of these moments, pedagogy is only relevant insofar as the spiritual discussions and interventions related to Lighthouse School's aims – though bearing in mind that for the learners it was the language learning that was paramount, while the religious matter was 'incidental', as Ania put it.

By the same token, though, the regular pedagogy of the school *is* of interest, the more so because it has been suggested that in mission-based schools there is a danger of privileging spiritual over pedagogical effectiveness, and that poorly trained teachers will discredit the profession of TESOL. It's also the case that evangelical authors such as Snow (2001: 72) make a strong appeal to mission teachers to be qualified and to ensure that above all they do a professional job at their teaching, because otherwise they will not be able to offer 'effective Christian witness'.

That said, and though I do not wish to dwell on purely pedagogical matters, it seems appropriate to make a few comments.

Overall, Sydney's pedagogy was solid and unobjectionable. She used a variety of games and other activities, many of which were embedded in the materials. It was evident from observing her at length that she had extensive experience and had learned from it well – this was apparent, for example, in her clear diction, her awareness of how her English was understood by low intermediate Polish learners (examples of this can be seen in the excerpts from classroom discourse shown above) and her ability to provide synonyms and paraphrases. The range of games and activities, in turn, revealed that she and Taryn had made extensive use of text- and web-based teaching resources. And, of course, Sydney's remarkable classroom manner was not the product of pure charm, but had been honed over several years – a perfect example of how an innate disposition needs to go hand in hand with experience.

That said, there were definitely also elements of Sydney's pedagogy that revealed a lack of extensive training of the kind offered in any good-quality master's program. Sydney herself confessed that she still struggled with grammar, grammatical concepts and grammatical explanations. The class meetings focusing on grammar were, by her own account, the ones where she felt most nervous having me in the classroom, and though she did the best job she could, I always had the sense that she was uncomfortable in her role as teacher of grammar. It was also, by the way, a major concern of the learners – in the first semester especially, Ania had struggled with grammar and I met with her on one occasion to try and help explain certain concepts; her struggles continued in the second semester. In general it can be said that Polish middle-class learners are fond of clear grammatical explanations, and often judge their language teachers in part on their ability to provide them.

Beyond this, and despite the fact that Sydney and Taryn both took very seriously their goal of providing 'quality language instruction', the lack of training also emerged in broader-scale issues. When one examines the materials, for example, though most of the activities taken in isolation were pedagogically justifiable, in their sequence and arrangement it was hard to discern a broader plan – for example, building small units into larger ones; moving from receptive to active knowledge, for instance from reading to writing; or using concepts such as schema theory to organize and systematize lexical work. Rather, the sequence of vocabulary activities, for instance, merely seemed like an attempt to offer a variety of ways of incorporating recently encountered lexical items, and often bordered on busy work. Likewise, because Sydney and Taryn were unfamiliar with work in second language acquisition, their general psychological empathy with the learners was not matched by an in-depth understanding of the language learning processes the latter were going through, except at a general level. And a lack of detailed knowledge of the workings of language itself meant that Sydney felt perpetually out of her depth in explaining, for example, verb tense and aspect to her learners.

Once again, I say these things not to suggest that the quality of instruction in Sydney's class was poor – I hope that through the examples shown above I have made it clear that I do not believe this to be the case, and, as I have also shown, nor did the learners – but to point out that, even with a gifted and experienced teacher like Sydney, a lack of in-depth teacher education impeded the larger-scale pedagogical effectiveness of her work. Since many mission teachers (like many other language teachers) are unqualified, the point extends to numerous teaching contexts. What can be learned from Lighthouse is that even large amounts of goodwill, experience and dedication are unlikely to replace training and know-how.

Allie: 'Knowing English will change their lives'

Allie was an American in her mid-twenties from northeast Texas. She was a lifelong evangelical Christian, and a graduate of a southern US Bible institute. She described herself on several occasions as 'conservative' in her social and religious views, and self-identified as a fundamentalist in terms of how she viewed, for example, the creation of the world.

Allie had wanted to be a missionary since an early age. Soon after graduating from the institute, Allie became an employee in Jean's organization (see Chapter 4) and taught children in Mexico for five years, an experience she spoke of fondly. She came to Poland with Jean in September 2008 to work with her at Lighthouse. In the fall semester, she taught three twice-weekly classes, including the intermediate adult class that Sydney took over in the spring. Allie was gracious enough to permit me to observe and eventually record her classes, but she was nervous about being observed, and asked me explicitly not to make her 'look bad' in what I wrote.

I observed Allie's class from the very beginning of the semester on September 22 and, aside from one 10-day absence in the US in October when I missed three class meetings, I was present at every class until the last one on December 11. To begin with, to get the students used to my presence I did not record or take notes but only sat in; I wrote notes immediately afterward in my research journal. After a month and a half, on November 4, I began to audio-record the classes, and recorded every class from that moment on, taking simultaneous notes in a small notebook.

The class was tiny. Only three students were registered, and one of them, Marysia, attended only sporadically; as a result only two students were usually present, and frequently Ania alone was there. This of course made my presence all the more noticeable. However, familiarity soon dulled concerns, and as I made an effort to get to know Allie and the students both inside and outside of class (for example, before and after class, and in the coffee breaks that were a time-honored custom at Lighthouse), they began to feel more comfortable with me and did not object when I asked if I could start recording the classes. It was also the case that, though I hardly ever personally intervened in class of my own accord, Allie occasionally called on me to take part in a game or other activity that required two people, especially when Ania was the only student present.

Allie was a large presence in the classroom, both physically and socially. She was tall and rather thickset, and had a loud voice; in the relatively small space of the Caribbean Room, she dominated proceedings. However, as a rule, middle-class Polish women are not shrinking violets, and Allie's students were no exception. I never had the sense that Allie's domination was in any way oppressive to them; even those who were linguistically hesitant, like Ania, were rarely afraid to make active contributions to the class.

Allie taught the first half of the *Robinson Crusoe* materials. Much of her teaching was fairly standard in terms of its content – there were numerous games, vocabulary and grammar work, reading aloud of the chapters and so on. Yet Allie's use of the materials was somewhat chaotic, and, as she admitted to me, she omitted quite a lot that she did not wish to cover in class.

Rather more frequently and overtly than either Sydney or Taryn in the following semester, Allie carried out what was clearly 'mission work' in the classroom. An early example of this came in one of the classes I observed but did not record, on October 30. This was the last class before All Souls' Day, which is one of the most important events in the Polish Catholic calendar. On this day, Poles visit cemeteries, clean the graves of their family dead and light funerary candles. Though I don't know how much Allie knew about this, since it was her first year in Poland, my guess is that she had heard something about Polish All Souls' Day, because at the end of class she brought the matter up. She quoted a line from the Bible in which Jesus says (in her words), 'Remember that God is a God of the living, not of the dead'.[5] She repeated the line, and asked the students to remember it in the coming days; she also asked them if they thought Poles would be surprised if they were told that this was a line from the Bible. This perceived 'cult of the dead' in Poland and other countries is a perennial concern for many evangelicals, and Allie's remark was a message she wished to convey to her students about the desirability of focusing on life rather than on death. (To some extent this concern parallels the evangelical desire to emphasize the joyfulness of faith, and their concomitant criticism of forms of worship like

Catholicism that, in their eyes, place an undue stress on guilt, disapproval and punishment.)

On numerous occasions, Allie gave more or less impromptu mini-sermons – I counted at least nine of these in the 11 classes I recorded. In class on December 9, the penultimate class of the semester, an activity involving the lighting of Advent candles turned into a series of lecture-like sermons. On another occasion, on November 27, Allie gave three such mini-sermons in a single class at which only Ania was present. The third of these was triggered by the Digging Deeper section of Chapter 7, which the class was reading at the time, and which comprised the following questions:

(1) Do you think Crusoe is losing hope? Why?
(2) Would you be losing hope if you were in Crusoe's situation? Why?

In response to the second question, Ania said with a laugh, 'I think I will be, lose my hope in the first day'. Allie laughed too, then responded as follows:

Allie: I can't imagine, I can't imagine; I'm not sure if I would, you know, I don't know. We're not in that situation. But if we look at it and compare it to our lives
Ania: Mhm
Allie: things happen to us different, but they make us lose hope, you know. Things happen. Your mom dies, you know. Um, you're in a terrible accident. It, it's easy to lose hope; it's easy to, it's easy to lose hope and feel like nothing good is going to happen. And also, if your hope is in for example, if you have hope in a person, if you, if your hope is in that person
Ania: Mhm
Allie: and then, that person fails
Ania: Mhm
Allie: then you have no hope. Or if you have only your hope in that person and they die, you know, or if you, all of your hope is in, um, your house, you know, having a good house, and then your house burns down, what's going to happen? You know, or if all of your hope is in your family and something happens, you know. If we put all of our hope in some thing, it will always fail.
Ania: Mhm
Allie: Because we live in a world where things fail, you know? The car stops running. Our children, you know, act really bad in front of everybody, and you feel really bad and you're like, oh gosh,

	you know. Or our husbands don't do what we want them to do. Or blah blah blah, or dah dah dah dah, dah dah dah dah, dah dah dah dah. So if our hope is in something that is *destined* to fail, then we will always lose hope. So it, if that's true, is there anything in this world that we can put our hope in? Is there anything that won't fail?
Ania:	God.
Allie:	Yeah.
Ania:	[???]
Allie:	Exactly. Cause the Bible says, 'God never fails'.⁶ You know, God never fails, and that's, that's nice to have when everything else fails. You know? And so Robinson at this point, he doesn't, his hope is in things that always fail him. His hope was in the house, in his house. And what happened? What happened in his house?
Ania:	Destroyed.
Allie:	It was destroyed. His hope is in this; his hope was in his plantation, and what happened? [*pause*] He left it behind, right? It's gone. His hope was in adventure. OK. He has adventure [*laughs*], he is, he is up to here with adventure [*laughs*]
Ania:	Mhm
Allie:	you know. I mean, when we put our hope in things that, they're going to fail. They're going to fail. But there is one thing that will never fail no matter what. And that's true, in God. In God.

This extract, which was typical of Allie's mini-sermons, comprises what I would see as a rather naive or simplistic form of sermonizing that is grounded in generalities rather than the particular individuals in the classroom. Ania does a solid job of following along and, where she can, taking part; but it remains the case that Allie is doing virtually all of the talking across a three-minute stretch of classroom discourse (recalling that this was the third such intervention in the course of one lesson). There is little pedagogical focus or purpose in this passage and others like it; rather, proselytizing is the only goal.

Though Allie strove to fulfill her missionary duty through such moments, her pedagogical skills left much to be desired, and the learners knew it. Her lack of training in language pedagogy was much more telling than with Sydney or Taryn, who over many years had come to learn numerous techniques through short training workshops, professional resource books and extensive mindful experience. Allie's limited experience with small children in Mexico had not prepared her for the demands presented by middle-class Polish adult learners and their expectations. She often struggled to clarify vocabulary items – I once witnessed her unsuccessfully striving for a long time to explain the word 'dirt'. She used bizarre grammatical terminology, for example describing the subject of a sentence as 'the form'. In a long discussion of the word 'instead', among other things she described it by saying, 'It's a good word that explains what happens; it's an explanation word'; and 'It's normally something that happened in the past'. On another occasion, when Ania used 'generous' in place of 'generosity', Allie explained, 'generous is the verb, generosity is the noun'.

Many of the problems Allie faced in explaining language in the classroom arose because she did not prepare thoroughly for class. The Teacher's Notes for *Robinson Crusoe* contained all the answers to the exercises and activities in every chapter, but Allie still struggled in class to figure out many of the answers. (It transpired very late in the semester that she was in fact unaware of the existence of the Teacher's Notes, though even without them she could have gone through the exercises and figured out the answers in advance.) It seemed to me that, like many inexperienced native speaker teachers, she relied heavily on the ability to 'wing it' – that is, to get by in the lesson during her first encounter with the materials.

The learners in Allie's class were not blind to the instructional problems. Both Ania and Marysia diplomatically but distinctly conveyed their concerns. Ania told me that though she liked the activities, she found Allie's explanations difficult to understand; she said that if she hadn't known Sydney would be coming back for the second semester she would have quit the school. Marysia sensed Allie's lack of education, and attended only infrequently in the first semester. Interestingly, neither objected to the overt religious content of Allie's classes. Ania expressed her acceptance as follows: 'When she talks about God, I have the sense that it's the only God who does after all exist […] that it's our Bible, the same one'. But pedagogical problems remained.

It transpired that Jean too had concerns about Allie. In December, after the end of the semester, Jean asked to have coffee with me in town rather than at the school, so we could talk 'off the record'. We met in a cafe in the old town. Though initially hesitant to do so, Jean explained to me that for a while – since Allie's time in Mexico – she had had concerns about Allie's work, attitude and disposition, and had decided to let her go from her organization. She pointed out that I had been observing Allie all semester, and she knew I was a TESOL professional. She apologized for the teaching I had observed, saying that it didn't reflect the 'striving for excellence' that Lighthouse embraced. She asked me if I thought she had made the right decision. This, of course, put me between a rock and a hard place – as a researcher, I was not supposed to interfere more than was absolutely necessary in the setting, certainly not to the extent of helping to get a teacher fired. I had an ethical obligation toward Allie (though of course I had just such an obligation toward Jean too, and equally toward Allie's students), and I did not feel comfortable revealing what I had observed in Allie's classroom. (It should be explained that the way the timetable was organized, Jean taught at exactly the same time as Allie and so had not been able to observe her at any point in the semester.)

Jean told me more about her decision and the thinking that had led up to it. Realizing that her mind was made up, I explained that it was hard for me to comment on the situation, but that I did feel her concerns were justified. I still feel bad about this incident; on the other hand, it represents many such moments that qualitative researchers encounter in their work, and, especially given the small scale and intense social relations of Lighthouse, it may have been inevitable in some form in this setting. It certainly was not the only time in which I found myself wrapped up in the affairs of the school much more than I would have wished or planned – for other examples see Chapter 7.

In any case, Jean released Allie from her position with Jean's organization, and Allie returned home to the US. She subsequently entered a program in elementary teacher education.

Taryn: 'I like to make things very interactive'

On Tuesday and Thursday mornings in the spring semester, Taryn taught a class that was designed around William P. Young's 2007 novel *The Shack*. This book, published just a year before I began my research at Lighthouse, had caused something of a furor in evangelical circles and was being widely read. It had also been translated into numerous languages, and at the time of my research a Polish translation was planned (it appeared the following year.) Taryn decided to use it as a class text for an 'upper intermediate to advanced' class in which she would also do extensive language work. The language work was concentrated in the Thursday classes while the discussion of the successive chapters of the novel was scheduled for Tuesdays, so I attended the Tuesday class only, curious to read the book, and to see how Taryn taught it and what Polish readers thought of it.

Unfortunately for my research (and possibly for Taryn's missionary work), the only students to attend the class were two Poles who were already members of evangelical churches – Dominika and Ola – and Jan, a middle-aged man. Jan's level of English was significantly lower than the other two, and he attended only sporadically. Since there were no Catholic learners regularly attending, I realized that the class could only be peripherally related to my main focus of interest – the Catholic–evangelical encounter. Yet, I decided to continue attending the Tuesday discussions so I could get a sense of Taryn's teaching, and also to extend my experience and understanding of Lighthouse School overall. Last but by no means least, I was curious to see how Polish readers responded to what I came to think of as a very American text. In the present section, then, I reflect briefly on my observations in Taryn's class.

The Shack is not what might be described as 'typical' evangelical literature. Set in the Pacific Northwest, it tells the story of Mackenzie or 'Mack', a middle-aged family man. Some years before the story begins, Mack's youngest daughter Missy was abducted. At the start of the novel, Mack receives a mysterious invitation to 'the shack', an abandoned building in a remote area where years before, evidence was found that Missy might have been murdered. Mack travels to the shack, and finds himself spending a few days in the company of the Holy Trinity. God is a Black woman who goes by the name of 'Papa', Mack's family's name for God; Jesus is a Middle Eastern man; and the Holy Spirit is an ethereal Asian woman called Sarayu. The central part of the book is part allegory, part theological treatise and part psychological healing from the trauma Mack suffered when his daughter vanished. The mystery of what happened to Missy is resolved at the end of the book, after Mack returns home from the shack.

The portrayal of God as a large Black woman making cookies in the kitchen is only one of many aspects of *The Shack* that evangelical readers have found stimulating and controversial. It's certainly been a popular title – it was the top-selling adult fiction book of 2008 (The Nielsen Company, 2008), despite having been essentially self-published. While this is not the place to discuss the book itself, it should be observed that, partly for the very reason that it is controversial, there is much in it that could serve as material for spiritually centered conversation, as Taryn planned.

The three students differed widely in terms of age and English ability. Ola, the most capable and comfortable English speaker by far in the group, was a married mother of about 40. Dominika, a young woman in her mid-twenties, was able to convey her ideas in English, but she needed help with grammar and vocabulary. Jan, a man in his fifties (and the husband of Ela from Sydney's class), struggled to compose even basic sentences, and found the reading concomitantly hard.

Objectively speaking, Taryn's class had many similar elements to those observed in Sydney's class. There was extensive use of pair work and games to teach vocabulary and (to a lesser extent) grammar; a lot of discussion organized around questions that Taryn provided each week, and that resembled the kinds of things that appeared in the 'Digging Deeper' sections of the Crusoe materials; some quasi-preaching; and a closing prayer at the end of each class. In the present section, I'll look briefly at learners' perspectives on *The Shack*; an example of Taryn's moments of preaching; and some problems that Taryn encountered in encouraging in-depth conversations.

For Dominika, as for many readers used to a more traditional patriarchal understanding of God, the idea of God as a woman was the most striking thing. As she put it in class, 'I think, yes, that the most complicated is that the Papa is woman [*laughs*], not black... because in the Bible often says, Father, yes? This is Jesus, Jesus turns to God [=addresses God as] "Father". So that's why it's very complicated and difficult to imagine'. Yet, after spending more time with the book, she stated: 'The things is described so interesting, and I think it's um, it's um, right thing to describe God; I think that many Christians not, cannot, um, tell in that way about God'. At the same time, she was concerned as to whether God had shown the author these things, since she heard that Young was not a 'believer'. For Ola on the other hand, who converted to evangelical Christianity as a result of the influence of American missionaries in Poland in the early 1990s (see Chapter 2), spoke fluent English and generally was more conversant with American cultural norms, it was precisely the racial question that was notable; she observed interestingly that if the book had been written by a Pole the ethnicities of the Holy Trinity would likely have been 'a Gypsy, a Russian', to mirror mainstream prejudices in Poland.

The questions that Taryn provided were often capable of stimulating extensive language use on what were for the learners engaging topics. For example, in Chapter 7 of *The Shack* (Young, 2007: 109), Mack and Jesus sit on the landing dock outside the shack at night, and Jesus looks up at the stars and says, 'Incredible'. One of Taryn's questions for the March 3 class was:

> Jesus lies on the dock with Mackenzie looking at the stars. He says he never gets tired of looking at them and that they are incredible. Why do you think Jesus would love looking at stars? Can you imagine him saying they are incredible?

In this part of the class, the learners had been put into pairs in separate rooms to discuss the questions. Ola was paired with the Lighthouse teacher Louise, who had joined the class for that lesson to make a pair activity possible. Ola laughed as Louise read the question aloud, was silent for several seconds, then began speaking:

Ola: Yeah, it's, it's funny because, and even Mack says this, that he created the stars and now he says, you know, that they are incredible. [*coughs*] Hm. I think maybe, I don't know any more, it's so hard to think what would God think [*Louise laughs*] or say; aaand, um, I could imagine God being, you know, happy, with what He created, like you know, but it would be, but it would be making Him as a human, because we are like this, you know, sometimes when we do something nice we, you know, we are proud of ourselves and we are just happy that you know –

Louise: 'That's a good one, that's nice'. [*laughs*]

Ola: 'Oh, yes. That's, that's, you know, my job [=my handiwork]'; so, so I wonder, you know, if God is doing this. So I, sometimes I think that He is happy when he looks at us, when he looks, you know, when he, when we do, when do something good, you know, that, um, he likes. And he is like a parent, you know, saying, 'Well that's my child', you know, 'good for you' and 'good girl', whatever.

Thus, Taryn's questions about Young's novel did serve to stimulate extensive discourse in this particular instance, as in several others. At the same time, Ola happened to be both talkative and more fluent than the other students in the class; she was willing to speak on many occasions. With Dominika and especially Jan, it was much more difficult for Taryn to enable good conversation.

Part of the problem, as Taryn herself admitted to me during a coffee break in one of the classes, was that when she asked a question, she often knew what answer she expected and so the conversation was not truly open-ended or student focused. For example, in class on April 28, Taryn asked a series of questions on the subject of happiness and sadness. The initial prompt was, 'What do people do to control emotions?' After this question was discussed in pairs, Taryn pulled the group together and asked: 'Do many people in Poland take anti-depressants?' She followed this up with: 'Well, now it's easy to get anti-depressants. Fifteen, twenty years ago you couldn't. What did people use twenty years ago?' Dominika responded with a laugh, 'Alcohol?' to which Taryn immediately replied, 'Often. Often they would use alcohol'. In looking at these questions, it's possible to see why Taryn was having problems stimulating discussion. The first question –

What do people do to control emotions? – is general and rather vague, and requires a high degree of abstract language (and thought) to respond to it. The second question, about antidepressants, is in turn a fairly simple yes-no question that demands, first of all, general knowledge, and secondly additional discursive work on the part of the learner if it is to stimulate more than short answers. The third question in turn, on how people dealt with emotional problems in the past, may seem open-ended, but it feels more like the kind of classroom question sometimes referred to as 'GWTW' or 'Guess What Teacher Wants'. Dominika seems to think that this is the case, and from her response and Taryn's confirmation, she appears to be right.

The same tendency to control the content of classroom discourse was manifest in Taryn's moments of preaching in the class. Like Sydney (and Allie), Taryn often gave 'mini-sermons' in the course of the class. Unlike Sydney's mini-sermons, however, Taryn's were less focused on the students in the class, and partly no doubt for this reason seemed less spontaneous and less personal. For example, on March 31, Taryn was talking with Dominika about how the basis of right and wrong varies from one country to another. One question read: 'What happens when there is no absolute truth to defining good and evil?' Dominika was somewhat stumped to come up with much to say in response. After a silence, Taryn began talking:

Taryn: Without an absolute truth, then I can say anything is good that I want
Dominika: Mhm
Taryn: and so can you. And so I think is where, this is an extreme example. But you look at people like Stalin or Hitler or Pol Pot, those kinds of people, they can say what they want is good.
Dominika: Mhm
Taryn: And if, if they have, if we do not have the same truth base, I can't say to them, no, you're wrong. Without that truth base they can say, no, this is, this is what I say is good
Dominika: Mhm
Taryn: and I say, no no, this is what *I* say is good. And so there's no way to agree on what is good and what is evil. And I think that's, um, part of the dilemma with the, in so many situations, people have different ideas what is good and what is evil. And they talk, and they can't agree, because they have a different source for truth. And that's what they're talking about in this chapter [Chapter 9 of *The Shack*], was, if you don't have an absolute source, and the same source, you won't agree on what is good and what is evil.

As Taryn spoke, it was clear that this was the main point that she wanted to come from her question. It's a standard argument that evangelicals make – that without an absolute point of moral reference (i.e. the Bible and the Word of God), human morality is doomed to be irredeemably relativistic. By the same token, though, the formulation of this question, like many of those posed in Taryn's class, showed that rather than aiming to explore the views of the students, the question was written with the ultimate goal of conveying a message – a message that Taryn eventually conveys herself in the passage quoted above, with only minimal backchanneling from her student. It seemed clear to me that in this instance, as in many others in the class, the ulterior motivation of the pedagogy was hindering an in-depth engagement with the students in the room.

As with the case of Allie, it's impossible and unnecessary to draw any broader generalizations from Taryn's class. Indeed, since all the students were already evangelicals, the class took on something of the character of a book club or even a Bible study group, rather than serving any kind of proselytizing function (though of course it fitted Lighthouse's broader mission of catering to the spiritual needs of Poland's middle classes, whatever their denominational affiliation). Nevertheless, the more directive nature of Taryn's teaching (in comparison with Sydney) for me was reminiscent of numerous instances I have read or heard about in which religious or spiritual content was introduced more directly and forcefully by missionary teachers. It served as another reminder that Sydney's Crusoe class was, all told, a rather unusual thing.

Conclusion

This chapter has shown three different evangelical language teachers at work in Lighthouse School. Sydney's lessons, and to a lesser extent those of Taryn, demonstrate that the vision Taryn and Sydney had of a mature, open adult classroom, in which spiritual and religious issues can be openly and honestly discussed, was in fact attainable. Despite the Polish love of privacy in such matters, it was possible to enable such conversations among Polish middle-class learners. Furthermore, I have argued that there is inherent pedagogical value in creating a space for learners to address such deeply personal matters.

At the same time, not all evangelical language teaching is going to be so effective. Though three teachers is too few to make any kind of generalization, it is immediately apparent that there were significant differences in the kinds of classroom environments created by these teachers, and that the resulting opportunities for spiritual discussion also varied. In particular, it strikes me that in any teaching situation where a teacher has an absolute truth that he or she wishes to convey to the students, the opportunities for truly student-centered pedagogy are going to be limited. It is to Sydney's great credit that she was frequently able to achieve this feat.

Notes

(1) In the original text the passage reads as follows: 'All this labour I was at the expence of, purely from my apprehensions on the account of the print of a man's foot which I had seen; for as yet I never saw any human creature come near the island, and I had now liv'd two years under these uneasinesses, which indeed made my life much less comfortable than it was before; as may well be imagin'd by any who know what it is to live in the constant snare of the fear of man; and this I must observe with grief too, that the discomposure of my mind had too great impressions also upon the religious part of my thoughts, for the dread and terror of falling into the hands of savages and canibals, lay so upon my spirits, that I seldom found my self in a due temper for application to my maker, at least not with the sedate calmness and resignation of soul which I was wont to do; I rather pray'd to God as under great affliction and pressure of mind, surrounded with danger, and in expectation every night of being murther'd and devour'd before morning; and I must testify from my experience, that a temper of peace, thankfulness, love and affection, is much more the proper frame for prayer than that of terror and discomposure' (Defoe, 1719/1968: 132).
(2) From Chapter 12 of the Lighthouse version of Robinson Crusoe. In the original text: '...and which I take notice of here to put those discontented people in mind of it who cannot enjoy comfortably what God has given them, because they see, and covet something that he has not given them' (Defoe, 1719/1968: 106).
(3) Thessalonians 5:17-18.
(4) In the King James Version, this reads: 'For he is not a God of the dead, but of the living' (Luke 20:38); 'He is not the God of the dead, but the God of the living' (Mark 12:27).
(5) Philippians 4:11-12.
(6) Isaiah 40:28; 'hast thou not heard, *that* the everlasting God, the LORD, the Creator of the ends of the earth, fainteth not, neither is weary?'

7 False-Bottomed Friendships?: Relation at Lighthouse School

Almost every evangelical missionary and teacher I have ever spoken to has emphasized 'relationship building' as the primary goal of their work. Most have learned to talk with extreme caution about 'conversion', and many claim that conversion is in fact not their aim. Rather, they seek to build relationships that mirror the personal relationship with Jesus Christ that they hope to enable for others. Alvin, a pastor with a large Baptist mission in N., described the mission's purpose as finding different ways to 'make relationships with people'. Dan, a pastor and one of the leaders of the Mennonite mission in the small town of K. near Warsaw, explained that the mission had decided to focus on English teaching because 'we felt like that was a good way to build relationships with people'. Throughout the country, I heard similar language from those involved in mission programs.

Lighthouse School was no exception. Virtually every aspect of the school's work was oriented toward the making, sustaining and strengthening of relationships among the teachers of the school, their learners and the broader community. In the present chapter, I explore some aspects of this process, in particular how it appeared from the perspectives of the various actors, and how it manifested itself in the classroom and elsewhere in the school and beyond. I will pay particular attention to relations between evangelicals and non-evangelicals in the school, focusing especially on one adult learner, Ania, and her involvement with the school; I will tell the story of a tragic personal loss that Ania suffered, and explain how this tragedy was dealt with in the school.

At the same time, relation as conceptualized in the context of evangelical mission work does not fit neatly into prior theoretical understandings of friendship. An ancillary goal of this chapter, then, is to reflect on what 'relation' actually means in this setting.

It is worth remembering also that a concept closely related to that of relationship is community, which might simplistically and somewhat misleadingly be defined as a network of relations. I mention this because one important way that the missionaries of Lighthouse sought to create and nurture friendships was through what they described on frequent occasions as community building, a notion which referred partly to the environment of the school itself and partly to the neighborhood in which the school was situated. While on this subject, it should be remembered that within evangelical Christian churches, community is a crucial feature of church life. As mentioned in Chapter 2, in the course of my conversation with Pastor Alvin, I asked whether he agreed with the four-part definition of evangelicalism cited in Chapter 2 (the centrality of Christ, the Bible, the experience of being reborn and witnessing to one's faith). He accepted this description, but said that he would add a fifth defining component, that of 'fellowship': Membership in a church is not merely a passive thing, but necessarily involves active participation in the church community through outreach activities, youth groups, Bible study, summer camps and so on.[1] Indeed, it is worth bearing in mind that, as Wanner (2007) points out in her analysis of conversion to evangelical Christianity in the Ukrainian context, it is almost by definition that conversion involves adopting new friends and new social circles (primarily those of the church), along with new ways of talking and acting, all of which serve to mark the evangelical community off from the surrounding society. I will look at the community building work of Lighthouse School later in this chapter.

It is important to always bear in mind the linguistic slippages that are part and parcel of transcultural encounters. In this case, the words 'relationship' and 'friend' have no direct equivalents in Polish. For 'relationship', the Great English-Polish Dictionary (Jassem, 1982) offers 'związek', which is closer to 'connection' (it's also the word for 'union' as in 'trade union'), or 'stosunek', which is also a one-way relation that can be rendered as 'attitude'. The dictionary offers, in parentheses, the qualifying adjective 'wzajemny' or 'mutual', thus making 'stosunek wzajemny' or 'mutual relation' the nearest and rather clumsy Polish equivalent to the evangelical idea of relationship. 'Friend' is even harder. The Polish word 'przyjaciel' is reserved for close intimate friends – in over 30 years of speaking Polish, I've rarely if ever heard anyone refer to someone they know as 'mój przyjaciel' or 'my friend'. (The female equivalent, 'przyjaciółka', when used by a man, can only mean 'girlfriend' in the sense of someone you are dating.) Rather, Poles will say 'mój znajomy/moja znajoma', meaning 'someone I know' (more or less the equivalent of 'acquaintance'), or less formally, 'mój kolega/moja koleżanka', a word that is cognate with 'colleague' and is in fact often used to refer to someone one works with or knows from work. There are other terms less formal still – for example, 'kumpel' or 'buddy' – but none of them indicates the intimacy of 'przyjaciel/przyjaciółka'.

All this, of course, is in stark contrast to English, in which 'relationship' automatically includes the meaning of mutuality. 'Friend', in turn, is widely used to mean little more than 'someone I know', as shown in its use on social networking websites such as Facebook. These deep cross-cultural differences in social terminology further complicate the missionary goal of relationship building, and add an additional, important layer of interpretation on either side of relations between Poles and non-Poles in contexts such as that of Lighthouse School.

Setting this aside for a moment, for many non-evangelicals the basic question asked about relations with evangelical Christians is whether these relationships are fundamentally like 'regular' friendships, or whether the ultimate underlying goal of conversion renders them suspect or even invalid. (In the course of this chapter, I will pick apart many of the questionable assumptions underlying the previous sentence.) In my first interview with Ania, when I asked her about this issue she used the term 'false bottom', as in a suitcase with a false bottom to hide smuggled goods, and said it had occurred to her sometimes to wonder whether the people of Lighthouse School, whom she liked very much, were so nice because they had an ulterior motive. (I'll say more later about her response to her own question.) The notion of 'false-bottomed friendships' stuck with me, and it will be woven throughout this chapter, always with the implied question mark I have included in the chapter title.

The body of the chapter is divided into three main parts. In the first, I look at the creation and maintenance of relation in the classroom, focusing on Sydney's Crusoe class that was described in the previous chapter. In the second part, I extend this examination to include the life of the school outside the classroom, including formal extracurricular activities, informal interactions at Coffee Central and elsewhere and relations between Lighthouse School and the church with which it was affiliated and which held its services and meetings in the school. This discussion will extend the notion of relationship building to include community building as it was conceived and attempted in and through the school. In part three, I tell the story of Ania and her relations in the school. As a coda, I describe two close relations with evangelicals I developed over the course of my year at the school, using these experiences to reflect on evangelical–non-evangelical relations at Lighthouse and beyond.

Relation in Class

At Lighthouse School, the classroom was the primary locus for relationship building, and it was here that much of the work was done. In this section, I will look at a variety of ways through which relation was nurtured and manifested in classroom interaction.

More than a warm-up: Pre-class chat as relationship building

Like many teachers, Sydney would almost always begin class with some informal chat with the learners. Sometimes, this would be merely a few short exchanges: How are you, how was your weekend, how did X go the other day, how is your sick relative and so on. Yet, much more frequently than in other classrooms I have observed, the opening chat session would sometimes stretch to several minutes. To begin with, probably unconsciously I associated this practice with bad teaching – where I've experienced it before, it was usually with a teacher who was either unprepared and so killing time, or who cared little about getting through the day's lesson, or both. As time went on, however, and I gained respect for Sydney's abilities as a teacher, I came to realize that the opening chats were not a filler, icebreaker (though the short ones often served this function) or an idle passing of time, but that they were an integral component of Sydney's pedagogy. The opening chats, of course, did serve to relax the beginning atmosphere in the classroom and get the learners back into speaking and hearing English. But they also jibed with the general emphasis at Lighthouse on using English for purposes of genuine communication (see Chapter 6 for many examples of this aspect of teaching in the school). And above all, these chats constituted moments in which relationships were nurtured and grown.

One of the most dramatic examples of such 'introductory' chats occurred on February 17. In this class, it was almost 20 minutes before Sydney began the planned business of the lesson. Only two students were present, Marysia and Ela. Sydney began by asking Marysia, 'So how are you?' Marysia replied, 'Oh, I'm very tired today, I don't know. I have a headache'. Sydney responded, 'Why are you tired? What kind of day was it? Tell me'. It was this kind of turn that made the pre-class chat much more than a warm-up activity, and turned it into an integral component of relationship building. The direct imperative 'Tell me' is particular notable here – it reminds me of therapeutic dialogue more than anything else, but in a non-therapeutic context such as that of Sydney's class it served as a decisive invitation to converse. In this regard, it's also significant that Marysia accepted the invitation.

After a few turns, the topic shifted from Marysia herself to her German boss, who had been seriously ill. In an earlier bout of the illness, Marysia had helped this man by arranging medical care for him in Poland and helping with language problems (Marysia was fluent in German). A couple of aspects of this part of the conversation struck me. First, it was clear that Sydney was well oriented to the situation, and made reference to the earlier illness as Marysia described recent developments. This emphasizing of shared history – of the temporal dimension of relation – was an important part of relationship and community development at Lighthouse, especially in N., where Sydney and Taryn were still in the process of 'building a past' with their learners. An additional facet of the same process was the fact that Sydney at several points asked for factual clarification of details concerning the course of the illness and the participants in the story, indicating distinctly that these details were important and were of interest to her – in other words, her participation was marked with several aspects of 'high-involvement style' (Tannen, 1984/2005). Also, throughout the exchange, which was dominated by Marysia describing her boss's condition, Sydney repeatedly made supportive comments directed specifically at Marysia herself. At one point, Marysia described how her boss, who was divorced, had a Polish girlfriend. The exchange continued as follows:

Sydney: So are you still taking care of him, really?
Marysia: Um
Sydney: Or is this other woman taking care of him?
Marysia: Um, I have never take care of him in this, um, sense, because, um, it, um, I think [2 secs] [laughs] I couldn't do, do it. But I have have, um, helped him really.
Sydney: Well.
Marysia: Because um, I think when, um, I know, but I think when [= if], um, when I, uh, don't find for him the help by Polish doctors, by professors, um, he would be died.
Sydney: He would have died.
Marysia: Have died. Yes.
Sydney: Wow.
Marysia: Because the German doctors had said, [emphatically] *You will die*. And I think, um, be-, because of this had he, had, uh, was he back to Poland.
Sydney: Mhm.
Marysia: It was very difficult.
Sydney: Very difficult for him, for sure; but I think it's also been very difficult for *you*.
Marysia: Yeah, it was.
Sydney: Because—
Marysia: Because—
Sydney: This is a a—
Marysia: It's a foreigner.
Sydney: It's a [??] It's beyond your job, right?
Marysia: Yeah.
Sydney: So.

Marysia: But I have make because I, I think, uh, I had to.
Sydney: Because you're compassionate.
Marysia: Uh? yeah? [laughs]
Sydney: Yeah.
Marysia: Because I, I, he had, um, nobody to—
Sydney: Mhm.
Marysia: to help him.

Sydney's high-involvement style is clearly evident here. Of particular significance are the supportive and sometimes flattering comments she makes about Marysia: 'I think it's also been very difficult for *you*'; 'Because you're compassionate'. Lastly, the idea that these parts of the lesson were in fact regarded by Sydney as being an integral part of her pedagogy is lent credence by her frequent correction of the speaker, even at moments in which she was clearly focused on content – an example can be seen above, where she corrected Marysia's 'he would be died'. There were several such corrections of both students in this part of the class, as in other pre-class chats during the semester.

After Marysia finished talking about her boss, Sydney asked Ela how she was doing. After Ela talked for a short while, about 12 minutes into the lesson Sydney began making some announcements, but then Marysia initiated a completely new topic – she had been to see a tango concert at the Opera House – and the conversation continued about this concert and related topics for another six and a half minutes. Finally, Sydney said, 'Well, I'm happy you got to do that', and moved on to the substance of the lesson.

Thus, a common feature of language classes – the pre-class chat and warm-up – in Sydney's classroom became a significant component of the relationship building that was the missionary goal of Lighthouse School.

Self as pedagogy: Self-revelation as strategy and symptom

Another key aspect of relationship building in Sydney's classroom was the extent of Sydney's self-revelation – what I called in the previous chapter, after Brian Morgan, 'identity as pedagogy'. During another opening chat, on February 26, Sydney spent over 15 minutes recounting the hilarious story of a faulty washing machine in her first Polish apartment in the town of D.; then the entire second half of the class after the break took place in the cafe as Sydney told more amusing stories about her first encounters with Polish ways of doing things. Among other things, Sydney was a consummate storyteller, and had further mastered the art of telling stories to second language learners. Throughout the stories, the students smiled and laughed, and it was evident that they were following the ups and downs of Sydney's narrative very closely. (Incidentally, it is in such cases that the inadequacies of written transcription become particularly glaring—a printed transcript of the story would completely fail to convey Sydney's intonation, her self-irony, her smiles and of course also the rapt attention of her listeners.) Though the stories in themselves were not particularly self-revelatory, aside from showing Sydney's one-time ignorance of Polish realia, such moments still served to create relation by making the substance of the class the sharing of personal experiences rather than, say, spending time on grammar exercises or vocabulary learning. At other times, Sydney revealed information that was much more personal. For the class on February 17, learners were asked to prepare a timeline of their life with critical moments. In order to demonstrate what was expected, Sydney prepared and shared her own timeline, which she talked through in class. Along with various personal items of information, she stated clearly and straightforwardly:

> Then in 1978 I met Jesus. This was when I had my first experience where I understood that Jesus loves me. For the first time. And then it began to grow from there. Then in 1980 I went to Bible college, because I wanted to learn more about Jesus.

She continued with some other key moments in her life, many of which also involved a significant degree of self-revelation, such as breaking up with a boyfriend she had originally thought she would marry, and also the death of her oldest brother at a young age. In another class, on March 5, she spoke at some length about her father and her close relationship with him. At all these moments, her own openness was an invitation to the others present to reciprocate – and, as will be demonstrated in this chapter, many learners accepted this invitation.

As seen in the previous chapter, much of the classroom discussion was designed explicitly to encourage the exchange of personal opinions and experiences. The examples in that chapter concerning romantic husbands, attitudes to prayer, and envy offered good examples of this. In these cases, the personalized topics arose from occasions such as Valentine's Day, or from the Crusoe materials. Even when language work was the focus of the class, Sydney still left room for personalized language use. Part of class on March 5, for example, was devoted to the differences among 'for', 'since', 'while' and 'during'. As part of this work, Sydney gave the learners a set of topic prompts, asking them to create a sentence about the topic using one of the four focus words. One of the prompts was 'Something special about your mother while you were a teenager'. Marysia's response, in which she described how her mother would advise her to be careful and good, led to an extended discussion lasting seven minutes in which Sydney and the two learners present that day, Marysia and Ania, swapped stories about their relationships with their mothers. It was clear to me that Sydney was not merely allowing such digressions from the purported language focus of the class, she was actively encouraging them, whether for personal, pedagogical or missionary reasons (and most likely a combination of all of these). Earlier in the same activity, Marysia chose a prompt that concerned her last vacation. The ensuing discussion began as follows:

Marysia: Mmm... During my last vacation, um, [3 *secs*] I went to Croatia, and um, we spent a very great time with, I spent a very great time with my family.
Sydney: Super. How long were you there?
Marysia: Um, f- we were there for, um, two weeks.
Sydney: Good job.
Marysia: Two weeks.
Sydney: For two weeks.
Marysia: For two weeks.
Sydney: Mhm. And, um, Ania, you've been to Croatia.
Ania: Yes.
Sydney: Yeah.
Ania: Twice.
Sydney: So where, whereabouts were you? Were you in a similar place?
Marysia: I, I don't think so. We were near Zadar [*rising intonation*]. It's, um, I think in the middle of the shore [=coast] of Croatia.
Sydney: Mhm.
Marysia: I, might know how to--
Ania: I was on, on island, on the island.
Sydney: [??]
Marysia: On the island?
Ania: On the island. Um, Loshni [=Lošinj?].
Marysia: Loshni?
Ania: This is named this island.
Marysia: And, um, how, uh, have you get this island?
Sydney: How *did* you get *to* the island?
Marysia: How did you get to the island?

From this point, the discussion, which had already lasted almost a minute and a half, continued for another two and a half minutes until Sydney called for a new topic – which, as mentioned above, led to an even longer digressive conversation of this kind.

A number of observations can be made about this extract from the perspective of relationship. First, Sydney's initial 'digressive' question: 'Super. How long were you there?' – is in fact a further prompt for Marysia to use another one of the four focus constructions of the lesson (*for* two weeks), hence Sydney's 'Good job' when Marysia gets it right. And, as was frequently the case, later in a conversation that was nevertheless clearly focused on meaning, Sydney still offered corrections of learner errors ('How *did* you get *to* the island?'). This said, though, it is remarkable that it is Sydney herself who initiated the true digression when she said: 'And, um, Ania, you've been to Croatia'. While this was evidently a move to include Ania in the conversation, it's equally evidently a shift away from the linguistic focus of the class and toward relationship building. Sydney even hesitated for a moment ('Um'), as if for a split second wondering *how* to digress in the way she sought. This closer analysis confirms my impression that such departures from the linguistic and pedagogical material at hand were nevertheless tied closely to the core goal of the program.

It's also interesting to see that Marysia and Ania both embraced Sydney's approach. Neither complained about such digressive pedagogy in their interviews. Quite the contrary – both, in different ways, expressed satisfaction with the teaching, and great admiration of Sydney (Ania described Sydney as being 'really warm' and having 'a certain charisma', while Marysia said Sydney was 'an authority' for her). In the extract quoted above, both learners were happy to engage in 'off-topic' conversations – indeed, Marysia herself initiated the part of the discussion about how Ania got to her island, and also, when Sydney asked Ania if she was in the same place as Marysia, Marysia usurped Ania's turn – but in a rather supportive way, leading to the co-construction of a response to Sydney's question. Seeing how hard both learners struggled with the linguistic resources available to them to convey information, as on previous occasions, one is struck by the powerful motivation that can be summoned by a sustained and in-depth interest in what the learners themselves bring to the classroom. No doubt, this too was a source of Marysia's and Ania's satisfaction with the program at Lighthouse – they sensed that at moments like this, they were being given opportunities to stretch their linguistic capabilities in a supportive atmosphere and on topics that were inherently interesting to them. In fact, Marysia spoke explicitly about the way in which learners were 'obliged to talk in English about a wide range of topics', and said this was infinitely preferable to what one normally encounters in Polish schools. Lastly, as mentioned elsewhere, it is significant that when we talk about relation in this context we are not only talking about teacher–student relations: as so often in this class, at numerous points the conversation was among the learners, and student–student relations were clearly a major aspect of the relational landscape at Lighthouse. More will be said below about this aspect of relation at Lighthouse School.

During the March 10 class, in turn, there was a conversation about the position of women in Polish society that also led to an exchange of personally meaningful stories and views. Sydney introduced this topic by recounting a detail from her morning class, which was also studying the Crusoe text, and in which the same topic had been discussed. One of the women in that class, Jolanta, was pregnant with her sixth child and was going for an ultrasound scan in which she would learn the sex of her baby. Another woman in the class had asked Jolanta whether she would rather it was a boy or a girl (she already had four boys and one girl). As Sydney recounted the story to her evening class: 'Her response was [*snapping her finger*] instantaneous. And she said, "I would like to have a boy, because the life of a boy when he grows up to be a man will be much easier than the life of a woman"'. In using this prompt as a springboard for discussion in her evening class, Sydney extended 'relation' to include not only relations within her own class, but more broadly in the school. She thus emphasized a wider sense of community and an ongoing conversation within it.

Lastly, there were numerous moments in which relationship was built through words of kindness and encouragement. In the very first class of the spring semester, on January 15, the learners were paired with American visitors on a short-term mission trip to N. Toward the end of class, after the pair discussions, the visitors left the classroom, and Sydney asked the learners what aspects of their language learning and use they felt good about, and what 'challenges they faced' – which parts of learning English they were particularly worried about at this stage in their learning. In response to the second question, Magda said, 'speaking', joking in Polish about how the conversation she had just had was 'masakra' (a disaster) from her point of view. Sydney responded as follows, addressing Magda directly and exclusively:

> **Sydney**: Now listen. I have to tell you, and I'm going, I am going to be very honest with you, as I stood over here and you were talking about your knee surgery and you were talking about the things that we have on the board, I was thinking, Oh my goodness! Magda is speaking! [*general laughter*] I'm so excited! Magda, you were doing very very well. Really. And you're with people that love you. You know what, really. You're doing super.

Similarly, in the class on February 12, in the course of a board-based exercise about verb forms focusing on the contrast between simple and continuous forms and the present and past tenses, Sydney commented in the course of going through an exercise:

Sydney: See, 'will have been there'. So Ania is very stressed about the present perfect tense, and we have not even studied this tense and she gets it right. Ania, you just need to relax [*laughter*]. [*She gives a short explanation of the answer*] That was a bonus. Good job on the bonus!

Such things are heard in many classrooms, of course, and are not peculiar to evangelical teaching. Nevertheless, in the context of the other relationship-building features of Sydney's class, these expressions of concern, affection and support must be read as further indications of the relational dimension of the pedagogy.

At the most general level, all of the preceding instances are examples of Sydney's person-centered pedagogy. This philosophy, which also manifested itself in the personalized prayers discussed in Chapter 6 as well as in all the other aspects of the class described in this and the preceding chapter, underlay the nurturing and intensifying of relations among all those involved in Lighthouse School. An interesting example of this occurred in a class on Thursday, February 19. In 2009, this was the last Thursday before Lent; this day is traditionally known as 'Tłusty Czwartek' or 'Fat Thursday' in Poland, and is a day when donuts are eaten (it is the start of the last week of Carnival). The following Tuesday was Shrove Tuesday, known in some English-speaking countries as Pancake Tuesday, which in turn is the last day before Ash Wednesday, the start of Lent (which in Polish is called 'Wielki Post' or 'the Great Fast') in the Christian calendar. Sydney had begun the class with a game of hangman in which the concealed phrases were 'many doughnuts' and 'Pancake Tuesday'. Sydney explained Pancake Tuesday, and then began asking the two learners present, Marysia and Ela, about their practices during Lent. The exchange with Marysia ran as follows:

Sydney: So do you fast during this Lent period, during the Great Fast? Do you, do you fast?
Marysia: Mhm, yeah.
Sydney: Yeah.
Marysia: I fast, um, I fast. I must say I fast also, um, one day in the week.
Sydney: Mhm
Marysia: Always on a Friday.

Sydney: Uh huh.
Marysia: I, um, don't eat meat.
Sydney: Mhm.
Marysia: And it it um, this day, it's um, tradition from my fadder, father. We don't, um, eat meat on Friday.
Sydney: Mhm. So when you're fasting, and you are fasting from meat – we usually say we say we fast *from* something –
Marysia: Mhm
Sydney: – if you're fasting from meat on Friday – you said it's a tradition of your parents –
Marysia: Mhm
Sydney: – and it became your tradition.
Marysia: Yeah.
Sydney: Is there, is there any, do, on Fridays do you think about this particularly?
Marysia: Mm, I would say I know it's Friday, I don't eat meat.
Sydney: Aha.
Marysia: But I, I, I, I ...
Sydney: Does it have any other significance for you?
Marysia: Yeah, I know that Jesus was died on Friday.
Sydney: Mhm. OK.

What is striking about this interaction is that Sydney's questions don't focus on Catholic practices in general, but on what Marysia's *personal* practices are, and what significance they have for her in particular. This passage contrasts interestingly with Allie's comments about All Souls' Day quoted in the previous chapter. There, Allie put out a general appeal to 'think about' the fact that God is 'a God of the living'. Here, though the situation is in many ways parallel—just as evangelicals eschew celebration of All Souls Day, they also do not practice weekly fasting in the way it is traditionally done in the Catholic Church—still, Sydney eschews broader issues of differences between Catholics and Protestants to ask about personal meanings and practices. In this regard, it's significant that she subsequently posed the same question to Ela, who was an evangelical. Also noteworthy is the way in which Sydney uses open questions. In this respect, her teaching puts me in mind of Nelson's (1999) 'pedagogy of inquiry', in which delicate and potentially divisive issues are explored not in a confrontational way but through a process of exploratory questioning. Here too, Sydney succeeds in personalizing the matter at hand, and by the same token creates a space in which students can and do open up to using English as a means for self-expression and also self-exploration.

Lest it be thought that all these initiatives came from Sydney, it needs to be pointed out that the learners themselves frequently and willingly also took part in the process of relationship building. Numerous examples of this have been seen over the last two chapters—for example, Marysia's taking the floor after Sydney's 'mini-sermon' as described in Chapter 6; there were plentiful others, including one we will see in the section below on Ania. Many of these instances involved students sharing personal information and opinions of their own accord. One such moment occurred in class on April 21. As Sydney went round the five students present asking how they were and how their weekend was, Ela started talking about her hobby of decoupage (the decorating of objects with paper cutouts and other adornments). She spoke at some length of the powerful creative urge that overcomes her when she engages in this occupation, and of how engrossed she can become in it; she said, 'this time is very exciting for me'. It was noteworthy that she was prepared to speak of her enthusiasm so frankly in the class, and also that she was supported in turn not just by Sydney's encouragement but by comments from the other learners – Ania, for example, exclaimed at one point, 'She's so creative!'

This last turn shows a final side of relationship building in Sydney's classroom – that of student–student relations. Though none of the learners in the class knew each other before coming to the school, there were many signs of growing closeness over the semester of Sydney's class. On numerous occasions, learners interacted with one another, usually in English, in ways that indicated an ongoing relationship. This took many forms, examples of some of which we have already seen. Sometimes, as in Ania's comment about Ela in the preceding paragraph, the interaction was in the form of a compliment. There was also a lot of teasing – in the same class, a few minutes earlier Ela had arrived late and Ania had said jokingly, 'What happened? Do you have a good excuse?' Such playful comments were common in Sydney's classroom. It was also interesting that, perhaps encouraged by Sydney's often extensive questioning of the learners about 'off-topic' issues like what they did over the weekend, the learners themselves often asked one another questions during these conversations – an example of this can be seen above in the conversation about Croatia, during which Marysia of her own accord, and presumably out of simple curiosity, asked Ania how she got to the island that she stayed on.

Lastly, there were also times when the closeness was manifested in ways that I read as not being as cordial as the preceding examples. One such moment occurred during the class of March 10, in the later part of the discussion about gender roles in Poland referred to earlier. To begin with, Ania, who was raising two small children, told the story of a childless friend of hers who made her feel small because Ania was sometimes unaware of current events or popular television shows since she was too busy looking after her children and didn't have time to keep up with the outside world. Ania was amused when this friend and her husband adopted three children and suddenly came to realize how very time-consuming it is to look after young children. After Ania had finished her story, Sydney asked Marysia: 'What do you think, is it good for women to work outside the home?' Marysia, who herself was a working mother, responded:

Marysia: Mm, firstly I will say to Ania, you have so many opportunities [??] when you are at home. [??*laughter from Ania?*] And I was, um, two years at home, when Maja was born, and I have, um, start my study, um [*laughs*] I have done many things, and I think, um, it's, it's a hard work if you are at home, but it's, it's really up to you how to, how do you manage your time [Sydney: mhm], how do you plan your time [Ania: [??]].

Already in the course of this speech, Ania could be heard trying to protest. Marysia then went on to tell the story of a woman she knew in Spain who worked mostly from home but said she liked to spend two days a week in the office so that she would have some social contact. Marysia then resumed her (to my mind) rather moralizing comments aimed at Ania the stay-at-home mom:

Marysia: And I think, um, it's, um, very hard to stay with children at home, but um, I think it's, um, it's really up to us. Because we have much more opportunities, um, to do something.
Sydney: Mhm.
Marysia: Really.
Ania: [??]
Marysia: Ania, I know that –
Ania: Because you have opportunity when you have money. When you have this money you have opportunity because –
Marysia: Ania, if you want have money you must learn.
Ania: I know but [Marysia: ??] you must have a money.
Marysia: No it's not true. Because I, um, my education, I, I, I have, um, make my own [??], how to say it in English, high school? Economic high school?
Sydney: College. Mhm.
Marysia: And then I, I tried to study, um, tourismus [Sydney: Mhm], and then, um, was over, because I started to work. And, um, when Maja was born I, I thought, Oh, I must do something [Sydney: Mhm] because I would, um, had no work, because

	I had my children, and I, um, all people would thinking, um, it's a mother, um, and I will have, um, it, it would be difficult to find a job for me. With one child. Because of this I start to study [Sydney: Mhm] and I think it work. [Sydney: Mhm] Because I had really no money.
Ania:	But you must paid for this study.
Marysia:	Yeah, I have paid.
Ania:	Mhm.
Marysia:	Mhm.

In this passage, Marysia and Ania challenge one another in ways that were not frequently encountered at Lighthouse, yet were consonant with the closer personal relationships fostered at the school. Such exchanges make me think of the wise aphorism that 'When people get close, they sometimes bump into one another'.[2] Here, lurking beneath the surface of a disagreement about the possibilities available to young mothers is a more personal conflict in which, as I read the situation, Ania takes Marysia's comments as a patronizing and somewhat judgmental criticism of her complaints about the difficulties of bringing up children as a stay-at-home mom. It's certainly true that Marysia's tone is a little sententious when she says things like, 'it's really up to us', and even more directive, 'it's really up to you [...] how do you manage your time'. Most patronizing of all in this context is Marysia's double use of Ania's name as a vocative, something that both in Polish and English often connotes condescension. Her offer of herself as an example is a little disingenuous, and can be read (at least I read it) as rather self-promoting and self-satisfied – a form of social one-upmanship. Ania understandably feels criticized and lectured to (it might be worth remembering here that Marysia is about 10 years older than Ania), and responds by pointing out that individual effort is not the whole picture – that financial resources are also needed. The conversation ended, a few turns after the last ones quoted above, without any particular resolution.

Thus, numerous signs of relationship building were observed in class meetings, from forms of self-revelation and support to more conflictual aspects of relation. In the next section, I'll look at some of the relationship-oriented non-classroom activities at Lighthouse School.

Relation Outside of Class

As already mentioned, Lighthouse School saw itself as much more than an institution offering language classes. Above all, Sydney and Taryn were originally invited to Poland to set up a school in D. as a major part of the outreach program of the church there, with the ultimate goal of attracting more members to the church. The same goal underlay the school's symbiotic relationship with the new church in N. More generally, as missionaries Sydney and Taryn saw their role as ministering to the spiritual needs of Poles, and specifically of middle-class Poles in N., particularly those living in the neighborhoods immediately adjacent to the school in the northwest suburbs of the city. This goal was pursued in a variety of ways, the most important of which will be surveyed in this section.

First of all, numerous extracurricular events were organized throughout the year. Some of these were activity-based sessions aimed at children, notably a monthly series of Saturday sessions entitled 'Get Creative', during which the children took part in various hands-on activities often revolving around a theme such as animals or as a tie-in with an adult-oriented event such as 'Out of Africa' (see below). Others were intended to be family events, remembering that in many cases adults and children from the same family attended classes at Lighthouse (this was the case, for example, with Zosia from Sydney's class, whose son was in one of the children's classes). There were usually two or three such events each semester. In the fall, on October 31, there was 'Cookie Night', for which both the school and attendees provided cookies (there was a competition for best cookie); then, on November 22, Allie led 'Mexico Night', which included a taco dinner, language games (such as an activity in which participants had to match Spanish and Polish sentences) and presentations about Mexico and Colombia, the latter given by a Colombian evangelical who was living in N. and was involved with the Baptist church. In the spring, on January 30, there was an 'Evening of Music and Discussion' at which the music was provided by two young men visiting with a Youth With A Mission (YWAM) missionary team organized from England. Then, on March 20, there was 'Out of Africa', an evening devoted primarily to Kenya and led by Louise, who had lived in Kenya for many years with her missionary parents. On another occasion, Louise's graduation from Bible school in Canada was marked by a surprise celebration.

I attended almost all of the events involving adults, and some of those aimed at children. None of the events involved overt proselytizing, though religious–spiritual elements such as prayer were present at all of them. Typically, around 40–60 people attended, filling the rather small cafe space. Many of the attendees were already members of the church – this was partly at the bidding of Rysiek, the pastor, who at Sunday services often urged church members to support the school in this way. Other attendees included Polish evangelicals who were members of other churches, such as Dominika and her husband Darek. On some occasions, numbers were swelled by visiting short-term missionary teams from the US, Canada, Britain or elsewhere (the YWAM group, for example, consisted of almost 20 young people). I was never sure what the attendees thought about these events, but many kept coming. It seemed clear that it was gatherings of this sort that were seen by the school leadership as prime venues for the nurturing and celebration of 'community' at the school – that is, an understanding of the school not merely as a quasi-educational institution but as a social one whose participants felt a sense of belonging, a groupness (Cooper & Brubaker, 2000) that produced and affirmed a sense of identity and connectedness.

All the events described above took place in Coffee Central, the cafe-cum-meeting space at the heart of the school. The cafe was staffed at any time that classes were going on, and participants and their families were invited to hang out there before, during and after class, whether or not they ordered a coffee or other drink (many often did). The teachers were also encouraged to be present in the cafe when they were not teaching or doing other work; they could often be found there playing card games with some of the children or chatting with the adults. As mentioned in Chapter 4, the cafe was a clean, bright, attractive area, and the seating arrangement was changed frequently, which created an atmosphere of freshness. It was evident that such 'hanging out', much like Sydney's extended warm-up chats, was regarded as an important component of relationship building in the school.

The Lighthouse team was also eager to see itself as part of what it referred to as 'the community' in the neighborhood where the school was located. Efforts in this direction included wooing local businesses to encourage their employees to attend the school: I knew at least one man, Łukasz, who worked in the auto parts distribution company housed in the same building as the school and who attended classes there; there were also others. The school also offered coffee at the local bus stop from time to time, something I never actually saw, though I did wonder how Poles, customarily very circumspect and inclined to 'mind their own business' in public places, must have looked upon young foreign women handing out coffee on a suburban street.

The younger teachers also made occasional visits to local high schools to take part in conversations with students learning English. While overtly publicizing Lighthouse School's mission was not permissible at these meetings, it was hoped that in this way the school could at least advertise its presence, though during my time there I was not aware of any learners who had been attracted to Lighthouse by this method. I did, however, attend a teacher training workshop offered by Jean and Allie at New Hope School, the only 'Christian' (i.e. evangelical) elementary school in N., which was housed within a regular elementary school in a residential neighborhood on the other side of town.

Another way in which Lighthouse sought to integrate itself into the life of N. beyond the school was by offering business seminars. None of these took place during my time in the school, but Taryn in particular talked about them quite a lot, and the school occasionally promoted business-related talks and other events being organized by other evangelical churches and missions in N. In fact, some of the 'advanced' curriculum offered by Lighthouse was business oriented. It's worth noting that a similar emphasis on linking evangelical Christianity with good business practices is discussed quite extensively in Wanner's (2007) study of evangelical mission work in Ukraine (see e.g. Wanner, 2007: 141–146).

Lastly, to return to class-related activities, the Lighthouse teachers were always interested in expanding the relationships developed in class to arenas outside the classroom. This took various forms, with a greater or lesser emphasis on spiritual matters. For example, in class on March 5, Sydney apologized for having taken up so much time the preceding week with her stories (see above), and announced that 'we' had decided to hold a supplementary class meeting in Sydney and Taryn's apartment for an additional evening class. During the subsequent conversation, Ania pointed out that the coming Sunday was International Women's Day (a widely celebrated occasion in Poland), and Sydney offered to have the women over for pizza and an English-language movie. It was decided to watch *Mamma Mia!*, which Sydney described as 'the best girls' movie I have ever seen'. As these arrangements were made, I was struck both by their spontaneity, and the active and willing participation of the two learners present, Ania and Marysia – Marysia volunteered to bring ingredients for pizza and to make it in the apartment, and both she and Ania were excited by the plans being made.

This was another of those moments that reminded me of the relative 'worldliness' of Sydney and Taryn – in these arrangements, aside from the unspoken certainty that alcohol would be absent there was little hint of any 'missionary' dimension. Yet, not all invitations of this kind were so secular – in the following section we shall hear Ania talking about a meeting that, for her, crossed the line into the invasive.

Thus, in various arenas from extracurricular class get-togethers, to school events, to community and city, Lighthouse School sought to forge and nurture relationships beyond the language classroom. Whatever the spiritual or religious results of these efforts, it was clear that at an interpersonal level relationships were indeed enabled through Sydney's teaching and more broadly through the work of the school. In the following section, we will take a closer look at relations between the school and one learner in particular.

The Story of Ania

Ania was in many ways a perfect example of the kind of middle-class professional person that Sydney and Taryn were aiming to serve. She was 30 years old, married, with two small children; her husband was a schoolteacher. Trained as a dancer, she had at one time taught dance, but was currently not working, only partly out of choice. She was a practicing Catholic. She lived within walking distance of the school, and had chosen it for convenience – most of the other language schools were located in or near the center of the city, necessitating a long commute. Ania's mother was living and working in England, and Ania wanted to learn English, among other reasons, to be able to function in England when visiting her mother; she was also more broadly interested in learning the language for travel and general communication.

Ania had begun attending Lighthouse School the previous year, and had liked it. She signed up for the follow-up course in the fall 2008 semester, which happened to be the course taught by Allie, that was then taken over by Sydney in the spring. During the fall semester, as mentioned above, the other learners' attendance in Allie's class was spotty, and often Ania was the only one present in class. (At the end-of-semester awards party, she received a certificate for regular attendance, having missed only one class during the whole semester.) She was also an extremely regular attendee in Sydney's class. Thus, as we have seen in this chapter and the preceding one, she appears frequently in the classroom data.

It became clear to me from fairly early on in my time at Lighthouse School that Ania was an object of particular attention and concern on the part of the mission. Magda, for instance, was an evangelical and a member of Rysiek's church. When I asked her about Ania, Magda described her as 'deeply spiritual', 'different from the the majority of Catholics' and 'on the right road as far as thinking about God, accepting him, is concerned'. I heard similar things from other evangelicals at the school.

Given Ania's pattern of regular attendance, it was unusual that on February 17 and 19 she missed two successive classes. When she came back to class on February 24, we learned that she had suffered a terrible tragedy – her younger brother, with whom she had been close, had died. Much of the following few weeks of Ania's involvement with Lighthouse played out against the backdrop of her loss.

The first inkling I had that something was amiss came before class, when I saw Ania talking intently with Sydney and then Rysiek, the pastor of the church, in another room. Then, at the beginning of class, after going around the other three women present and eliciting their news, Sydney announced that Ania's 29-year-old brother had died on February 13, and that the funeral had been the following day. Unusually, she then said an opening prayer, explaining that 'we need God to help us in these situations'. Significantly, she concluded by saying that 'we know this is more than an English class'.

During the break, I sat in a group with Ania and some others, and she spoke about her brother. It transpired that he had suffered from depression for a long time, and that he had taken his own life.

It seemed to me remarkable, first that Ania had chosen to come to class so soon after this terrible event, and second that despite the fact she was in deep mourning, she also did not hesitate to speak about her brother's death and about her own feelings to Sydney, Rysiek and her classmates and me. This strongly indicated that not only did she feel comfortable among the group, but that she actually drew strength from being there. It may well also have been the case that she needed the routine of the school, such as it was, to cling to as part of the agonizing process of going on living; my guess is that Sydney sensed this too, for despite her evident compassion (the opening prayer was said teary-eyed), she opted to hold a fairly regular class, with grammar and vocabulary activities and work on the text of the present chapter of *Robinson Crusoe*. Interestingly, though, toward the end of class, she embarked on a short mini-sermon about fear, sparked by the episode in the book in which Crusoe builds several barricades of trees around his dwelling. The conclusion of the sermon, deriving again from the book, was that in the case of Crusoe, 'his fear replaced his Christian faith and hope'. As I listened to the recording I made of the class, it occurred to me to wonder whether in some sense this message was intended for Ania in particular. I don't know if Sydney was planning on addressing this matter anyway; but at any given moment in any class, she was aware of exactly who she had in front of her, and I would not have been surprised to learn that she was thinking in particular of Ania and her recent loss as she said these words.

In fact, in the second interview she gave me, on May 5, Ania confessed that she herself had been surprised at how easily she had opened up at the school and talked about her brother – to the point that she worried afterward that she might be misunderstood. Once again, she ascribed her openness to the special atmosphere created by the school.

The subject of Ania and her brother recurred numerous times throughout the following weeks. For example, in class on March 5, in response to a prompt about 'something you remember from your childhood', Ania spoke for three minutes about playing soccer with her brother and his friends, and other memories of playing games with him. At other times too she shared memories of her brother. It was also a major topic in the interview I conducted with Ania in early May.

The amount of attention that Rysiek, Sydney and others paid to Ania was no doubt due in large part to their desire to help her through such a difficult time in her life. However, I felt sure that there was also an unspoken hope that Ania might come into the church. I myself was also very curious about whether this was a possibility. It was hard for me to judge – like many Poles, though outwardly friendly Ania very much played her cards close to her chest, and it was extremely difficult to gauge the extent of her interest in evangelical Christianity. Certainly there were signs – numerous subdued conversations with Rysiek that I had noted from a distance; the fact that she felt so comfortable at the school; her enthusiastic acceptance of many of the religious and spiritual elements of the classroom. Yet I could not read her, and in the end I simply asked her point-blank in the second interview that I conducted with her. I have to confess that her answer surprised me. To begin with, she told me that her brother's suicide had not caused her to move away from her own faith, as can happen to survivors in such situations, but had reinforced it. She said prayer had helped her, as had a conversation with a priest who, in light of the Catholic belief that suicides cannot receive redemption, suggested to her that in the case of her brother, it was the illness – depression – that had killed him, and that thus he could not be held responsible for his own death.

I asked Ania if the church attached to the school (and, by implication, the form of Christianity it represented) had any influence on her or interested her in any way. Ania paused to think, saying she hadn't given it much thought. Then she said:

> No, maybe it's just that I've gotten used to the idea that you go to church on Sunday, there's the priest, the priest can't have children, that's how it is; there are nuns that dedicate their lives to God, to the Church. It's hard to say, hard for me at least to know if it's that way because our faith says it has to be so, or if it's just that you spend all those years that way, subconsciously to begin with. [BJ: Mhm] But; um, but that suits me more than this, I don't know, that there's a pastor who has his own family, and who, who, I don't, services where people just gather in some place, like here [in the school] for example, and talk and discuss things together. Something isn't right for me in that [BJ: Mhm]. No, no. In some way, in some way I have my own faith and I feel comfortable in it. That's how I'd put it. The same way that I have my own country and I feel comfortable in it. I wouldn't want to go abroad—well, to work maybe, but I'd never be able to emigrate, and, and abandon everything here.

In fact, though Ania was very fond of Lighthouse and its teachers, she mentioned one moment when she had felt uncomfortable. In the year before I conducted my study, which was Ania's first year in the program, at some point she had been invited to join a Bible study group in Sydney and Taryn's apartment. She told me: 'This for me was too much, an invasion of privacy'; Ania was not attracted to the idea of reading the Bible with others she did not really know. The invitation was not repeated.

It transpired, then, that Ania had no interest in leaving the Catholic Church and joining Rysiek's church, or any other evangelical church. I had been seriously misreading the signs; I wondered if Rysiek and Sydney would be equally surprised to hear Ania talk in these terms about her strengthened faith in Catholicism. Of course, there exists a possibility that Ania was not being entirely open with me, or that her attitudes were more complex; yet a year later there had been no change in her situation, and furthermore, from everything I had learned about and from Ania after spending almost a year with her in the school, I had no particular reason to think that she was not being frank. It seems that, however much the conversations with Rysiek and Sydney may or may not have helped her, they were not going to translate into membership of the church.

Yet, at the same time, Ania was very much interested in deepening her friendship with Sydney. In the same interview, she said to me that her contacts with Sydney were 'sporadic', that she would like more, but that she was afraid of imposing. She said that at this time in her life she had a little more free time that she could devote to social contacts, which she further felt would do her good. Thus, Ania herself seemed to have come to the conclusion that this was not a 'false-bottomed friendship' – either that, or she had decided that for her purposes and from her perspective, the purely interpersonal dimension of the relationship could be separated from its missionary aspect. In this way, while religious changes for Ania seemed unlikely, her relation with Sydney was continuing and deepening.

Is Relation Possible?

When non-believers like myself spend time with evangelicals, especially missionaries, they can be absolutely sure that their souls are being prayed for in their absence, and this may well happen in their presence too. Many of my more staunchly anti-Christian or anti-evangelical friends find this offensive. Personally, I find it hard to understand why they get so upset – it's simply a question of someone who doesn't know you closely but wishes you well in a way that feels most comfortable and meaningful to them. This said, the expression of concern and hope that you will see the light – which is to say, come to know Jesus Christ – can be irritating. It often comes over as patronizing, superficial and thus insulting. I had this feeling a couple of times in the course of my research. For example, toward the end of the last interview I conducted with Allie, when I asked her if there was anything she would like to add for herself, she said outright:

> You must know, I mean, I, I have to say this, that my hope for you is that you would come to [??] a knowledge of Christ. Because I truly love you and I care about you [...] But you've heard all of these different things, and I, I, my prayer for you, and I am praying for you [...] as you listen to all of these times that we've spoken, that your heart will be pricked; and so I'm praying for you, and I want you to know that.

This was the first time during the study that such wishes had been explicitly voiced, and I was somewhat taken aback. Yet, the language Allie used was, for want of a better word, generic – the same desire in the same terms could have been expressed toward any non-evangelical Allie had contact with – and her words did not really affect me. The moment when I felt most disturbed and at the same time most distant – or perhaps distanced – from the people and the world I was researching, was on another occasion. As explained in Chapter 4, as the teachers and staff of Lighthouse grew more familiar with me and comfortable with my presence, along with observing classes and hanging out in the cafe I also started to attend the weekly Friday team meetings at which the school leadership – Jean during the first semester, Sydney and Taryn in the second – would lead a long (up to four hours) get-together that served several different functions: It was used to sum up the preceding week, make plans for upcoming events and also provide spiritual guidance for the young women teachers and staff. Of course, a regular component of the meeting was prayer. In March, my sister, whom I had not seen for several years, decided to visit N. with her husband. I mentioned this to Sydney and Taryn, adding something to the effect that my sister and I were not especially close. During the prayer session of the meeting immediately preceding my sister's visit, on March 13, Taryn included the following prayer:

> Father, it's really, it's really great that Bill's sister has time to come and stay for more than just a day or two, but to really be here for a while. Use this time for her as a time to refresh her and, um, give her the rest she needs; that she and her husband would have a, a nice time and a good vacation. And father, we especially pray that as she and Bill talk and visit and see things together, that you would restore and renew and

refresh and heal their relationship in ways that they can't even imagine. That there be great conversations, and understanding, that there be a new openness, and that, um, you would take their relationship really to a new place; that there be closeness; and father, you would watch over them, put a hedge and a wall [??] of protection around their time together; that they wouldn't become distracted, or argue over things that aren't important, but really that the conversations would just resonate with the enjoyment of being with each other and of learning and understanding each other better.

I was, frankly, outraged. I experienced this as a gross violation of my privacy, as well as a hurtful misrepresentation of the actual state of things (relations with my sister were not close, but they were by no means conflict-ridden as was suggested by words such as 'argue' and 'restore'). I also found it immensely patronizing that Taryn's god could 'heal' my relationship with my sister 'in ways that we could not imagine'. Of course, I simultaneously appreciated the fact that Taryn was concerned, and that her prayer showed solicitude. Nevertheless, it felt like an invasion of my private life that I had never sanctioned, despite my quite close relations in other ways with Taryn. The effect was intensified because a few weeks earlier, Taryn had made another prayer about me that had irked me. On that occasion, on January 30, just before I left on a short trip to England to visit my mother and brother, Taryn had wished among other things that 'there would a healthy time for them as a family [??] move to the next level, and change their relationship in a way that would just be more positive and more hopeful, and more joyful, and a little deeper in the way they understand each other'. This too, while well intentioned, seemed hugely presumptuous – I resented the implication, first, that my family relationships needed to be 'deeper' and more 'hopeful' and 'joyful'; second, that Taryn presumed to know or suppose this to be the case; and third, that divine intervention was necessary.

Like Allie's wish, these prayers (especially the one concerning my sister) brought home to me the very different perceptions that researcher and researched were bringing to the encounter, and by extension how concern and interest shown by evangelicals may be perceived very differently by non-evangelicals. In a word, it revealed radically different perspectives on relation, and perhaps even the *possibility* of relation, between the two groups.

It is precisely accounts of moments like this that seem to produce gooseflesh in so many of my non-evangelical friends and colleagues. Such moments precisely mark the cultural fault line that runs between evangelicals and non-evangelicals. They indicate the points at which the possibility of dialogue fails, and are, I think often unconsciously, taken as proof that dialogue in fact *must* fail in this cross-cultural encounter.

In the course of my research project, however, I came to question whether this failure is in fact so inevitable. Two friendships in particular (and I use the term 'friendship' mindfully) led me to see other possibilities. In this closing section, I'd like to reflect briefly on these two relationships.

One deeper relationship that I developed in N. was with Victor, a pastor at the American Baptist mission. I originally met him through his wife Carol, whom I interviewed because she had been involved in an eventually abandoned attempt to set up English classes through the mission. I also knew Victor from several sermons I had seen him preach at the church, and from his participation in other services. One thing led to another, and Victor and I ended up having a couple of lunches together. As always with friendships, though Victor was a very nice person, it was still difficult to pinpoint exactly what it was that I found so sympathetic in my interactions with him. On reflection, I believe that a major part at least was played by Victor's openness to exploring my own point of view, and his willingness to allow me to probe his beliefs in a way that was searching but not hostile. We spoke, for example, about the evangelical hostility toward homosexuality, which I have always seen as a complete red herring. One of the good things about talking with Victor was that, though he presented his arguments, I never felt that either one of us was trying to persuade the other – we were simply listening to each other's point of view and seeking to understand and acknowledge it, while being prepared to admit that another perspective exists. What Victor found interesting in me – aside from my general interest in evangelical Christianity and my willingness to dialogue where other non-evangelicals might not be, or appear, so open – was a genuine curiosity he had about what I might call my secular humanism – that is, my belief in the importance of moral values uncoupled from any belief in a supreme being or a sacred text. In any case, I valued my friendship with Victor – for I believe that that was what it was – and I wish I could have continued to talk to him (soon after I left Poland he did too, and we have not been in touch since).

The other person who made me sense the possibility of dialogue between evangelicals and non-evangelicals was Sydney. Obviously, I spent a lot more time with Sydney than with Victor, including many hours in the classroom, and almost as many in informal chats, recorded interviews and numerous social situations. We came to know each other rather well. As in the case of Victor, it is hard to identify precisely what it was about Sydney, or my relationship with her, that made it seem that dialogue was possible.

In the end, as with Victor, it may have been the fact that I felt listened to and safe; I felt as if Sydney was not coming at me with a fixed agenda, but encountering me as a person. Ultimately, in human relations this may be the crucial ingredient – to accept the other as a full human being, without an initial impulse to want to change or improve. It might be the lack of just such a quality, on either or both sides, that impedes evangelical–non-evangelical communication. But it may also be the case that, even allowing for generally favorable dispositions on either side, true friendships require a further indefinable sympathy that cannot be planned or guaranteed. No doubt it is these kinds of relationships that many evangelical missionaries hope for; yet the naivety of much missionary work makes this unlikely. On the basis of my relationships with Sydney and Victor, however, I can confirm that such sympathy is indeed possible, and that when it occurs, it is a powerful experience.

Conclusion: What 'Relation' Means

Lurking beneath all of the foregoing is a set of interrelated ambiguities about the word 'relation' – ambiguities made concrete in Ania's doubts about 'false-bottomed friendships'. What, exactly, do evangelicals mean by 'relationship building', and how might this be perceived from a non-evangelical viewpoint? Fehr (1996) compiles attempts by various social scientists to define 'friendship'; crucial differences among the definitions echo the uncertainties around the term 'relation'. Thus, for instance, Hartup (1975: 11, quoted in Fehr, 1996: 7) defines friends as 'people who spontaneously seek the company of one another', and Wright (1984: 119, quoted in Fehr, 1996: 7) describes friendship as 'a relationship involving voluntary or unconstrained interaction in which the participants respond to one another personally, that is, as unique individuals'. Reisman (1979: 93–94, quoted in Fehr, 1996: 7), on the other hand, says that a friend is 'someone who likes and wishes to do well for someone else and who believes that these feelings and good intentions are reciprocated by the other party'; and Berscheid and Peplau (1983: 12, quoted in Fehr, 1996: 7) argue that 'two people are in a relationship with one another if they have impact on each other'. The first two definitions address primarily the sheer sympathy that draws friends together – the pleasure of one another's company. This, I would argue, is how friendship is thought of outside of the evangelical mission setting. It's exactly this kind of pleasure that Ania is referring to when she talks about wanting to spend more time with Sydney; and it's what I have in mind when I think of the enjoyment I got from my discussions with Sydney and Victor.

Yet Reisman's definition adds a crucial component: a friend is someone 'who likes *and wishes to do well for* someone else' (emphasis added). It is this additional component – the desire to further another person's interests – that is present in the evangelical understanding of 'relationship' in the mission context. For the evangelical missionaries I spoke to, there was no contradiction between enjoying someone's company and wishing the best for them. If someone is your friend, naturally you want them to be as happy as possible; this necessarily includes their moving toward a more fulfilling spiritual life. In evangelical eyes, this is analogous to wishing that they would embrace, say, a healthier lifestyle or diet. It is not perceived as an abuse of friendship; it's what a good friend *should* do, because friends, in Berscheid and Peplau's terms, 'have impact on each other'.

That said, as in any developing relationship some people tread more lightly than others. Some hold back more than they should; some come on too strong. There were moments, both for Ania and me, when the teachers of Lighthouse went too far – Allie's 'prayer' for me was a rather naive example. But the sustained engagement of all Sydney's learners in her class discussions – and also Ania's tentative conclusion that her friendships at Lighthouse were not 'false-bottomed' but genuine – point to a much more nuanced understanding of the 'relationships' developed between evangelical missionaries and those they seek to serve. In theory, it's hard to conceptualize such relationships. Aristotle, the first recorded theorist of friendship, posited three kinds of friendship: friendships of pleasure, in which people enjoy one another's company; friendships of utility, which can serve mutual interests; and friendships of virtue, in which good people take strength from one another (Ross, 2015). It is hard to fit evangelical mission 'relations' – which are focused above all on the good of one friend as conceived and desired by the other – into Aristotle's framework. Can such relations in fact be considered friendships? Conceptually, this is problematic. But the evidence from Sydney's class is that, if handled in the right way, such relationships can be a great deal more than might initially be thought.

Notes

(1) One piece of evangelical literature I have is entitled, 'Don't Just Go to Church, BE the Church'.
(2) I always thought I remembered this quotation from Mary Midgley's (1984/2001) book *Wickedness*, but I have been unable to locate it there or elsewhere.

8 Empty Meeting Grounds?: The Cross-Cultural Encounter at Lighthouse School

At the beginning of this book, I described the project reported on here as an ethnography of contact. In the present chapter, I will examine directly some of the multifarious aspects of the cultural encounter that constituted a central feature of Lighthouse School and its work.

Like other academics working in the social sciences and humanities in the early 21st century, I have learned to be suspicious of the term 'culture'. I certainly do not believe that any individual is wholly or even largely defined by cultural factors, and I am extremely skeptical of 'culture' as a stand-alone explanation for any person's behavior. At the same time, also like many academics, I acknowledge that the term still has its uses. In the present chapter, I will do my best to follow Appadurai's (1996) practice of using the adjective 'cultural' while avoiding the reifying noun 'culture' itself wherever possible. In a social sense, I do believe that the phenomenon referred to in popular parlance as 'culture' is shorthand for a (socially and therefore humanly) real complex of values, practices and assumptions that play a highly significant role in social interactions, though I see it as an influence on, rather than as a determiner of, human actions, attitudes and desires.

It was certainly the case that Lighthouse School represented an encounter between at least two such complexes. One, which I will call imprecisely 'North American evangelical culture', found itself embedded in a second that (equally vaguely) I will call 'Polish Catholic culture'. These two complexes included differing and often competing values and practices. Each in turn comprised one important religious or spiritual dimension (evangelical, Catholic) and one regional and linguistic one (North American, Polish).

Yet in reality the picture is, of course, much more complicated. In the present chapter, I will describe the (sometimes hostile) encounter between these two cultural complexes; complicate and problematize this binary distinction with data and facts that do not match it neatly; and finally, ask to what extent a cultural account of what I observed and recorded at Lighthouse School retains any explanatory power for understanding the phenomenon of teaching-based evangelical missionary work in Poland, and also how else the encounter whose epicenter was Lighthouse School might be understood.

Lighthouse School can be conceptualized as forming part of a 'global contact zone' (Singh & Doherty, 2004). Singh and Doherty (2004: 11), drawing on the work of Clifford (1997) and Pratt (1992), define global contact zones as 'spatial, temporal locations that have already been constituted relationally and that enter new relations through historical processes of displacement', a slightly altered quotation from Clifford (1997: 7). Singh and Doherty also quote from Pratt (1992: 4), who defines contact zones as 'social spaces where disparate cultures meet, clash, and grapple with each other'. Lighthouse School was just such a location. At the same time, I have found myself returning to MacCannell's (1992) phrase 'empty meeting grounds' to describe such problematic encounters in which it is not entirely clear whether the two sides are altered in a meaningful way by the meeting. It is from MacCannell's work that I take the title of this chapter, which once again bears a question mark as an indicator of the central puzzle around which the chapter is organized: Is this encounter in fact empty, and if not, what content or processes does it generate?

While I was concerned above all with the work of the school in its narrow local context, the encounters at Lighthouse could also be seen as a microcosm of the cross-cultural encounters taking place between North American evangelical missionaries across Poland, and indeed elsewhere in Central and Eastern Europe; beyond this, as argued in Chapter 3, it can also be said to represent the human face(s) of globalization in general.

The chapter is organized into four parts. In the first, I will examine some of the obvious and less obvious differences between the two complexes outlined above, and some resulting misunderstandings. In the second part, I will describe some of the conflicts that arose as a result of cultural difference. In the third part, I'll look at some important instances in which the values, beliefs and attitudes on either side of this purported divide were in fact in curious harmony. And finally, in the fourth part, I will explore some of the many points at which the two sides bled into one another, troubling the neatness of the distinction and rendering the entire picture much more complicated and interesting.

Grounds of Difference

When speaking of the encounter between North American evangelical Protestant Christians and Polish Roman Catholics, the differences between the two sides are easiest to identify and write about. Indeed, many of these differences have come up in the preceding chapters. It should also be said at once that though these differences may seem at times to be broad 'cultural' generalizations, I have taken care in this subsection to include only the preferences, values and practices that were manifested in some way by the individuals included in this study, either in their actions or the perceptions of others that they expressed. I will make a particular effort to distinguish behaviors, attitudes and so on that I actually observed from behaviors and attitudes ascribed by one side to the other.

An initial word should be said about the term 'North American', which I use deliberately to refer to the personnel of the school. While Americans in the US are often rather ignorant on the subject of their northern neighbors, the same is not true of most Canadians, and the majority of the latter are well aware of the cultural differences between the two countries. Nevertheless, in the context of Lighthouse School it seems advisable to talk of 'North American' culture, for several reasons. First, though Taryn and Sydney were both Canadian, others involved in the school were from the US, including Jean, the interim director of the school in fall 2008 and Allie, who taught there in the same semester (both hailed from Texas). Second, and perhaps most importantly, the kind of evangelical Christian mission work represented by Lighthouse is strongly associated with the English language, and many of the leading mission organizations are based in the US; as already stated, the largest mission group in the city of N. was entirely composed of Americans and was sponsored by the US-based Southern Baptist Convention. For this reason, it would be misleadingly restrictive to call Lighthouse a 'Canadian' mission. Third, many of the Polish learners I spoke to seemed unaware that Taryn and Sydney were Canadian, not American, and moreover were not unduly concerned with the differences between the two countries; for the Poles, Lighthouse was 'amerykańska' or 'American', that term serving in Polish to indicate 'North American' just as much as referring exclusively to the US. Ania, for example, said that to her all those working at the school were simple 'obcojęzyczni' or 'foreigners' (literally, 'speakers-of-a-foreign-language'), and asked me if there were differences between Canadians and Americans. (Lest this seem surprising, I might mention that when I taught English in Poland in the 1980s alongside both Britons and Americans, many Polish learners could not perceive the differences between those two groups even in their pronunciation, which for native speakers of the two varieties of English is a highly salient distinction.) For all these reasons, then, the cultural complex represented by Lighthouse School is referred to in this chapter as 'North American', however imprecise and excessively overarching that term might be.

Many of the cultural differences between North American evangelicals and Poles that could be observed in the work of the school were more connected with national and linguistic than with religious identity. To a significant extent, these differences played out along the axis of openness versus privacy. North Americans are typically a lot more open in their social contacts on the surface; Poles tend to be more reserved in surface encounters. The best example I can think of is that, when walking down the street in a pleasant, safe suburb, many Americans will not hesitate to greet a passing stranger with 'Hi', and will not be fazed if so addressed. In Poland, such a greeting would be shocking and suspicious. Along with such attitudes to strangers in public, Poles are more wary in initial social contacts, and will nearly always use the formal V form (*Pan/Pani*) with new acquaintances until an explicit move is made to shift to the T (*ty*) form, something that may take years or may indeed never happen.[1] (Interestingly, one of the few exceptions to this is in Polish evangelical Christian circles, where the T form is often used at once, as happened when I first met Rysiek, the pastor of the Lighthouse church.) Lastly, Poles are very careful about which personal information they share, and unspoken codes regulate what kinds of personal information are and are not appropriate for use in casual conversation – there is a marked preference for neutral topics, and an avoidance of anything that might be considered overly intimate. Ania, for example, said: 'I value the quiet of my home, my family... I value my privacy'. At one point, she was invited to a Bible reading at Sydney and Taryn's apartment (see Chapter 7), and in recounting this encounter and explaining why she chose not to accept further invitations, she said: 'That was too much for me, it was an intrusion on my privacy [...] I didn't need to read the Bible with people I don't really know'. In my initial expectations of the encounter taking place at Lighthouse, I had wondered what would happen when North American 'openness' came into contact with Polish 'privacy'.

There were indeed moments when these two preferences came into conflict. At a team meeting on November 21, Jean and the other teachers reviewed attendance in the adult classes. One male student, Jacek, had missed class for the first time. The school had a policy of calling a learner if that learner missed two classes, but Jean asked Agnieszka, the Polish administrator, to call Jacek at home about his absence. I instantly felt that this would be a significant breach of privacy in the sense described above. Agnieszka was clearly unhappy about this request, and, with Mavis' encouragement, explained to Jean that this would not be an acceptable step to take:

Jean: And our prayer was that, you know, there would be some new revelation and, and what happened was he didn't come. It's the first time he's missed.

Agnieszka: Hm.

Jean: So, I would like you, Agnieszka, even though we call after two times, I'd really like you to call because this is the first time he's ever missed. I want you to call him, make sure he's OK, and, if you would do that please ma'am. Just say, Wow, you've never missed! Jean was so amazed. [laughs] I was like, where is he?

Mavis: Are you comfortable with that?

Agnieszka: Not really.

Jean: Oh, I thought that was what you did.

Agnieszka: [No it –]

Jean: I thought that was your –

Agnieszka: It's really like. See, you need to understand like, yesterday we talked about the Polish culture thing [Jean: Mhm], um, and how Jerzy has never come back [Jean: right], and you were thinking about, like, I don't know, kind of, going to his home [laughs] and checking up. [Jean: Yeah] This is completely [1 sec] beyond [1 sec] like [Jean: Uh huh], it's just stepping into someone's, um, territory [Jean: Uh huh] in my culture. [Jean: Uh huh] So you need to be really careful. I'm not comfortable in calling someone where there are, after they [???] class

Jean: OK. Because it's like, in the thing that Sydney and Taryn gave me, that we do.

Mavis: After two.

Jean: After two.

Agnieszka: After two. He's not been here two times.

Jean: I know, I wanna know what's wrong with him now! I wanna know if there's, there's a problem now.

Briana: I mean, it could be something minor, maybe he like –

Jean: Well right.

Mavis: We'll find out after

Briana: – On Tuesday –

Jean: Right.

Briana: We'll just ask him on Tuesday.

Jean:	If he comes on Tuesday.
Briana:	And if he doesn't –
Mavis:	And if he doesn't we'll call him.
Jean:	OK. OK.
Agnieszka:	Thanks.

In this extract, Jean, who had only been in Poland some two and a half months (though she had visited before), asked Agnieszka to do something that runs counter to Polish cultural norms. It is noteworthy that Mavis, who had lived in Poland for longer and was also a friend of Agnieszka's and so probably sensitive to her reactions, asked her, 'Are you comfortable with that?', no doubt sensing that Agnieszka was not, and prompting her to speak up. In this particular case, Agnieszka was able to express her misgivings clearly from the point of view of cross-cultural (mis)communication, and a faux pas was avoided; but this incident was emblematic of many others that may have caused greater or lesser offense on either side. Yet it is also the case that Poles tend to be equally private in their criticisms. Even when they are offended, they often will not say anything except to family or very close friends. Thus, there may have been any number of such moments of tension in the encounters at Lighthouse. (Indeed, the mention of Jerzy and his failure to come back to the school hints at just such a possibility.) At the same time, the very hiddenness of these reactions makes it possible for the cross-cultural encounter to continue to take place.

Other differences that at moments became salient in the encounter were more religious in nature. Generally speaking, knowledge of the Bible is much greater among evangelicals, for whom the Word of God is central to faith, than among Catholics.[2] Taryn and Sydney were well aware of this fact, and much of the Lighthouse curriculum was aimed at (re)acquainting Polish Catholics with their own Holy Book. As seen in the preceding chapters, Bible quotations and stories found their way at numerous moments into the Crusoe materials. Zosia, a Catholic participant, commented explicitly on Sydney's knowledge of the Bible as something she would like to emulate. Another major difference between evangelical and traditional Catholic practice is the use of spontaneous prayer, as discussed in Chapter 6. As mentioned there, Ania confessed to being a little embarrassed by this at the beginning, though she said she got used to it eventually; Zosia was impressed by it, and associated it with recent calls in the Catholic Church for greater spontaneity in prayer. This latter connection will be touched upon later in the present chapter when we shall look at the points of overlap between Protestant and Catholic practices that at first blush seem so distinct.

Lastly, it was often the case that each side revealed a perhaps surprising lack of knowledge of the other – something that might seem somewhat less remarkable in the Poles, few of whom had ever traveled to North America, let alone spent any length of time there, and more striking in the North Americans working at the school, most of whom had spent a considerable amount of time in the country at the time of my study. Ania's ignorance of differences between Americans and Canadians, mentioned above, was one example. On the part of the Lighthouse teachers, I was sometimes taken aback by their lack of knowledge of some quite basic aspects of Polish life – for example, at a team meeting toward the end of the school year, on April 24, it turned out that some of the younger teachers were unaware of how Lighthouse's curriculum related to what was studied in English classes in Polish high schools, something I found surprising given the number of high school teens who attended Lighthouse classes (and spent a great deal of time hanging out in the cafe), and also bearing in mind the visits that Lighthouse teachers had paid to local high schools. At the same meeting, other teachers turned out not to know about the 'third name' Poles have that honors their special saint – something that, given the nature and frequency of their conversations with their Polish participants, I would have expected to come up. In such instances, the cultural encounter seemed sometimes to be taking place in a darkened room.

Grounds of Conflict

There were also times when some combination of the differing values, practices and perceptions outlined above led to clashes, and even open or concealed conflict.

The situation of missionaries in post-1989 Central and Eastern Europe has rarely been easy. Missionaries of all stripes – Mormons and Jehovah's Witnesses as well as various brands of evangelical Protestants – have encountered administrative and social hostility across the region from Russia and Ukraine to Poland and elsewhere (see e.g. Baran, 2006, 2007; Wanner, 2007). The missionaries of Lighthouse School were no exception. Though their time in the town of D. was over by the time I commenced my study, I heard much from Sydney, Taryn, Agnieszka and others about the problems that they had faced in that city. Their school was criticized from the pulpit of the local Roman Catholic church, whose priest warned his congregation against the 'sekta' represented by Lighthouse (we have seen elsewhere how this Polish perception of evangelical Christianity is widespread); parishioners subsequently repeated around the community the idea that the school was an 'evil place'. No such accusations appeared to have surfaced in N. after the school moved there in 2007. Nevertheless, many of those attending the school or sending their children to it told me that they or their friends or family had had similar misgivings: Marysia, for example, told me that her mother had specifically been concerned that the school was run by a 'sekta'. Though the Polish Catholics attending the school did not have worries of this kind, I heard stories of potential learners who were put off by the religious affiliation of Lighthouse.

As already mentioned, though, the kinds of conflict I heard about or observed more frequently were those across cultural, national and linguistic divides rather than denominational ones. Alvin, one of the pastors at the large Southern Baptist mission, told me that there continued to be an uneasy relationship between the leadership of the Polish Baptist church that hosted the mission, and the North American leaders of that mission. Even though the two parties shared a religious faith, they often differed in terms of goals and practices, and even though there had been a significant American Baptist presence in N. for many years and the current arrangement was well-established, I still heard several reports of friction between the American and Polish sides. More generally, I heard a number of stories of missionaries at odds with their host churches. Pippa, a British missionary language teacher, told me stories of conflict between one of the Baptist churches in the city of R. and the language school it sponsored – a conflict that also played out as being between the Polish church leadership and the often non-Polish teachers at the school. Wanner (2007), in her study of Ukrainian Baptists, reports similar clashes between the more traditional, formal, hierarchical structures and practices of the Ukrainian Baptist churches on the one hand, and the more free and easy, less hierarchically inclined Western (mostly US) missionaries on the other. Many of these tensions revolved around issues such as how the women dress; the American missionaries' promotion of material success; and American preaching styles. According to Wanner (2007: 178–184), the perception of American Baptism held by many (though by no means all) Ukrainian Baptists was that the Americans had been extensively and negatively influenced by the broader American culture, and thus endangered the 'purer' form of Baptism that existed in Ukraine.

Interestingly, tensions akin to those mentioned above also surfaced in the small and rather intimate world of the Lighthouse church. Rysiek, the pastor, who was also officially the director of the school, was very much concerned about integrating Taryn and Sydney and their work into the life of the church community. Nevertheless, my interview with Ola, a Lighthouse learner in Taryn's *The Shack* class who was also an evangelical Christian and a member of the Lighthouse church community, revealed that the picture was not quite as rosy as it might have seemed. While acknowledging the 'potential' of the missionaries' presence, Ola expressed her disappointment at certain aspects of relations between the Polish and North American members of the church, in particular what she saw as a 'lack of openness' and a distance maintained by Taryn and Sydney. She was critical of the fact that as a church member she had never been invited to Sydney and Taryn's home, stating generally that while some missionaries have open homes, for others like Sydney and Taryn 'their home is their castle'. She also resented the fact that she and other church members were not actively involved in helping with joint school–church projects such as the special evenings (Mexico Night, Out of Africa Night and so on, as described in Chapter 7) – that all the organizing was done by Sydney and Taryn and the school. And perhaps most significantly, she criticized the fact that at the church, the Polish members were obliged to speak in broken English to Taryn and Sydney, while the latter were unwilling to use their own broken Polish (and thus to render themselves vulnerable). As she said: 'For several people in the church it was kind of a hard pill to swallow: that they don't make an effort. At least not that you can see'. This, of course, is only one person's perspective, and there may be personal factors involved. Nevertheless, Ola's objections suggest the possibilities of conflict that are always present in cross-cultural encounters like those taking place at Lighthouse School.

Grounds of Convergence

If there were major points of difference and sometimes discord between the cultural complexes brought into contact at Lighthouse School and elsewhere in the evangelical mission field in Poland, there were, equally, points at which the two sides converged. In this section, I will examine two of these, one the result of a careful strategy on the part of the school, the other a fascinating overlap in values between the two purportedly incommensurable sides.

Ecumenical discourse

Well aware as I was of the great theological and other differences between Catholicism and evangelical Christianity, the gulf between the tendency toward spiritual openness among evangelicals and the strong preference for privacy among Poles, and the suspicion of evangelical forms of Christianity often encountered in Poland, I was initially very surprised to see the willingness with which Polish Catholic participants like Ania, Marysia and Zosia participated in discussions on religious and spiritual topics.

Eventually, I realized that one of the ways this was being achieved was through Sydney's deployment of what I came to call *ecumenical discourse*. By this, I mean a way of using language to address religious and spiritual matters that carefully eschews any reference to denomination-specific terms, practices or values, and that restricts itself to words, phrases and concepts that can be readily understood and accepted (even if in different ways) by anyone who thinks of himself or herself as a Christian. Thus, in leading the class in discussion, Sydney would use terms such as 'God', 'prayer', 'church', 'faith', 'Bible', 'Jesus' and so on. These are all terms that exist and are widely used both in evangelical and Catholic traditions, and thus create a common language around which a discussion can be built. As a small example, at the beginning of class on March 12, Sydney announced a couple of events being held at a camp run by Proem, an evangelical Christian organization. She presented the two events – a women's meeting, and a weekend devoted to personal fitness – without any reference to their evangelical background; the only hints of this that she gave were that the camp is interested in the 'spiritual dimension' of life, and that at the women's meeting there would be a delegation from a 'very large church' in the US – she didn't say what denomination the church was. This careful effort to maintain discourse in the common ecumenical arena was a foundational feature of Sydney's classroom throughout the semester. (Another more extensive example appears below.)

To be clear, I do not mean that the concepts or practices indicated by the terms mentioned above were in fact the same for all parties. Both theologically speaking and in terms of personal practices, the meaning of 'prayer' or 'church', for instance, can be vastly different for an evangelical and a Catholic, or indeed for two different Catholics or evangelicals. The point is that both *terms* are recognizable – that they mean *something* to each one, a meaning that furthermore has a significant overlap, and thus can be used as a basis for conversation.

It is an open question, of course, to what extent in the resulting conversations the participants were *actually* speaking about the same thing. When prayer was discussed, for example, it may well have been the case that each person in the room was engaging in the talk on the basis of her own denominational and/or unique personal conception of what 'prayer' is, can be or should be. Nevertheless, that the talk was possible at all was due to Sydney's consistent deployment of ecumenical discourse. Many examples of this strategy can be found in the excerpts from classroom discourse presented in the previous two chapters – for example, in Chapter 6 the extensive discussion about prayer, which from a discursive point of view took place exclusively in the non-denominational discursive space that Sydney created (by this I mean, for example, that at no point did anyone make any kind of reference to prayer practices specific to particular denominational traditions, nor was any attempt made to differentiate prayer-related issues according to denominational background).

Perhaps the most extreme case of ecumenical discourse, and one of the most extensive instances of spiritual issues taking center stage in Sydney's classroom, occurred on March 31. In this class, after 20 minutes of chat at the beginning of class, Sydney referred back to a discussion in the previous class (which I had missed, having been out of town on a research trip) about the Holy Spirit, and about the question of whether one can read the Bible without the help of someone to interpret what one reads. Sydney brought in a handout with some of what she described as her 'favorite' Bible quotations. The first two of these, from John 14 in the Contemporary English Version of the Bible, were from the words of Jesus. The second was verses 16-17. Verse 16, in the version used by Sydney, read as follows: 'Then I will ask the Father to send you the Holy Spirit, who will help you and always be with you'. After clarifying one or two vocabulary items from the passage, the discussion proceeded as follows:

Sydney: OK So we have [*writing on the whiteboard*] God. And we have God as the Father, we have God as the Son, and we have God as the Holy Spirit. [*stops writing*] Do we agree on this?
SS: Mhm.
Sydney: Yes? OK. In English we call this [*writing on the board*] the Trinity. [*stops writing*], because there are three in one. Right? OK. So, we have the Father, God the Father, creator of all things; we have the Son, who is our Savior. And then we have the Holy Spirit. What is his job? Right, because God has these roles, right? God the Father: we see him as the protector, as the creator, as the one who made everything. We understand that Jesus is the one who came to save us. But what is the role of the Holy Spirit?
Marysia: [???]
Sydney: Do we talk about the Holy Spirit much?
Marysia: No.
Sydney: No.
Marysia: But
Ania: He helps us to understand God.
Marysia: Yeah.
Sydney: He helps us to understand God.
Marysia: Yeah.

Sydney: For me this is a very interesting thing, because so many Christian traditions do not speak that much about the Holy Spirit.
Marysia: Mhm. Yeah.
Sydney: And yet, if we believe that they are equal, we should, we should talk about the Holy Spirit. So, in, in verse 16, what does it say that the Holy Spirit will do? Two things. [*12 secs*]
Ela: the Holy Spirit will help us –
Sydney: OK.
Ela: – about everything
Sydney: OK, So why don't you, why don't you circle that. The Holy Spirit will help [Marysia: [???]] us, and...
Ela: Always be with us.
Sydney: Always be WITH us. OK, now when you think of someone being with you, what do you think? [*5 secs*]
Ela: 'Always'?
Sydney: Yeah, when, because, you know, we're using these words, 'with', 'by', 'in', 'at', 'to' – when you, when you think of 'with', what do you – ha, see there's grammar even in the Bible! Oh my goodness.
Ela: Oh, oh [*Sydney laughs*] no way!
Sydney: 'I'm done! Never reading it again!' [*laughter*]
Marysia: Um, someone who is very close to me.
Sydney: Yes, some who's very close to me.
Marysia: And to God.
Sydney: [*intrigued tone*] Mhm.
Marysia: And, um, for me, Holy Spirit, um, is like a bridge, because I can [?=can't?], can see the God [*questioning tone*], I can, um, I can't, understand, but if, um I ask Holy Spirit to help me, it works [Sydney: Yeah], I think.
Sydney: Yeah. OK, so we have two things in the first verse. He will help [Marysia: Mhm], and he will be with us [Marysia: Mhm]. So this is, I mean, this is Jesus. This is obviously a promise. Jesus doesn't say things and then, 'Ah, I changed my mind'. [SS: Mhm] Right, so when Jesus says something we can believe it, we can trust it. So he says, I'm sending you the Holy Spirit. He will help you, and he will be with you. When I think of being WITH someone, I think of a friend, someone I want to talk to, someone I can walk down the street beside. OK. Let's continue to verse 17.

Of all the discussions that went on in this class, this was probably the most directly religious or even theological in nature. In all, this part of the class continued in a similar vein for about 40 minutes. There are several notable points to comment on here. First and foremost, such a conversation – between two evangelical Christians (Sydney and Ela) and three Catholics (Ania, Marysia and Zosia) – was only possible because of shared ground. Belief in the Holy Trinity is shared by both denominations, of course, as is the importance of the Bible and the text taken from it around which the discussion developed. Second, the discussion was equally enabled by the fact that Sydney carefully shaped it in discursive terms within the parameters of ecumenical discourse – that is, by exclusively using terms and concepts that make sense to both sides. Third, the participants' evident engagement in the discussion is remarkable. Marysia, for example, can be heard just aching to speak – her eventual contribution is signaled far ahead of time by her unusually active backchanneling. All the other students were intent on the discussion throughout its duration. Last, the leading role that Sydney took throughout is perhaps the clearest indication seen so far of her charisma, and of the acknowledgment of it by all the participants. Let us remember that none of these participants was shy in class – none was afraid to present a challenge whenever they saw fit. The fact that they allowed Sydney to introduce this topic and that they actively participated, under Sydney's leadership, in developing it speaks volumes about the regard in which they held her.

To further emphasize the point being made about ecumenical discourse in the passage above and in all similar discussions in this class, as with the curious behavior of the dog in the nighttime, we should also be mindful of what was *not* said. Thus, in these discussions I rarely if ever heard mention of denomination-specific terms or ideas such as, for instance, 'being born again', 'pastor' or 'witnessing' on the one hand (two of these three, of course, forming the very foundation of evangelical identity), or 'confession', 'priest' or 'Pope' on the other (equally central notions in Catholicism). There was a similar absence of other terms and concepts peculiar to one 'side' or the other.

In this way, Sydney created a discursive middle ground in which something like dialogue was possible. As I suggested earlier, I am not in fact convinced that this was dialogue in the truest sense of a conversation in which the views of the other are acknowledged, explored and challenged (Burbules, 1993; Noddings, 1984). Indeed, I think that in this case it is precisely the *illusion* of common ground that kept the participants from engaging with their actual differences in many crucial aspects of faith. In other words, the mechanism of ecumenical discourse in this instance is such that, in creating the appearance of discursive concord, it masks and thus effectively denies divergent beliefs. Nevertheless, as a discursive strategy it is fascinating because it makes it possible to raise issues that otherwise would be unlikely to be addressed.

The success of this strategy can clearly be seen in the ensuing conversations (see above, and in Chapter 6, for example). It was also confirmed in interviews with the Catholic participants. Zosia for example said, 'I don't see any big differences [...] things match up' from a religious point of view between the two denominations. Ania went even further. When I interviewed her after the first semester and asked about the many times when Allie had spoken about religious or spiritual issues in the classroom, she said:

> She talks about God, and it seems to me that it's about the one God that does in fact exist; it wasn't that it was presented, I don't know, in some other light somehow; and they seem to believe in the same thing that we do [...] Last year the classes were about, about Joseph – yes, they were stories about Joseph – and it was, it's practically speaking our Bible, it's the same thing. So there were no distortions, or; it seems to me it's really, really, if not the same then a very similar faith to ours.

Such statements confirmed that the strategy of ecumenical discourse had paid off, at least with these learners. Thus, ecumenical discourse proved a major mechanism of convergence, enabling evangelicals and Catholics to discuss purportedly 'common' issues across the denominational divide. As such, it constituted a central strategy in the ongoing denominational encounter that was Lighthouse School.

Where values meet

Ecumenical discourse was clearly a conscious and concerted strategy on the part of the school's leadership, and of Sydney in particular. But there was another significant area of convergence that was much more incidental, yet which also exerted a powerful influence on creating a sense of shared values and beliefs. It is to this that I turn in the present subsection.

The moments in class that most took me aback were those in which the conservative views of North American evangelicals chimed with the conservative views of Polish middle-class Catholics. While in retrospect I perhaps should not have been so surprised, it still came as a shock to me to find out the extent of the ideological overlap between the two supposedly so different 'cultures' represented in the classroom.

The most striking occasion on which this became apparent was during a class on April 28, focusing on Chapters 19 and 20 of the Lighthouse adaptation of *Robinson Crusoe*. Toward the end of the novel, Crusoe finds himself on the island with Friday, Friday's father and a Spaniard Crusoe has rescued. At one point in Defoe's original, Crusoe describes with self-irony 'how like a king I look'd' (Defoe, 1719/1968: 194) and how his people were 'perfectly subjected' (Defoe, 1719/1968: 194). Defoe (1719/1968) goes on:

> It was remarkable too, we had but three subjects, and they were of three different religions. My man Friday was a Protestant, his father was a pagan and a cannibal, and the Spaniard was a Papist: However, I allow'd liberty of conscience throughout my dominions. (Defoe, 1719/1968: 194)

In the Lighthouse rendering, this became:

> My three people were also all different religions. My man Friday was a Christian, his father was a wild man, and the Spaniard was a Roman Catholic. However, I allowed freedom of religion on my island.

(The change from 'Protestant' to 'Christian' is of course striking, and is noted here, though I will not comment on it at this point. I return to this issue in the next section.)

After giving a mini-lecture on the Reformation, Luther, the indulgences and related topics in an effort to give historical context to the passage, Sydney focused on the 'freedom of religion' line and elicited from the learners the word 'tolerance'. She then asked: 'Is tolerance a positive or a negative word?' At this point, Ania said quietly, 'positive'. Sydney acknowledged Ania then turned and addressed Magda directly: 'For you, Magda?' Magda, one of the evangelical students, immediately responded: 'I hate this word'. The conversation continued as follows:

Sydney: You hate this word.
Magda: Yes.
Sydney: Why do you hate this word?
Magda: Because, um, in this day –
Sydney: Mhm.
Magda: Today, it's, um, so popular word, but I feel like a person which is not tolerance [=tolerant]. Because people around me, um, try, um *zmusić* [to force], try –
Ela: press. press.
Magda: press me be tolerance.
Sydney: To be tolerant.
Magda: To be tolerance, um, about?

Sydney: Mhm.
Magda: Um, strange things. [*2 secs*] I don't know, for example homosex –
Sydney: Homosexuality.
Magda: Yes, and, and I think this word is, we use this word not correct.
Sydney: Mhm.
Magda: I think this word, um, in the past was good, but right now is not good.
Sydney: Aha.

This was by no means the first time that the issue of homosexuality had been raised in the context of the school or the study in general (see below), but it was the first time it had come up in class. After Magda had spoken, Sydney asked Ania, reminding her that she had said it was 'positive'. Ania revised her statement, saying, 'Yes, I think positive, but I, I don't must, um, agree with everything, because I have all my soul, my heart, my mind, and my val, value, which, but, I think tolerance, um, you must be tolerance to be good people, to be good person'. (Soon after this, Sydney attempted to clarify the grammatical distinctions among 'tolerance', 'tolerant' and 'tolerate'.) Then Ania explained further: 'I accept homosexualism, but I don't toler, tolerate it. Not accept, but I, I, um, I know that it is [=exists]. But I not agree with'.

Ela, the other evangelical member of the class, was even more vehement than Magda in her criticism of the idea of 'tolerance'. In what she said, she drew on a common Polish objection to the phenomenon of gay pride marches – the so-called 'Marches of Equality' that had taken place in major Polish cities in the immediately preceding years:

Sydney: Ela – positive word? negative word? nothing word?
Ela: difficult to say
Ania [?]: difficult [*laughs*]
Ela: because, um, I'm not tolerant
Sydney: You're not tolerant?
Ela: No.
Sydney: Mhm.
Ela: But I, I have my opinion about, um, everything. But it's no, it's no place to tolerant. Because I have very clear, um, think, thoughts about, about, um, many things about being [in?] our world. For example, why people who are, for example, who are, new heart or transplantated heart, or, or another illness [Sydney: Mhm] don't, don't go to the street and shout, I'm, I'm sick in heart, um, I'm, I'm, I am pregnant,

for example women who is pregnant. But homosexual people go during [=along] the street and, 'we are normal people'. It's very amazing for me, and very funny, and strange. Where is the line? [Sydney: Mhm] Tolerance.

As the class progressed, initially I had assumed that this discussion was something of a moral dilemma for Sydney, of the kind described by Edge (1996a: 21), who writes of the difficult choice that teachers face when their professional respect for the views and beliefs of others – what Edge calls 'the right to be different' – has to include respect for the views and beliefs that are themselves intolerant of the difference of others. But, as Sydney followed on from Ela and took the floor again, I realized that in fact her own views were, though perhaps more diplomatically couched, in essence close to those of her Polish learners. The extract above continued as follows:

Sydney: This is, this an interesting point, um, because, where is the line? You know, you talk about you have your, your values, and the things that are important to you; where, where do you say to your children, you know, as, as you are raising your children, where do you say, you tolerate to this point and after this point, we are intolerant?

At this juncture, Zosia pointed out that people may be less tolerant when there is a threat to their family, than when they merely see something on television. Sydney picked this up, talking about AIDS and about poverty in Africa, summing things up by saying, 'the only way we ever change anything in the world is to be intolerant of something'. After talking about religious tolerance in Poland, she then began to speak about Canada, which she said is in 'big trouble' because 'we had a moral foundation that was based in Christianity', but that Canadian immigrants are encouraged 'to keep their culture, to keep their religion', unlike the US, which is more assimilationist. The result, she explained, is that there are pockets of different cultures and languages all over Canada, and that 'these are really wonderful things, keeping your culture, keeping your religion'. She went on:

Sydney: But what has happened is that as Canada has become more and more tolerant, Canada has given up its own foundation, and it has said, oh, we must be tolerant of the Muslims, we must be tolerant of the Buddhists, we must be tolerant of the homosexuals, we must be tolerant of the dah-dah-dah-dah, all these groups that want us to be more tolerant. And yes we need to be tolerant towards those people, but they don't share the same values. And so now in Canada people are coming from all over the United States to Canada, homosexuals are coming to Canada to get married, because it's legal to get married as a homosexual in Canada. The government of Canada has changed the definition of what marriage is. Marriage used to be between one man and one woman, now marriage is between two people.

Sydney went on to speak about the disappearance of prayer in Canadian schools, and the ban on saying 'Merry Christmas'. She concluded: 'And so I think there's this really interesting conversation about tolerance, and I don't have the answer, like where do you draw the line, I have no idea. But I know that once you cross the line you can't go back. It's almost impossible to go back'. A short while later, she talked about having numerous homosexual friends during her college years and afterward in her work, and said that she loved those people, 'though I didn't agree with their lifestyle'. Then she said:

Sydney: But when this [gay rights] gets pushed, and pushed, and pushed, and pushed, and pushed, it makes it seem like everybody wants this. Well, you know, when you talk to the average person in Canada, the average person doesn't agree with the homosexual lifestyle. If you said, 'Oh, would you like your son to grow up to be gay?' everyone says, 'No, I want my son to grow up and have a wife and kids, I want my daughter to grow up and have a husband and kids'. I mean, you don't say I want my children to grow up to be gay, right? I don't know anybody who's ever said that. Maybe, maybe there are people who would say that, but I've never known anybody. So, what do you do with that? How do you, how do you treat those people? How do you draw the line?

Though, as I suggested, Sydney's comments are couched in a more nuanced way than those of, say, Ela, they were nevertheless clear to read, especially for an audience that was evidently predisposed to understand her and agree with her. The essence of the matter is that certain ideological presuppositions were present in both speaker and listeners, meaning that the message was understood because its ideological underpinnings were shared (Edwards & Potter, 1992). In the present case, the discursive construction of homosexuality as a lifestyle, as a sickness and as a choice seems to be shared by both sides; likewise, the heteronormativity evident in Sydney's comment about what the 'average Canadian wants' for his or her children finds a response in the Polish listeners. In the case of this particular issue, both in North American evangelical discourse and in middle-class Polish Catholic discourse such an understanding of homosexuality is a largely unquestioned norm, and so no counter-discourse is either necessary or possible. Each side is simply expressing things they know to be true and self-evident. Further, they join in in expressing their perplexity and frustration at fellow citizens who think otherwise.

In retrospect, I should not perhaps have been so surprised at this discussion. Evangelical opposition to homosexuality is well-established; it occupied a significant part of my conversations even with liberal-leaning Pastor Victor, and is known to occur in much more virulent forms, such as the local church here in Indiana that occasionally organizes demonstrations by the Indiana University gates, holding up signs that say 'God hates fags'. Of course, no one at Lighthouse would espouse such hateful practices. Nevertheless, there is a persistent and relentless thread of homophobia that runs throughout evangelical Christianity, and indeed other Protestant denominations, as seen in the fracturing of the Episcopal Church over the election of Gene Robinson, an openly gay priest, as a bishop in 2003, and several ongoing controversies within the Church of England.

Polish homophobia, too, is well-established. At the time of the study, Poland was known to be one of the most homophobic countries in Europe. According to two 2005 surveys by the leading Polish polling organization (CBOS, 2005a, 2005b), 89% of Poles believed that homosexuality is 'not normal'; 58% of Poles believed that gays and lesbians should not have the right to engage in political demonstrations; 78% thought gays should not have the right to openly show their lifestyle; 40% did not 'tolerate' gay people, period; 72% were opposed to homosexual marriage; and 90% were opposed to adoption by gay couples.[3] As mentioned above, in the years immediately prior to the commencement of the study, issues of gay rights were prominent in Poland and in the Polish media. In 2005, Lech Kaczyński, the mayor of Warsaw (and later president of the country), banned a March of Equality (a gay rights march) from taking place in the capital (this is the kind of march that Ela refers to in the extract above). Leading right-wing politicians have been known to make public statements denigrating homosexuals (see e.g. a 2006 BBC report by Adam Easton [2006]). Indeed, the campaign against homosexuality was and remains part of Poland's larger culture wars, which have also included such issues as abortion, immigration and anti-Semitism. At the time of writing in 2016, the country remains unwelcoming to homosexual people: A CBOS study in 2013 found that 68% of respondents did not accept gay marriage, while 87% were against adoption by gay couples (CBOS, 2013).

While there are numerous thought-provoking parallels between the culture wars of the US and Poland, one difference is that many socially conservative values are much more deeply ingrained in the educated Polish middle classes than in the equivalent social groups in America, at least in non-evangelical circles. Evidence of this was the conversation in the Lighthouse classroom on April 28. My guess is that most educated middle-class Americans would be embarrassed to express publicly such ideas about tolerance, even if they happened to believe in them. In Poland, such views and comments are widespread and normative, and needed neither justifying nor explaining.

This, in turn, means that such issues constitute a fascinating, perhaps unexpected and resonant ground of confluence between Polish Catholic and North American evangelical values and beliefs. Other developments around this time jibed with such a convergence. Two examples will suffice. First, in 2006, Polish Member of the European Parliament (MEP) Maciej Giertych, a prominent member of the Liga Polskich Rodzin (League of Polish Families) or LPR, an extreme right-wing political party, led a seminar in Brussels on creationism (Kutschera, 2006). Giertych, a Catholic, is a member of the UK-based Catholic creationist organization, the Daylight Origins Society. Thus, creationism or 'intelligent design', a credo that in the US is almost exclusively associated with evangelical Christians, in Poland has entered the picture through the work of a right-wing Catholic politician. It should be noted in this regard, by the way, that since 1950, successive popes have grown increasingly comfortable with evolution as a compelling explanation of many natural phenomena that is not in conflict with the basic spiritual teachings of the church – the current Pope, Francis I, has made statements to this effect (McKenna, 2014). Evolution is taught in Catholic schools around the world. It should also be pointed out, though, that some Catholic leaders have spoken out against evolution, and the Daylight Origins Society is not the only unofficial Catholic organization that opposes evolution and argues for creationism or intelligent design – others include the Kolber Center for the Study of Creation, based in Mt. Jackson, Virginia, and the Faith Movement based in England.

Second, another evangelical 'import' has also made inroads into Polish Catholic life. 'Post-abortion stress syndrome' or PASS (modeled on post-traumatic stress disorder) is an alleged mental illness suffered by women after having an abortion. The concept, promoted as being 'pro-woman, pro-life', and purporting to have the best interests of women at heart, has been much trumpeted by pro-life activists such as David C. Reardon, director of the Elliot Institute, an evangelical Christian organization based in Springfield, Illinois. Reardon has written numerous books about PASS. Yet PASS is not recognized either by the American Psychological

Association or the American Psychiatric Association, and recent research has failed to demonstrate any causal link between abortion and mental illness (e.g. Charles *et al.*, 2008). In 2004, however, the Polish Ombudsman for Children's Rights, along with two scientific institutions (the Polish Academy of Science's Committee for Demographic Studies and the Institute for Psychiatry and Neurology), hosted a conference in Warsaw devoted to PASS (Włodarczyk, 2010). As Włodarczyk points out, the imprimatur conferred on this, to say the least, questionable concept by the Polish academic authorities is remarkable. The fact that (unlike in the case of creationism and intelligent design) the Catholic Church has a long-standing record of opposition to abortion does not in the slightest justify (though it may explain) the involvement of these scholarly bodies. It seems clear that the pseudoscience of PASS touched a nerve in Polish academia, which, perhaps allied with an apparent lack of suspicion of the concept's origins, gained an acceptance there which it would probably not have obtained at any mainstream American university or comparable institution.

Thus, in these two different areas, ideological positions associated with North American evangelical conservatism can be seen to have entered Polish Catholic conservative discourse. As with hostility to homosexuality, so in the case of creationism and anti-abortionism there proved to be powerful resonances between frequently expressed evangelical positions and prominent Polish Catholic positions. I do not believe that this convergence necessarily aided the missionaries of Lighthouse School, or indeed any other evangelical missionaries in Poland, in recruiting new members for their church – perhaps precisely because such conservative views were already affirmed by many voices from within Polish Catholicism (and in some cases from the central Roman Catholic Church). Nevertheless, the discussion on April 28, along with the other examples outlined above, show that while in theological terms the gulf between evangelicals and Catholics may be large, in social and cultural matters the two sides were often extraordinarily close.

Grounds of Encounter

There were, finally, spaces – some connected with Lighthouse School, some not – where the 'two cultures' encountered one another in ways that caused them to some extent to interpenetrate.

My first inkling of the gulf between evangelical Christians and Roman Catholics came many years ago, in 2003, when I was conducting an interview with Elisabeth, an American student teacher in an ESL teacher education program at a small evangelical university in the American Mid-South. Near the beginning of the interview, I asked if Elisabeth had ever been abroad, and she told me she had been to Hungary, where she had stayed with a host family. I asked how that had been. She indicated that at the beginning there had been some problems because 'My family that I lived with wasn't, wasn't Christian – they were Catholic'. This statement shocked me profoundly at the time, since until then I had always thought of Catholics as Christians (as, indeed, do most Catholics). I began to understand that among many evangelicals there is a perception that Catholicism is not 'true' Christianity since, foremost among many reasons, Catholics generally cannot be said to have a personal relationship with Jesus Christ. It was at this point too that I began to notice how the term 'Christian' is used by evangelical Christians exclusively to refer to their own form of Christianity, and is used contrastively with 'Catholic' and other such terms. We saw an example of this earlier in the present chapter, in the way that Defoe's text about tolerance was rewritten by the Lighthouse materials designers such that the word 'Protestant' was replaced with the word 'Christian'.

These perceptions were reinforced as I began preliminary work on the present project in 2006 by surveying various evangelical websites devoted to missionary work in Europe, and specifically Poland. In those early stages, the working title of my project was 'From Mary to Jesus'. This title was taken from an evangelical electronic newsletter entitled 'thE-TASK' devoted to 'student missions'; the April 2005 issue of this newsletter included a focus on Poland and spoke of 'Leading Poles from Mary to Jesus' (thE-TASK Newsletter, April 2005), in other words, leading them away from a mistaken adoration of the Virgin Mary and toward a personal relationship with Jesus Christ. Numerous other websites that I surveyed in the course of this preparatory research expressed similar sentiments. A Greater Europe Mission page devoted to Poland said that many in Poland are 'mired in empty tradition' (Greater Europe Mission, 2006). A SEND International Christian World Mission page about Poland quoted the Bible: 'Like the Jews of Paul's day, Poles have "a zeal for God not in accordance with knowledge" (Rom 10:2)' (SEND International, 2006). A web page called www.christforpoland.com said, 'the Poles are very religious yet many are missing out on a personal relationship with God through Jesus Christ' (ChristForPoland, 2006). At the time of writing in October 2015, many similar kinds of materials may be found on the internet.[4]

Thus, entering the study I saw evangelical attitudes as profoundly inimical to Catholicism – that is, east is east and west is west, and that the two versions of Christianity were fundamentally irreconcilable. Yet as often happens in the course of sustained research, many of the things I subsequently heard and observed made me question my initial assumptions.

First, I became aware of a movement within the Catholic Church called Charismatic Catholicism. This will be no news to theologians and those in religious studies, but from my own perspective it was something new that complicated the neat division I had created in my mind. The charismatic movement in numerous denominations borrows from Pentecostalism a renewed interest in the gifts (Greek, 'charismata') of the Holy Spirit,[5] and in practice it can bear a close resemblance to aspects of evangelical Christianity, including lively services, the incorporation of such elements as healing and prophesying, and above all an emphasis on a personal relationship with Jesus Christ. Charismatic Catholicism, which began in the 1960s and 1970s, is now a significant minority movement within the Roman Catholic Church. It has been recognized by several recent popes, including Paul VI, John Paul II and Benedict XVI.

Several Poles I met who were members of evangelical churches had come to evangelicalism through involvement in charismatic activities within the Polish Catholic Church. Indeed, some evangelical Poles continued this involvement after their evangelical baptism. Others attended evangelical services while still being members of the Catholic Church. It was stories like this that made me realize that the boundary between Catholicism and evangelicalism was in fact not a boundary at all, but a permeable border zone.

Some of the evangelical missionaries I spoke to had active contacts with charismatic Catholic priests: one of these was Jean, Lighthouse's interim director in the fall semester. In the city of R., about 180 miles west of N., I also met with Sarah, an American who was the longest-serving missionary of all those I encountered in the country (at the time of the study, she had been living in R. for almost 20 years). Sarah was also one of the most fascinating people I spoke to during my study. She worked at one of the few evangelical seminaries in the country. She explained that the longer she served in her role, the less concerned she had become about denominational designations and the more interested she was simply in the life of the spirit. Sarah told me that she had become quite heavily involved in meetings with charismatic Catholic priests in R.

But perhaps the most surprising example of all was that of Pippa, a British woman who for 15 years had served in R. as a missionary for the Navigators, a missionary organization whose UK website declares that its goal is 'to help individuals and communities of believers to know Christ and make him known' (Navigators UK, 2015). At the time of the study, Pippa was director of studies at a small language school affiliated with a Baptist church in R. Near the beginning of my interview with her, I asked Pippa about her 'religious background', expecting to hear the story of when she was reborn and became a 'Christian', that is to say, an evangelical

Christian. However, to my considerable surprise it turned out that almost a year before the interview, Pippa had formally become a member of the Catholic Church. What was more, she was still working for the Navigators as a missionary. Of all my moments of encounter during the study, this was the one that most deeply rocked my sense of the two 'cultures' being separate. The full story was as follows, as explained by Pippa:

> **Pippa:** [*laughs*] My religious background is Protestant [BJ: Mhm]. But I'm actually a Catholic. I, I became a Catholic, um, just a little less than a year ago [BJ: Really]. After, I mean, after a very very long, I mean several years of [*1 sec*], because I'm not, I'm a missionary supported by an organization which in Britain is Protestant [BJ: Mhm] and I wasn't really, um, ready I think to take the risk of, you know, showing my true colors. But actually, um, the Navigators is an ecumenical organization, and –
> **BJ:** So they're OK, they're OK with you –
> **Pippa:** And I mean in Catholic countries most people in the Navigators are Catholics [*laughs*]
> **BJ:** Oh really. OK.
> **Pippa:** And we have, we have another, we have a missionary, a British missionary, who's um, he's um, he's in, he's in the Coptic Church because he works in Ethiopia. [BJ: Mhm]. And I think, um, I mean I, I changed churches, it wasn't connected with what I do as, with my mission [BJ: Mhm] it was connected with my relationship with God. [BJ: Mhm] Um, and, you know, what, what, um, the, the, the kind of, um, I think I just, for me personally I discovered a much richer, um, a much richer and deeper spirituality in the Catholic Church [BJ: Uh-huh]. And the Catholic Church in Poland is, um, is very active, very evan-, not, I mean not all of it [BJ: Mhm], but it's much more evangelical and much more active I would say. And because it's the national church then it has, there are doors that have opened to me since I've been in the Catholic Church less than a year which just never would have opened if I w-, w-. In the Protestant Church I just didn't do very much. I went to church on a Sunday [BJ: Mhm, mhm]. Um, I don't think women do a lot of teaching in the Protestant Church in Poland, but I've done a lot since I've [*laughs*] been in the Catholic Church [BJ: Uh-huh]. So I think, it just has opened doors to me that. But I, that wasn't my reason, um, for, for, for making that decision [BJ: Mhm], but um the, the Catholic Church in Poland, a certain

> part of the Catholic Church in Poland is very evangelical, does a lot of outreach; um, and [*3 secs*] a lot of [*2 secs*] – they do Alpha[6]. I don't know if, I don't know, I didn't come across Alpha in the Protestant Church here. Maybe, maybe it is [BJ: Mhm], but, um, the Catholic churches are very, very you know, involved in Alpha [BJ: Mhm, mhm] and, um, so, yeah. [BJ: Hm]. So that, yeah, that's my religious background [*laughs*].

Of the numerous striking aspects of Pippa's story, two stand out. First, the idea of a Protestant missionary organization accepting a missionary's membership in a non-Protestant church is remarkable – though it should also serve as a reminder that not all missionaries are Protestant, and that ecumenism is indeed possible in the mission field as well as elsewhere (though such a notion has not been apparent thus far in the present study). Second, when Pippa stated that there was much more evangelism and outreach in the Catholic Church than in the Baptist church she was affiliated with, one cannot but be struck by the seeming paradox – is it not the case that the evangelical missionaries described in this book were present in Poland precisely because the Catholic Church was allegedly not offering its adherents a true version of Christianity? Of course, Pippa did qualify her claim by acknowledging that only some parts of the Catholic Church engaged in these activities. Also, we should remember that her perspective was very intra-Polish, and she was talking about a Polish Baptist church with Polish leadership, not a foreign-led mission. Nevertheless, Pippa's mention of Catholic evangelicalism and ecumenical mission work is a powerful reminder that the neat binary opposition between evangelical and Catholic, American (or Canadian, or British) and Polish, is in many cases untenable, and that Protestant mission work in Poland over the last 20 years has led in some cases to such interpenetration that new categories are needed – though such conceptual work must remain beyond the scope of the present book.

Conclusions

Where does all this leave us? Is Lighthouse School indeed a 'global contact zone' (Singh & Doherty, 2004) where 'disparate cultures meet, clash, and grapple with each other' (Pratt, 1992: 4)? Or is it rather, in MacCannell's (1992) terms, an 'empty meeting ground'? Does the concept of 'culture' help us understand what was observed at the school – in other words, can it be said to have any explanatory power?

It is certainly the case that the evidence presented here confirms the fact that even such apparently distinct and antithetical categories as 'evangelical' and 'Catholic' can never ultimately serve to distinguish individuals from one another. The existence of Poles who found themselves in both 'camps' at once, and even more the case of Pippa and her simultaneous identity as a member of the Catholic Church and an evangelical missionary, give the lie to this absolute categorization. Less extremely, the contacts that evangelical missionaries Jean and Sarah had with Catholic charismatics show the interbleeding of the two theologies.

Along the same lines, I was repeatedly struck by the eagerness with which the Polish Catholics in Sydney's class engaged in discussions on deep spiritual issues such as prayer and the Bible. Their enthusiasm was confirmed by interview comments from all the Catholic learners – Ania, Marysia and Zosia – expressing their enjoyment of the class and its spiritual dimension, and their admiration of Sydney. In other words, the individual 'culture' of the Catholic participants was undeniably affected by their encounter with the North American evangelicals running the school.

Yet, within the world of Lighthouse School itself, it can also be said that the notion of 'culture' served to maintain boundaries. While Ania, Marysia and Zosia were changed by their experiences at the school, none of them can be said to have changed their identity in terms of the labels they would attach to themselves. As Ania said, 'I have my own faith and I feel comfortable in it'. As shown in the previous chapter, while Ania appreciated many aspects of her classes from a personal and relational point of view, she had no interest in leaving the Catholic Church and becoming an evangelical. Likewise, though Sydney and Taryn had undoubtedly been profoundly changed by their experience of being in Poland, it cannot be said in any meaningful way to have been in the direction of 'becoming Polish'. Furthermore, as shown above, some of the points of 'contact' (on issues such as homosexuality) were a kind of cultural serendipity in which views happened to coincide, rather than arising through any process of actual mutual influence. Lastly, along similar lines, while 'ecumenical discourse' enabled conversation to take place, it is debatable whether what each side actually understood by such terms as Jesus Christ, prayer, Bible, church and so on, was significantly changed by the encounter. In any case, relatively little evidence of major changes of this kind could be seen in the data. Thus, in the context of Lighthouse School the notion of 'culture' in fact has some validity.

Finally, one key feature of the encounter at Lighthouse School was that it was in fact relatively one-sided. While the participants expressed admiration for certain 'American' traits such as openness and optimism, and in the context of the school at least may have tried to emulate them, I was not aware of parallel influences on the behavior, linguistic or otherwise, of the missionaries at the school. More broadly, the very fact that English was the medium of communication at the school, and that I never once heard any North American teacher[7] attempt to communicate with any participant in Polish, meant that linguistically speaking the 'influence' only went one way. In this, despite Taryn and Sydney's insistence that their mission was not a colonial operation, I perceived what I can only describe as a hegemonic colonial relation in which influence and change overwhelmingly moved in only one direction. To put this another way, in the course of the school's work it was very much more the case that the Poles involved were Americanized than that the North Americans were Polonized.

In sum, the cross-cultural encounter that took place at Lighthouse School influenced both sides, but unequally; and though there was mutual influence, it did not amount to significant interpenetration, at least in terms of gross identity categories such as 'evangelical' and 'Catholic'. For whatever reason, the compelling if troublesome notion of 'culture', of which I myself remain leery, came out of this encounter relatively unscathed.

Notes

(1) To some extent this is changing, especially among young people. But it's still largely true in formal encounters between strangers.
(2) Familiarity with the Bible is also common among Polish Lutherans. One contemporary Polish author I have translated, Jerzy Pilch, who was raised Lutheran, litters his books with biblical references and quotations, even though the subject of his prose is usually far from religious: See for instance his novels *His Current Woman* (2002) and *The Mighty Angel* (2009).
(3) To provide an interesting point of comparison, a 2001 Kaiser poll (The Henry J. Kaiser Family Foundation, 2001: 6) on attitudes to homosexuality in the US reported that: About three quarters (74%) of evangelical Christians believe homosexual behavior is morally wrong, compared to 48% of non-evangelical Christians, 40% of Catholics and 20% of those with no religious affiliation.
(4) See for example the SEND organization's page on Poland (SEND International, 2015); the Foursquare Missions International page devoted to the country (Foursquare Missions International, 2015); the European Christian Mission page on Poland (European Christian Mission, 2015); and the Poland Evangelical Mission page (Poland Evangelical Mission, 2015). Numerous other examples can be found.
(5) The nine charismata granted by the Holy Spirit are wisdom; the 'word of knowledge'; faith; healing; the working of miracles; prophecy; 'discerning of spirits'; the gift of tongues; and the interpretation of tongues (1 Corinthians 12:8-10).
(6) Alpha is a 10-week program, originating in Britain in the 1970s, that offers an introduction to Christianity. It is specially designed to be non-denominational, and is used by numerous Protestant denominations and also by the Catholic Church.
(7) The one person at the school who did try to use Polish was Mavis, who did not work as a teacher but ran the cafe and helped out in other operations of the school.

9 Conclusions

I began this study with certain questions, and indeed concerns, about the ways in which English teaching is being used for the purposes of mission work by evangelical Christian organizations. The study constituted a small way of gathering empirical data that can help to address these questions and find at least partial answers. Along the way, other questions that I did not anticipate arose and needed to be asked. Last, all along I have been touching on the matter of how my findings can be framed in conceptual terms, and what this might mean for future research. This concluding chapter will summarize the findings and look forward to future research and how it might be framed.

Concerns about the Use of English Teaching for Mission Work

Covertness? Coercion? Conversion?

The study described here was a small and intimate one. What it gained in looking in detail at the lives of relatively few participants, it lost in its capacity for generalizing. Of course, as has already been pointed out, qualitative studies like ethnographies are never intended to be generalizable. Their aim is primarily to explore the texture of a particular setting, and to try to understand it better. That was always my goal in the work described here.

Yet it is also true that the initial impulse to conduct this study arose from a desire to seek answers to some of the questions that had been raised generally about the use of English teaching in evangelical mission work. How do the findings of the study – what I observed at Lighthouse School – relate to those questions? Was the mission operation covert at Lighthouse School? Was coercion involved? Were the participants vulnerable?

In the case of Lighthouse, it cannot be said that the school's operations were covert. It's true that a certain amount of fudging went on. For instance, though Lighthouse's Polish-language website mentioned the school's 'Christian' (chrześciańskie) foundations, it did not explicitly describe these in terms of mission, nor did it give any denominational details or mention the church to which Lighthouse was attached. For Catholics consulting the site, the term 'Christian' is one that includes them – in Polish the word does not have the same meaning of 'evangelical' that it holds for evangelical Christians. Thus, the site chooses to obscure denominational differences. I noticed several other evasions of this kind in the school's dealings with potential participants.

Yet, the school's operations can hardly be called covert. Its religious dimension was abundantly in evidence, from the materials and the subsequent discussions in class, to the frequent presence of mission groups and the promotion of evangelical activities in the region, to the constant presence of Rysiek and other members of his church at school events. It is also the case that Sydney and Taryn saw their mission, not as bringing evangelical Christianity to their learners (see below), but much more broadly as ministering to the latter's spiritual needs. In this respect, a more general religious vocabulary seems in fact appropriate.

We should also remember that those on the receiving end of Lighthouse School's efforts are not to be thought of as helpless victims either. As we have seen, many chose to attend the school despite warnings from friends or family that it was run by a 'sekta'. These participants were capable of making a choice, and they chose Lighthouse because they liked it – they liked the classes, the materials, the teachers and the atmosphere. At the same time, they chose *not* to be interested in the mission work of the church – Ania, as we have seen, had no desire to join the church, though in all other ways she appreciated the school. At no time during my work at Lighthouse school did I see any behavior that might be considered 'covert' on the part of the teachers or staff of the school. By the same token, nothing like coercion was in evidence either. Indeed, Stevick's (1996) claim about offering teaching in the 'free market' was literally true here, since Lighthouse was only one of dozens of language schools serving the population of N.

The question of conversion was for me one of the most fascinating aspects of the mission work going on in Poland. To put it bluntly, if the missions were to be judged by the numbers they brought into their respective churches, the missionary teachers I encountered were not successful. In the city of N., the only baptisms that I witnessed during the nine months I was at the school were administered by the American Baptist mission. In April, a group of three adults – two young Polish women and the Colombian husband of a Polish evangelical – were all baptized together in the pool of a sports complex. No one from the school joined Rysiek's church during the study. In K., the Anabaptists had not had a single conversion in seven years.

As I got further and further into the study, though, it became ever clearer that for many missionaries conversion was not necessarily the goal. Time and again, the missionaries I spoke to reiterated the fact that they were there, not to convert, but simply to share the Word of God. Indeed, one of the sources of frustration that the church in D. had expressed was that Sydney and Taryn were not bringing enough new members into the church. Clearly, then, such thinking *did* exist among some church authorities, and it surfaced in some of the interviews I conducted – for example with Ray, who preached to the Roma and was very much interested in numbers. But equally, it was rejected by others, including Sydney and Taryn, who did not regard this as the guiding purpose of their mission work. In fact, the great majority of the missionaries I interviewed for this study echoed Sydney and Taryn's position. Thus, one of my founding questions – how can Polish Catholics be 'converted' to evangelical Christianity – turned out to be fundamentally flawed as a starting point. The matter of conversion is infinitely more complex than it seems.

Imperialism and neocolonialism

A further set of concerns raised about the use of English teaching for evangelical Christian mission work was its purported participation in, or at the very least alignment with, broader geopolitical agendas. Is it the case that evangelical Christian mission work is related in a meaningful way with US neo-imperialism? That missionaries re-enact colonial relations? That they encourage an unthinking adherence to capitalism and promote conservative values like militarism and homophobia?

In this regard, the picture is less clear. Certainly, when I raised the question of neocolonialism, Taryn said she had never considered such a thing, that as a Canadian she felt that this was alien to her thinking and that she did not think such a perspective reflected accurately what the school was about.

Yet in fact, in much of the mission work I observed there were indications both of neocolonial thinking and of an alignment with Western capitalist values. The clearest example of the former was Sydney and Taryn's continued use of English, not just in the school, where of course it was appropriate, but also in the church, as commented on by Ola (see Chapter 8). Unequal language relations, in which one side learns the other's language but not vice versa, are typical of hegemonic and indeed colonial relations. Of course, language schools all around the world reproduce such one-way relationships, and the hegemony of English is particularly marked. Yet, this does not diminish the fact that Lighthouse School at times felt like a colonial enterprise. As mentioned, the other teachers too largely failed to learn Polish even after relatively long stints in the country. In this sense, the colonial origins of Pratt's (1992) concept of the contact zone seem in fact rather appropriate. I also thought of such relations as I heard Ola's complaints about never being invited to Sydney and Taryn's apartment. They came to mind too when I visited K. Here, the Anabaptists running the mission lived in a compound that included houses they and other church members had built themselves. Furthermore, they homeschooled their children rather than sending them to Polish schools, and in other ways also were rather isolated from the Poles they lived among – again reminding me of colonial arrangements.

As concerns 'conservative values', it must be stated clearly that Anabaptists believe in a strict separation of earthly and spiritual powers, and do not take part in worldly politics – they do not vote and do not serve in the military. In this respect, they are interestingly different from many other evangelicals, some of whom can be quite bellicose. I did not hear any warmongering from the evangelicals I met in Poland. But other conservative values were indeed in evidence. As mentioned in Chapter 5, part of the Lighthouse curriculum revolved around business language, and the school often organized or promoted seminars on business topics. As explained earlier, both Sydney and Taryn came from business backgrounds, and it could be said that free-market capitalism was an unspoken default value in the school. And as for 'promoting homophobia' – as seen in Chapter 8, homophobic views were certainly expressed in class by both students and teacher; perhaps they were not vigorously 'promoted', but they were certainly encouraged and reinforced, a process considerably enabled by the fact that such views were already prominent and often unquestioned in the Polish setting.

A last observation might serve to mitigate the foregoing. At the risk of sounding patronizing, I have to say that at numerous moments during my research I was struck by the sheer naivety of some of the missionary efforts. The generalities of Allie's mini-sermons are a case in point (see Chapter 6). I also spoke to Ray, a Baptist missionary from upstate New York who had come to Poland to minister to the Roma population in the southeast. He knew very little about the Roma before he arrived in the country. He began his work by simply preaching the gospel on the street, in English. Such approaches reflect the 'innocence' that Zimmerman (2006) takes as one of his themes. Innocence in adults is a quality that can be both endearing and irresponsible: it can charm, but it can also reflect a lack of understanding – of the ways of the world, of how people are, of what constitutes persuasive rhetoric – that at times can be reprehensible. Both these facets of innocence were apparent in the words and actions of several of the missionaries in Poland.

Quality of teaching

Another of the concerns expressed about English teaching as mission work is the quality of the teaching being offered. Many TESOL professionals, including evangelicals such as Snow (2001), have expressed the worry that missionary zeal might in some cases be considered an adequate substitute for professional competence. Non-evangelicals suggest that such teaching will bring the field as a whole into disrepute; evangelicals are additionally troubled by the idea that the same will happen to their religion.

We need to remember, of course, that bad teaching is not the exclusive preserve of poorly trained missionaries. TESOL has wrestled for decades with its status as a 'profession', and a perennial concern is that, especially (though not always) in EFL contexts, it can be only too easy for an unqualified person to land a job as a teacher. The status of the native speaker is still frequently sufficient 'proof' of one's suitability for the position. Such matters have been written about extensively in the TESOL literature and need not be re-examined here; my point is simply that substandard English teaching remains a significant concern for the entire field of English teaching.

In pedagogical terms, the teaching I saw in Poland was mostly unexceptionable. The best instruction I witnessed was at the language school in R. that was affiliated with a Baptist church. Both classes I observed there were taught extremely professionally, with appropriate high-quality materials, good pacing and effective use of class time. Both teachers were well-trained and highly experienced, and it showed. At the other end of the spectrum was Allie, who, as mentioned, was often unprepared for class, and unable to offer accurate and helpful grammar and vocabulary explanations. Yet it also needs to be remembered that Jean was embarrassed at not having had the opportunity to observe Allie's teaching, and that Jean seemed aware of Allie's shortcomings and let her go after the fall semester.

For the rest, most of the teaching I saw was at least acceptable. As mentioned elsewhere, Sydney remained somewhat uncomfortable teaching grammar, and this was not necessarily her forte. Yet Sydney was mindful of this, and had worked hard to gain at least an adequate understanding of English grammar and how to teach it. I did not observe any egregious problems in the language-focused portions of her classes – rather, there were simply moments where I felt things could have been done a little differently (though that is of course always the case when one teacher observes another teacher's class). Overall, and with certain exceptions as mentioned, I cannot say that, pedagogically speaking, the standard of the teaching I saw differed significantly from a great deal of the language teaching I have observed over many years in the field. The same was not always true of the materials – as pointed out in Chapter 5, these often left something to be desired in both their overall arrangement and their specific wording. It was here that Sydney and Taryn's lack of professional preparation most showed. On the other hand, the liveliness of the class discussions that arose from these materials was definitely a pedagogical point in their favor.

Local Generalizations

Much of what was said above emphasized what Lighthouse School was *not*. But what *was* it then? What generalizations can be usefully made of this particular setting?

Lighthouse School was very definitely different from all the other language schools I visited, read about or heard of in Poland, and indeed in the region. The overt focus on spiritual subject matter, anchored in the Bible-based materials that Sydney and Taryn had created, was highly unusual. Furthermore, in pedagogical terms the materials were also successful. The learners' consistent engagement in classroom discussions showed that motivation was high, and the fact that the learners' linguistic resources were being stretched so consistently is a clear indication that they were repeatedly being given the most useful kinds of challenges for their growing competence.

From the point of view of content, and specifically the management of the Catholic–evangelical encounter taking place in the classroom, Sydney's deployment of what I have termed 'ecumenical discourse' was the key ingredient in making this encounter both possible and, in a certain sense, successful. Though its 'success' in terms of bringing new members into the church was questionable, nevertheless it made it possible for Catholics and evangelicals from across denominational and cultural divides to talk about spiritual matters in ways that were meaningful to each side and to all participants. As has been seen, the participants were highly appreciative of the opportunities for meaningful, interesting conversations that simultaneously helped them improve their English language skills in practical ways – through use, rather than for instance the memorizing of vocabulary and grammar rules or the completion of exercises.

It was also the case that the management of the Polish–Catholic encounter was facilitated by several key elements of overlap between the two traditions represented. Aside from the obvious religious commonalities – precisely those shared points of reference that Sydney exploited so ably through ecumenical discourse – there were also conservative political views that, whether or not by chance, aligned the two sides. In thinking ahead to possible directions for future research, such a confluence of views may well exist in other contexts, and might even help to explain the powerful rise of evangelical Christianity in numerous countries around the world.

Such occasional confluences of views aside, I sometimes had the sense that Sydney and Taryn were performing, rather skillfully, a multifaceted balancing act. They managed to be welcoming yet, apart from a couple of exceptions referred to early, without putting people off; they offered a pedagogical service that their learners valued highly while also being concerned above all for those learners' spiritual well-being; they juggled the needs of the school they ran and the church with which it was affiliated. Furthermore, they had to reconcile their own passion for, and commitment to, mission work with the varying levels of restrictions placed on women in evangelical ministry (see below). It is to their great credit that they survived and indeed thrived while juggling these multiple desires, goals and constraints.

At the same time, darker aspects of the enterprise cannot be overlooked. Two points can be mentioned. First, even in Sydney and Taryn I detected a certain a lack of awareness of the political dimensions of their undertaking. As mentioned above, Taryn seemed blindsided by the notion of a neocolonial dimension to the work of Lighthouse School. In Sydney's class, I was frequently surprised at the absence of any discussion of the racial, colonial and class dimensions of *Robinson Crusoe*. Likewise, Sydney and Taryn's failure to use Polish even in their dealings with their church bespoke the presence of certain underlying hegemonic values.

The second point is the notion of 'the truth'. This word cropped up frequently in the interviews I conducted with Sydney and Taryn, and even found its way into the teacher's notes for the materials (see Chapter 5). For me, each mention brought with it all the associations of zealotry and intolerance that it carries for many non-evangelicals. These were moments when my own openness was maximally under strain, and when the enterprise of Lighthouse School seemed most questionable. It seems to me that evangelicals' belief that they alone possess 'the truth' is the most problematic aspect of the use of English teaching in mission work, profoundly affecting as it does the multiple dimensions – spiritual, political, cultural – that are in play in a context like Lighthouse School.

Conceptualizing Lighthouse School

As stated at the beginning of this book, I chose not to use a strong theoretical framework for an exploratory study such as this. Rather, I wanted the lived reality of the school to come through. I've preferred merely to indicate interesting theoretical directions that others who pick up this line of research may wish to explore. I'd like to mention three in particular here: gender studies; critical pedagogy; and discourse analysis.

Concerns about gender have threaded all through this book. Those who inhabit the world of evangelical Christianity are ever conscious of gender identity. In the great majority of contexts, restrictions of one kind or another are placed on the part that women can play in ministry and in missions. At one level, the story of Lighthouse can be read as that of two dynamic women who kicked against the pricks – who found ways to engage actively and creatively in mission work on their own terms, often, as we have seen, struggling against authorities that did not accept such an active and independent role for women in the mission field. More broadly, the interplay among missions, gender and English teaching seems ripe for examination. In TESOL, a field in which the great majority of teachers are female, the gender and power dynamics of mission work are particularly complex and interesting. If one factors in certain other concerns in the field of gender studies, such as the issues of sexual orientation and identity that also cropped up throughout this study, it is clear that such a perspective could provide a fruitful conceptual base for further inquiry.

Another useful conceptual perspective is that offered by critical pedagogy. Pennycook and Coutand-Marin (2004) took the evangelicals to task for their lack of a critical perspective on the phenomenon of mission work. I suggested above that this criticism was justified in the case of Lighthouse School, and that there was a significant and troubling lack of how the mission project of Lighthouse might relate to unequal patterns of national and cultural relations across the globe. Specifically, the neocolonial dimensions of mission work need to be explored further. In Chapter 1, in explaining why I call this study an ethnography of contact, I quoted from Pratt's book, which is itself an account of 19th-century colonial travel writing. It should at the very least give us pause that a description taken from a book on Victorian-era colonial relations should resonate so strongly in the context of a 21st-century evangelical mission in Central Europe. The colonial dimensions of Christian missions have been extensively described and analyzed from a historical point of view (see e.g. Willinsky, 1998). The application of such a framework to present-day missions, linking them for instance to American neo-imperialism (as suggested by Edge [2003]

The discourse of the mission

Lastly, if I am a true believer in anything, it is in the usefulness of discourse analytic approaches to the study of language use. Since the first class in discourse analysis that I took from Julian Edge in the late 1980s, I've been convinced that a major key to understanding our assumptions, values, motivations, anxieties and passions lies in paying close attention to our use of language. Specifically, I believe that the insights of discursive psychology (Edwards & Potter, 1992; Potter & Wetherell, 1987) can be extremely helpful in teasing out the meanings of encounters such as those in classrooms. It was essentially a discursive psychological approach that allowed me to identify and describe what I call ecumenical discourse as it was deployed in Sydney's class. I believe that discursive psychology, and more generally the insights of discourse analysis, offer a fertile vein for future conceptual work on the topic.

I have to say, though, that, much as this conceptual work is interesting and can shed light on various aspects of teaching-based mission work, I still feel dissatisfied with the conceptual frameworks on offer, and I feel that none of them quite helps us get to the heart of what is going on. None, for example, really helps in conceptualizing the issues of relation explored in Chapter 7, or the anxieties about 'conversion' that run through this book. As I conclude this study, I continue to search for useful ways to organize and understand what I saw, heard and read during my year at Lighthouse School.

Future Research

The limitations of the present study are manifold and manifest. It was small in scale, and it looked in detail at only one setting in one national and cultural context. Furthermore, the targets of the evangelical Christian mission described here were middle-class white Europeans who had themselves been brought up in a Christian tradition.

It would be fascinating to read accounts of mission-based English teaching in contexts that differ significantly from that of Lighthouse School. How do things look in other continents? With less affluent populations? Across other, deeper religious divides?

Though the methodology of this study, like any other, has its limitations, I do think it crucial to go beyond interview data in researching matters of such delicacy and importance. One major complaint about the empirical research done so far – including my own previous work (Varghese & Johnston, 2007) – is that almost all of it revolves around teacher identity and its data comprise almost exclusively interviews with, or surveys of, evangelical teachers. This is true even of Baurain's (2013) dissertation-length study, and also of the studies collected in Wong *et al.* (2013). What teachers say is, of course, of great value, and even in the present study I spent a lot of time interviewing teachers at Lighthouse and elsewhere. Yet if we are to get a full and accurate picture of what English teaching in the mission field looks like, we absolutely have to include classroom data, materials, and other data sources, as well as interviews with learners and other stakeholders. It is such studies that are needed.

The other complaint I have about the empirical (data-based) research done so far is that, with the exception of Varghese and myself, it has all been conducted by researchers who are themselves evangelical Christians. I do not blame these researchers – far from it, I applaud their commitment to data-based inquiry. Rather, I call on non-evangelical researchers to play their part. If the worries expressed by Edge (2003), Pennycook and Coutand-Marin (2004) and others are of interest to us – and by us I mean precisely those researchers among us who are not evangelical Christians – it behooves us to go out and gather data. Otherwise, we will have little empirical evidence to justify (or allay) our concerns.

Final Thoughts

As I have repeatedly said, this study was from the beginning conceived as a first tentative exploration. There is no doubt that further research is needed. Ethnographic work is labor-intensive and slow, and it would be unrealistic to call for many more studies of the kind reported on here. Nevertheless, we also need more than just data from websites and from interviews with teachers if we are to gain a better understanding of the ways in which English teaching is actually used in mission work. It would be fascinating to see more materials, to gain the perspectives of participants, to peek into classrooms in other schools, countries and cultures. Such work would give us a richer picture of real settings, and no doubt, further challenge the claims and preconceptions of evangelicals and non-evangelicals alike.

On this last subject, I commented early on in the book about the virulence of non-evangelical attitudes toward evangelical Christianity. Though this is a huge topic in itself, and one that certainly cannot be dealt with adequately in a brief concluding chapter, a few words should nevertheless be said on the subject.

Where does this intense feeling come from? One answer is that to a significant extent, (mis)perceptions of evangelicals arise from the fact that the non-evangelical world overwhelmingly gets its information about evangelicals from indirect sources, primarily the mass media. And in the mass media, it is the most strident and extreme voices that dominate, while moderate or opposing voices, because they are less newsworthy, do not see the light of day. Thus, for instance, any American is familiar with the extreme religious views of Pat Robertson, whereas the sizeable progressive movement in evangelicalism (e.g. Wallis, 2005) is never mentioned.

There is no doubt that, for example, opposition to women's rights, gay rights, and environmental protection is frequently voiced in evangelical circles, both among the leadership and regular church members. Such positions are, of course, deeply antithetical to the beliefs of many non-evangelicals, especially the educated and often progressive-aligned circles from which many TESOL researchers and teachers are drawn.

Yet there is another facet to this situation. Non-evangelicals – in TESOL and elsewhere – are getting their information about (and hence attitudes toward) evangelicals from the media – but that is their only source. For reasons that in part have been touched on in this book, in real life evangelicals and non-evangelicals carefully steer clear of one another. This can be seen as part of a larger social change. In the last two decades or so, in the country I've chosen to call home there has been a disturbing tendency. Ideological opponents on both sides of the political spectrum are less and less willing to engage with one another in sustained, respectful, measured discussion. Increasingly, members of a particular political or other ideological group – whether it be political progressives, evangelical Christians or whatever – are choosing to restrict their discursive universe as much as possible to others of their own kind. The proliferation of TV channels and, especially, online news sites has facilitated this process. Indeed, it is even demographic: in his book *The Big Sort*, Bishop (2008) documents how like-minded people increasingly elect to live in communities where the great majority of the population thinks as they do. Bishop is right to suggest how easy it is to enclose oneself in a discourse community of one's choosing. And the 'big sort' that he describes is not restricted to the US – I see a similar separation happening in many other countries, including Poland, where for instance those on the far right and members of the more moderate parties seem less and less capable of meaningful dialogue.

I find this trend an insidious one. It condones and even encourages demagogy, lazy and complacent thinking, isolationism and intolerance, on all sides. Worse, it causes us to lose sight of one of the deepest truths of life – that we must exist in a world in which many people we come into contact with hold views that are radically different from, and often inimical to, our own. In a healthy society, each side in a given debate is strong and confident enough to actually listen to the perspectives and arguments of the other side, and, just occasionally, to admit that they might have a point. Yet, as Bishop suggests, many of us are in danger of losing our ability to properly listen to those different from ourselves. We – our whole society – do not seem strong and confident; rather, we appear anxious and even paranoid, fearful that the 'other' will take over, and perhaps that we ourselves will be changed. Interestingly, Bishop (2008: 286–287) cites work by Mutz (2006) indicating that '[t]he more educated Americans become – and the richer – the less likely they are to discuss politics with those who have different points of view. [...] Those who have suffered through graduate school have the most homogenous political lives'. I take that last sentence, in particular, as a meaningful caution to myself and others like me.

The making of this book did indeed change me; but not in the dramatic sense of my own identity. I was not converted, I did not become an evangelical. What happened was that my world was expanded to include the voices, views and wishes of those I worked with, evangelicals and Catholics alike. I did not embrace those views, but I came to understand them better. And it is my deepest belief that understanding and dialogue are the only valid ways to engage with those different from ourselves. The alternative is disrespect, dismissal, scorn, fear – and, eventually, conflict and violence. This book has been my small attempt to listen and to understand.

Appendix A: Transcription Conventions and A Note on Translation

In rendering interviews and classroom interaction, I have used broad transcriptions except in a few places where narrower information is helpful. My aim has been above all to concentrate on what is said. Where possible, speakers are identified by name. Otherwise, the following conventions are observed:

S:	unidentified student
SS:	more than one student
[??]:	inaudible matter
[9 secs]:	length of pause longer than one second
[laughter]:	'stage directions' indicating non-verbal actions, tone of voice, etc.
[=Here it is]:	translation of something said in Polish, or clarification of meaning of an English word or phrase misused and open to misinterpretation

All the Polish participants in the study elected to be interviewed in Polish. All the excerpts from their interviews that appear in this book were translated by the author.

References

'Abortion Laws', wiki article, 2 December 2009. See http://upload.wikimedia.org/wikipedia/commons/a/a5/Abortion_Laws.svg (accessed 10 February 2015).
Appadurai, A. (1996) *Modernity at Large. Cultural Dimensions of Globalization*. Minneapolis, MN: University of Minnesota Press.
Balmer, R. (2010) *The Making of Evangelicalism: From Revivalism to Politics and Beyond*. Waco, TX: Baylor University Press.
'Baptist Union of Poland', wiki article, October 27 2011. See http://en.wikipedia.org/wiki/Baptist_Union_of_Poland (accessed 2 July 2012).
Baran, E.B. (2006) Negotiating the limits of religious pluralism in post-Soviet Russia: The anticult movement in the Russian Orthodox Church, 1990–2004. *The Russian Review* 65, 637–656.
Baran, E.B. (2007) Contested victims: Jehovah's Witnesses and the Russian Orthodox Church, 1990–2004. *Religion, State and Society* 35 (3), 261–278.
Baurain, B. (2007) Christian witness and respect for persons. *Journal of Language, Identity, and Education* 6, 201–219.
Baurain, B. (2013) Religious faith, teacher knowledge, and overseas Christian ESOL teachers. PhD dissertation, University of Nebraska.
Bebbington, D.W. (1989) *Evangelism in Modern Britain: A History from the 1730s to the 1980s*. London: Unwin Hyman.
Berscheid, E. and Peplau, L.A. (1983) The emerging science of relationships. In H.H. Kelley, E. Berscheid, A. Christensen, J.H. Harvey, T.L. Huston, G. Levinger, E. McClintock, L.A. Peplau and D.R. Peterson (eds) *Close Relationships* (pp. 1–19). San Francisco, CA: Freeman.
Bielo, J.S. (2009) *Words Upon the Word: An Ethnography of Evangelical Group Bible Study*. New York: New York University Press.
Bishop, B. (2008) *The Big Sort: Why the Clustering of Like-minded America is Tearing Us Apart*. New York: Houghton Mifflin Harcourt.
Booth, W.C. (1988) *The Company We Keep: The Ethics of Fiction*. Berkeley, CA: University of California Press.
Bradley, C.A. (2009) Spiritual lessons learned from a language teacher. In M.S. Wong and S. Canagarajah (eds) *Christian and Critical English Language Educators in Dialogue: Pedagogical and Ethical Dilemmas* (pp. 235–241). New York: Routledge.
Burbules, N.C. (1993) *Dialogue in Teaching: Theory and Practice*. New York: Teachers College Press.
Canagarajah, A.S. (2013) Foreword. In M.S. Wong, C. Kristjánsson and Z. Dörnyei (eds) *Christian Faith and English Language Teaching and Learning* (pp. xxi–xxiii). New York: Routledge.
CBOS (2005a) *Akceptacja Praw dla Gejów i Lesbijek i Społeczny Dystans Wobec Nich*. See http://www.cbos.pl/SPISKOM.POL/2005/K_127_05.PDF (accessed 22 October 2015).
CBOS (2005b) *Prawo do Publicznych Demonstracji Gejów i Lesbijek*. See http://www.cbos.pl/SPISKOM.POL/2005/K_193_05.PDF (accessed 22 October 2015).

CBOS (2012) *Zmiany w Zakresie Wiary i Religijności Polaków po Śmierci Jana Pawła II*. See http://cbos.pl/SPISKOM.POL/2012/K_049_12.PDF (accessed 17 February 2015).
CBOS (2013) *Stosunek do Praw Gejów i Lesbijek oraz Związków Partnerskich*. See http://www.cbos.pl/SPISKOM.POL/2013/K_024_13.PDF (accessed 17 February 2015).
Charles, V., Polis, C., Sridhara, S. and Blum, R. (2008) Abortion and long-term mental health outcomes: A systematic review of the evidence. *Contraception* 78 (6), 436–450.
ChristForPoland (2006) 'Formal Religion'. See www.christforpoland.com/FormalReligion.html (accessed 30 August 2006).
Clifford, J. (1997) *Routes: Travel and Translation in the Late Twentieth Century*. Cambridge, MA: Harvard University Press.
Coetzee, J.M. (1986) *Foe*. London: Penguin.
Cooper, R. and Brubaker, F. (2000) Beyond 'identity'. *Theory & Society* 29, 1–47.
Cox, H. (1993) *Fire from Heaven: The Rise of Pentecostal Spirituality and the Reshaping of Religion in the Twenty-first Century*. Cambridge, MA: Di Capo Press.
Defoe, D. (1968) *Robinson Crusoe* (J. Sutherland ed.). Boston, MA: Houghton Mifflin Harcourt (original work published 1719).
Dudley, J. (2011) *Broken Words: The Abuse of Science and Faith in American Politics*. New York: Crown.
Easton, A. (2006) Fears of Poland's gay community. *BBC News*, 10 June. See http://news.bbc.co.uk/2/hi/europe/5068318.stm (accessed 22 October 2015).
The Economist (2016) Lexington: Franklin Graham's promised land. 418 (8971), 27.
Edge, J. (1996a) Cross-cultural paradoxes in a profession of values. *TESOL Quarterly* 30 (1), 9–30.
Edge, J. (1996b) Keeping the faith. *TESOL Matters* 6 (4), 1.
Edge, J. (2003) Imperial troopers and servants of the lord: A vision of TESOL for the 21st century. *TESOL Quarterly* 37 (4), 701–708.
Edwards, D. and Potter, J. (1992) *Discursive Psychology*. London: Sage.
European Christian Mission (2015) 'Poland'. See http://www.ecmi.org/europe/country/PL/ (accessed 22 October 2015).
Fehr, B. (1996) *Friendship Processes*. Thousand Oaks, CA: Sage.
Fetterman, D.M. (1989) *Ethnography Step by Step*. Newbury Park, CA: Sage.
Foursquare Missions International (2015) 'Poland'. See http://www.foursquaremissions.org/donate/country/poland/ (accessed 22 October 2015).
Glesne, C. and Peshkin, A. (1992) *Becoming Qualitative Researchers*. White Plains, NY: Longman.
Goffman, E. (1959) *The Presentation of Self in Everyday Life*. New York: Anchor Books.
Grabowska, M. (2008) Radio Maryja – polska prawica religijna. *Znak* 640 (9), 11–16.
Graves, K. (ed.) (1996) *Teachers as Course Developers*. New York: Cambridge University Press.
Greater Europe Mission (2006) 'Countries'. See https://www.gemission.org/Countries/Default.asp?ID=4 (accessed 28 August 2006).
Griffith, T. (2004) Unless a grain of wheat... *TESOL Quarterly* 38 (4), 714–716.
Guerrettaz, A.M. and Johnston, B. (2013) Materials in the classroom ecology. *Modern Language Journal* 97, 779–796.
Hartup, W.W. (1975) The origins of friendship. In M. Lewis and L.A. Rosenblum (eds) *Friendship and Peer Relations* (pp. 11–26). New York: Wiley.
The Henry J. Kaiser Family Foundation (2001) Inside-OUT: A Report on the Experiences of Lesbians, Gays and Bisexuals in America and the Public's Views on Issues and Policies Related to Sexual Orientation. See http://kff.org/hivaids/poll-finding/new-surveys-on-experiences-of-lesbians-gays/ (accessed 22 October 2015).

Instytut Statystyki Kościoła Katolickiego (2013a) 'dominicantes 2013'. See http://www.iskk.pl/kosciolnaswiecie/193-dominicantes-2013.html (accessed 11 February 2015).
Instytut Statystyki Kościoła Katolickiego (2013b) 'dominicantes 2009'. http://www.iskk.pl/kosciolnaswiecie/116-dominicantes-2009.html (accessed 11 February 2015).
Jassem, Z. (ed.) (1982) *Wielki Słownik polsko-angielski* [*Polish-English Dictionary*] (6th edn). Warsaw: Wiedza Powszechna.
Johnston, B. (2003) *Values in English Language Teaching*. Mahwah, NJ: Lawrence Erlbaum Associates.
Johnston, B. and Varghese, M. (2008) Neo-imperialism, evangelism, and ELT: Modernist missions and a postmodern profession. In J. Edge (ed.) *(Re)Locating TESOL in an Age of Empire* (pp. 195–207). Basingstoke: Palgrave Macmillan.
Kościół Jezusa Chrystusa Świętych w Dniach Ostatnich (2012) 'Polska'. See http://www.mormoni.pl/ (accessed 2 July 2012).
Kościół Zielonoświątkowy w Polsce (2012) Statystyka. See http://www.kzbb.org/ind.php?kzbb=statystyka (accessed 2 July 2012).
Kutschera, U. (2006) Devolution and dinosaurs: The anti-evolution seminar in the European parliament. *Reports of the National Center for Science Education* 26 (5), 10–11. See http://ncse.com/rncse/26/5/devolution-dinosaurs (accessed 22 October 2015).
Lausanne Movement (2016) 'The Manila Manifesto'. See https://www.lausanne.org/content/manifesto/the-manila-manifesto (accessed 12 February 2016).
Lincoln, Y.S. and Guba, E.G. (1985) *Naturalistic Inquiry*. Newbury Park, CA: Sage.
Literacy and Evangelism International (2011) 'Mission'. See https://www.literacyevangelism.org/mission/ (accessed 26 May 2011).
Literacy and Evangelism International (2015) 'History'. See https://www.literacyevangelism.org/mission/history (accessed 27 February 2015).
Loptes, K.A. (2009) A preliminary survey of Christian English language teachers in countries that restrict missionary activity. In M.S. Wong and S. Canagarajah (eds) *Christian and Critical English Language Educators in Dialogue: Pedagogical and Ethical Dilemmas* (pp. 53–59). New York: Routledge.
Luterański Kościół Ewangelicko-Augsburski (2012) Statystyka: Luteranie w Polsce. See http://www.luteranie.pl/pl/index.php?D=22 (accessed 2 July 2012).
MacCannell, D. (1992) *Empty Meeting Grounds: The Tourist Papers*. London: Routledge.
Marshall, C. and Rossman, G.B. (1989) *Designing Qualitative Research*. Newbury Park, CA: Sage.
McKenna, J. (2014) 'Pope Francis: "Evolution… is not inconsistent with the notion of creation"'. *Religion News Service*, 27 October. See http://www.religionnews.com/2014/10/27/pope-francis-evolution-inconsistent-notion-creation/ (accessed 22 October 2015).
Midgley, M. (2001) *Wickedness*. London: Routledge (original work published 1984).
Mitchell, J. (1994) Sex kills. On *Turbulent Indigo* [CD]. Los Angeles, CA: Reprise Records/Crazy Crow Music.
Morgan, B. (2004) Teacher identity as pedagogy: Towards a field-internal conceptualization in bilingual and second language education. In J. Brutt-Griffler and M. Varghese (eds) *Re-writing Bilingualism and the Bilingual Educator's Knowledge Base* (pp. 80–96). Clevedon: Multilingual Matters.
Mutz, D.C. (2006) *Hearing the Other Side: Deliberative Versus Participatory Democracy*. New York: Cambridge University Press.
Nation, I.S.P. (1993) *Teaching and Learning Vocabulary*. London: Longman.

Navigators UK (2015) 'Who we are'. See http://navigators.co.uk/who-we-are/ (accessed 22 October 2015).
Nelson, C. (1999) Sexual identities in ESL: Queer theory and classroom inquiry. *TESOL Quarterly* 33, 371–391.
The Nielsen Company (2008) The Nielsen Company Issues Top Ten US Lists For 2008. See http://www.nielsen.com/content/dam/corporate/us/en/newswire/uploads/2008/12/nielsen-top-tens-2008-final15.pdf (accessed 14 June 2011).
Noddings, N. (1984) *Caring: A Feminine Approach to Ethics and Moral Education*. Berkeley, CA: University of California Press.
Noll, M. (2002) Evangelicals past and present. In E.L. Blumhofter (ed.) *Religion, Politics, and the American Experience: Reflections on Religion and American Public Life* (pp. 103–122). Tuscaloosa, AL: University of Alabama Press.
Pennycook, A. and Coutand-Marin, S. (2004) Teaching English as a missionary language (TEML). *Discourse: Studies in the Cultural Politics of Education* 24 (3), 338–353.
Peshkin, A. (1986) *God's Choice: The Total World of a Fundamentalist Christian School*. Chicago, IL: University of Chicago Press.
Pilch, J. (2002) *His Current Woman* (B. Johnston, trans.). Evanston, IL: Hydra Books.
Pilch, J. (2009) *The Mighty Angel* (B. Johnston, trans.). Rochester, NY: Open Letter.
Poland Evangelical Mission (2015) 'About Us'. See http://www.polandem.org/about-us/ (accessed 22 October 2015).
Porter-Szűcs, B. (2011) *Faith and Fatherland: Catholicism, Modernity, and Poland*. New York: Oxford University Press.
Potter, J. and Wetherell, M. (1987) *Discourse and Social Psychology: Beyond Attitudes and Behaviour*. London: Sage.
Pratt, M.L. (1992) *Imperial Eyes. Travel Writing and Transculturation*. London: Routledge.
Prendergast, C. (2008) *Buying into English. Language and Investment in the New Capitalist World*. Pittsburgh, PA: University of Pittsburgh Press.
Purgason, K.B. (2004) A clearer picture of the 'Servants of the Lord'. *TESOL Quarterly* 38, 711–713.
Reisman, J.M. (1979) *Anatomy of Friendship*. New York: Irvington Publishers.
Richert, S.P. (2014) 'The New Translation of the Mass'. *About religion*, 10 December. See http://catholicism.about.com/od/worship/a/The-New-Translation-Of-The-Mass.htm (accessed 10 February 2015).
Ross, W.D. (trans.) (2015) 'Nicomachean Ethics by Aristotle: Book 9'. See http://www.virtuescience.com/ethics9.html (accessed 9 October 2015).
SEND International (2006) 'Mission: Poland'. See http://www.send.org/poland/index.htm (accessed 28 August 2006).
SEND International (2015) 'Poland'. See http://www.send.org/poland/?fullstory (accessed 22 October 2015).
Seweryn, A. (2008) Zarys dziejów baptyzmu w Polsce (1858–2008): Rozwój w okresie ostatnich 30 lat. *Kościół Chrześcijan Baptystó*, 21 June. See http://www.baptysci.pl/kosciol/1083-zarys-dziejow-baptyzmu-w-polsce-1858-2008?start=4 (accessed 2 July 2012).
Singh, P. and Doherty, C. (2004) Global cultural flows and pedagogic dilemmas: Teaching in the global university contact zone. *TESOL Quarterly* 38 (1), 9–42.
Smith, D.I. (2009) *Learning from the Stranger: Christian Faith and Cultural Difference*. Grand Rapids, MI: William B. Eerdmans.
Smith, D.I. and Carvill, B. (2000) *The Gift of the Stranger: Faith, Hospitality, and Foreign Language Learning*. Grand Rapids, MI: William B. Eerdmans.

Smith, D.I. and Smith, J.K.A. (eds) (2011) *Teaching and Christian Practices: Reshaping Faith and Learning*. Grand Rapids, MI: William B. Eerdmans.
Snow, D.B. (1996) *More than a Native Speaker: An Introduction for Volunteers Teaching English Abroad*. Alexandria, VA: Teachers of English to Speakers of Other Languages, Inc.
Snow, D.B. (2001) *English Teaching as Christian Mission: An Applied Theology*. Scottsdale, PA: Herald Press.
Spolsky, B. (2003) Religion as a site of language contact. *Annual Review of Applied Linguistics* 23, 81–94.
Stevick, E. (1996) Response to Julian Edge's 'Keeping the faith'. *TESOL Matters* 6 (6), 6.
Sutherland, J. (1968) Introduction. In D. Defoe (ed.) *Robinson Crusoe* (pp. v–xiv). Boston, MA: Houghton Mifflin Harcourt.
Tannen, D. (2005) *Conversational Style: Analyzing Talk Among Friends*. New York: Oxford University Press (original work published 1984).
Taylor, N. (ed.) (2008) *Daniel Defoe's Robinson Crusoe*. Harlow: Penguin.
thE-TASK (2005) Leading Poles from Mary to Jesus. *ThE-TASK Newsletter*, April. (accessed 28 August 2006).
Tournier, M. (1967) *Vendredi ou les Limbes du Pacifique*. Paris: Gallimard.
Tournier, M. (1969) *Friday* (N. Denny, trans.). Garden City, NY: Doubleday.
Varghese, M. and Johnston, B. (2007) Evangelical Christians and English language teaching. *TESOL Quarterly* 41, 9–31.
Vu, M.A. (2008) Europe mega-pastor gives tips for revival of US Christianity. *The Christian Post*, 24 April. See http://www.christianpost.com/news/europe-mega-pastor-gives-tips-for-revival-of-u-s-christianity-32082/ (accessed 17 February 2015).
Wallis, J. (2005) *God's Politics: Why the Right Gets It Wrong and the Left Doesn't Get It*. New York: Harper Collins.
Wanner, C. (2007) *Communities of the Converted: Ukrainians and Global Evangelism*. Ithaca, NY: Cornell University Press.
Watch Tower Bible and Tract Society of Pennsylvania (2012) 'Poland'. See http://www.jw.org/index.html?option=QrYQCsVrGlBBX (accessed 2 July 2012).
Willinsky, J. (1998) *Learning to Divide the World: Education at Empire's End*. Minneapolis, MN: University of Minnesota Press.
Wiśniewska, K. (2009) Mniej księży, mniej wiernych. *Gazeta Wyborcza*, 29 April, p. 8.
Włodarczyk, J. (2010) Manufacturing hysteria: The import of US abortion rhetorics to Poland. *Genders* 52. See http://www.genders.org/g52/g52_wlodarczyk.html (accessed 10 February 2015).
Wong, M.S. (2009) Deconstructing/reconstructing the missionary English teacher identity. In M.S. Wong and S. Canagarajah (eds) *Christian and Critical English Language Educators in Dialogue: Pedagogical and Ethical Dilemmas* (pp. 91–105). New York: Routledge.
Wong, M.S. and Canagarajah, S. (eds) (2009) *Christian and Critical English Language Educators in Dialogue: Pedagogical and Ethical Dilemmas*. New York: Routledge.
Wong, M.S., Kristjánsson, C. and Dörnyei, Z. (eds) (2013) *Christian Faith and English Language Teaching and Learning*. New York: Routledge.
Wright, P.H. (1984) Self-referent motivation and the intrinsic quality of friendship. *Journal of Social and Personal Relationships* 1, 115–130.
Young, W.P. (2007) *The Shack*. Newbury Park, CA: Windblown Media.
Zimmerman, J. (2006) *Innocents Abroad: American Teachers in the American Century*. Cambridge, MA: Harvard University Press.
Zuzowski, R. (1992) *Political Dissent and Opposition in Poland: The Workers' Defense Committee 'KOR'*. Westport, CT: Praeger Publishers.

Name Index

Appadurai, A., 126

Balmer, R., 19, 24
Baran, E.B., 132
Baurain, B., 25–26, 162
Bebbington, D.W., 12
Berscheid, E., 124–125
Bielo, J.S., 28, 53
Bishop, B., 163–164
Blum, R., 146
Booth, W.C., 65
Bradley, C.A., 26
Brubaker, F., 115
Burbules, N.C., 138

Canagarajah, S., viii, 25–26
Carvill, B., 24
Charles, V., 146
Clifford, J., 35–36, 127
Coetzee, J.M., 65
Cooper, R., 115
Coutand–Marin, S., viii, 4–5, 23–25, 31, 160, 162

Defoe, D., ix, 48, 55, 62–64, 67, 80, 98, 140, 147
Doherty, C., 35–36, 127, 150
Dudley, J., 20

Easton, A., 144
Edge, J., viii, 4, 21–25, 142, 160–162
Edwards, D., 143, 161

Fehr, B., 124
Fetterman, D.M., 32

Glesne, C., 30, 32
Goffman, E., 42
Grabowska, M., 17
Graves, K., 55
Griffith, T., 23

Guba, E.G., 36
Guerrettaz, A.M., 62, 68

Hartup, W.W., 124

Jassem, Z., 100
Johnston, B., 2, 22, 26, 28, 37–38, 62, 68, 162

Kutschera, U., 145

Lincoln, Y.S., 36
Loptes, K.A., 26

MacCannell, D., 36, 127, 150
Marshall, C., 30, 32
McKenna, J., 145
Midgley, M., 125 n. 2
Mitchell, J., 4
Morgan, B., 84, 104
Mutz, D.C., 164

Nation, I.S.P., 56
Nelson, C., 110
Noddings, N., 138
Noll, M., 12

Pennycook, A., viii, 4–5, 23–25, 31, 160, 162
Peplau, L.A., 124–125
Peshkin, A., 20, 26–27, 30, 32
Pilch, J., 152
Polis, C., 146
Porter–Szűcs, B., 16
Potter, J., 143, 161
Pratt, M.L., 35–36, 127, 150, 156, 160
Prendergast, C., 28
Purgason, K.B., 23

Reisman, J.M., 124–125
Richert, S.P., 15
Ross, W.D., 125
Rossman, G.B., 30, 32

Seweryn, A., 11
Singh, P., 35–36, 127, 150
Smith, D.I., 24–25
Smith, J.K.A., 25
Snow, D.B., 24, 85, 157
Spolsky, B., 19
Sridhara, S., 146
Stevick, E., 22–23, 154
Sutherland, J., 76–77

Tannen, D., 103
Taylor, N., 76–77
Tournier, M., 65

Varghese, M., viii, 2, 22, 26, 28, 37, 38, 162

Vu, M.A., 27

Wallis, J., 177
Wanner, C., 13, 20, 27, 100, 116, 132–133
Wetherell, M., 161
Willinsky, J., 19, 160
Wiśniewska, K., 16
Włodarczyk, J., 146
Wong, M.S., viii, 25–26, 162
Wright, P.H., 124

Young, W.P., 33, 69, 92–95

Zimmerman, J., 27–28, 156
Zuzowski, R., 15–16

Subject Index

9/11, 22

Alpha, 150, 152 n. 6
Anabaptists, 11–12, 24, 30–31, 99, 154, 156

baptism, *see* conversion
Baptist Church, 10–14, 27, 31–32, 99, 114, 123, 128, 133, 148, 150, 154, 156–157
Bible study, 13, 28, 45, 51, 53, 97, 100, 120

Cambridge English series, 48, 52, 61–62
charismatic Catholicism, vii, 148, 151
classroom ecology, 62, 68
coercion, 31, 35, 82, 153–154
colonialism, ix, 19, 35, 37, 65, 68, 152, 155–156, 159–160
community
    and Lighthouse School, 115–116
    discourse, 163
    evangelical, ix, 4, 12, 47, 49, 79, 99–101, 103, 108, 115–116, 132–133
    non-evangelical, 26
conservatism, viii, 8, 15, 20, 31, 49, 87, 139, 145–146, 155–156, 159
conservative values, *see* conservatism
conversion, ix, 1, 12–13, 23, 25, 31, 39, 54, 94, 99–101, 154–155, 161, 164
covertness, *see* deception
creationism, viii, 20, 87, 145–146
critical pedagogy, 25, 37, 160–161

deception, 4–5, 21–23, 25, 153–154
discourse analysis, 7, 160–161

ecumenical discourse, ix, 8, 67, 84, 134–146, 151, 158–159, 161
ethnography, ix, 5, 20, 27–28, 30, 32, 34–37, 126, 153, 160, 162

European Union, 16–17, 29
Evangelical Christianity
    and business, 116
    and gender, ix, 49, 133, 159–160, 163
    definition, 11–12
    in the United States (US Evangelism), 3, 27

fundamentalism, 11, 20, 27, 87

gender, 7, 37, 49, 88, 108, 111–114, 116, 133, 159–160, 163
global contact zones, 127, 150
Great Commission, 2, 12, 21, 27

hostility toward evangelicals, 3–4, 24, 132

innocence, 27–28, 124–125, 156–157
intelligent design, *see* creationism
Invasion of Iraq, 22–23

Jehovah's Witnesses, 11, 13–14, 132
John Paul II, *see* papacy

Lighthouse School
    affiliated church, 14, 45, 49, 119, 154
    alcohol, 41, 95, 116
    Bible-based curriculum, ix, 29, 31–32, 36, 46–47, 49, 51–53, 158
    Coffee Central, 41–42, 101, 115
    extracurricular activities, 113–116
    finances, 55
    grammar and vocabulary teaching, 33, 48, 52, 55–62, 65, 68, 69, 71, 74, 80, 85–86, 88–91, 93–94, 105, 118, 157–158
    move from D. to N., 30, 47–50, 132
    outreach, 47, 113–114
    pre-class chat, 102–104
    smoking, 41
Latter-Day Saints, *see* Mormonism

Literacy and Evangelism International, 46, 48

Manila Manifesto, 12, 21
Mennonites, *see* Anabaptists
mini-sermons, 71, 78–84, 89–90, 96, 111, 118, 156
Mormonism, 11, 13–14, 132

naivety, *see* innocence
Navigators, 148–149

papacy, 6, 15–16, 138, 145, 148
Peace Corps, 12, 27
Pentecostalism, 11–12, 14, 20, 27, 148
Poland and
    abortion, viii, 15–17, 20, 144–146
    All Souls' Day, 88
    Catholicism, vii, 8–10, 13–17, 85, 89, 134, 138, 146–148
    communism, vii, 6, 10–16, 20, 28–29, 40
    English teaching, vii, 1, 29–30, 36
    homosexuality, viii, 31, 123, 141–144, 146, 151, 152 n. 3, 155–156
    minorities, 9–10, 49, 148
    missionary activity in, 1, 12–14, 18, 28–29, 36, 127, 147, 154–155
    other evangelical language schools, 28–29, 39 n. 1

Post-abortion stress syndrome (PASS), 145–146
Protestantism, vii, 9–11, 13, 17, 19–20, 110, 128, 131–132, 144, 147, 149–150
    Solidarity post–1989, 15–16
    the Virgin Mary, 17, 147
postmodernism, 36
prayer, 38–39, 60, 70–73, 75, 79–80, 82–85, 94, 105, 109, 114, 118–119, 121–122, 125, 131, 135–136, 143, 151
    classroom prayer, 109, 118, 121–122, 143
    closing prayers, 70–71, 82–85, 94

Radio Maryja, 17–18

The Shack (novel), 33, 69, 92–96, 133
short-term missions, 28, 44–45, 108, 114–115

TESOL, 4–5, 19–26, 46–47, 85, 91, 157, 160, 163
    Christian Caucus, 24
teacher identity, viii, 2, 7, 21, 26, 84, 104, 162
tolerance, 3, 140–147, 159, 163
Ukraine, 13, 27, 45, 100, 116, 132–133
witnessing, 2, 12, 25, 38, 85, 100, 138
World War II, 9, 20

For Product Safety Concerns and Information please contact our EU Authorised Representative:

Easy Access System Europe

Mustamäe tee 50

10621 Tallinn

Estonia

gpsr.requests@easproject.com

www.ingramcontent.com/pod-product-compliance
Lightning Source LLC
Chambersburg PA
CBHW070613300426
44113CB00010B/1514